D0975805

THE
BIG
BOOK
OF FAITH

IYANLA VANZANT

A FIRESIDE BOOK
Published by Simon & Schuster

FIRESIDE
Rockefeller Center
1230 Avenue of the Americas
New York, NY 10020

First Fireside Edition 1997

FIRESIDE and colophon are registered trademarks
of Simon & Schuster Inc.

Manufactured in the United States of America

1   3   5   7   9   10   8   6   4   2

Library of Congress Cataloging-in-Publication Data is available.
ISBN 0-684-84999-2

Act on faith . . . even when you are in the valley! When you don't know what to do, or believe you don't know how to do it. There is no better time to challenge what you know, and when you believe, than when you are having a difficult time in your life. This is when faith is most effective! It's also when we can't seem to find the faith that we need. Even when we can find it, we sometimes doubt that it will work. Faith is not anything you must acquire. Faith is what you are! You are the living embodiment of God's faith in life, and in the strength of the human spirit. You are strong, and if you have nothing else, you must have faith in your own strength.

These two books, *Acts of Faith: Daily Meditations for People of Color;* and *Faith in the Valley: Lessons for Women on the Journey Toward Peace;* are faith guidelines. *Acts of Faith,* will guide you through a process of creating a shift in your thought patterns that will maximize your inner strength. *Faith in the Valley,* will help you identify what, or how you are thinking that causes your faith to dwindle. The key to keeping yourself and your faith strong, is to stand guard over what you think, see, hear, and say. All physical stimuli are like seeds being planted in the fertile soil of your mind. These seeds will grow roots and bear fruit. Faith-filled fruit, positive thoughts and words, support your inner and outer growth. Weeds, such as negative thoughts and words, strangle and stifle positive energy, causing your strength and faith to diminish. Faith born of productive thought patterns will kill off the weeds in your consciousness.

Acts of Faith will give you the theory for planting positive thoughts. *Faith in the Valley,* will provide you with a process for implementing the theory in your life. After reading the *Acts of Faith* message for the day, you may find it helpful to look up the major theme of the message in the *Faith in the Valley* glossary and index. The ideas expressed in both of these books will work hand in hand to help you in developing a new perspective, and approach to life. I know you have heard it, I know you know it. I must, however, remind you once again, it is not what happens in life that tests our faith, it is how we respond to an experience that makes all the difference in the world. My prayer is that as you move through this book, you will discover ways to respond to experiences that will fortify your strength, maximize your faith, produce miraculous changes in you, and ultimately alter the face of the world.

Acts of Faith

DAILY
MEDITATIONS
FOR
PEOPLE OF
COLOR

For

My Father
Horace Lester Harris, all you were and
all you were not;

My Brother
Horace Raymond Harris, Jr., all I needed you to be;

My Son
Damon Keith Vanzant, all you are;

My Grandson
Oluwalomoju Adeyemi, all you are becoming.

Acknowledgments

My heartfelt appreciation, love and gratitude to my daughter *Gemmia* for her contribution to ten of these pages;

My daughter *Nisa* for stopping my grandson from eating these pages;

Ralph Stevenson for putting up with my endless requests and taking me anywhere and everywhere while I was in labor with this book;

Kim Mickens, who typed and retyped and never once complained when I scribbled changes on the pages she had just retyped;

Dawn Daniels, my editor, who supported and trusted me enough to know it had to be done;

Shaheerah Linda Beatty, who loved and prayed me through the entire process by making arrangements with Detroit Bell so we could stay in touch;

BarbaraO and *Nana Korantemaa*, who never asked me a question they could not answer;

My *Godfather*, who prayed the power down and sent it to my house;

My *Transformation Station* family in Philadelphia and

Detroit, who never stopped praying, praising and pumping me up;

and, of course, God, who always knew I had it in me and finally convinced me, too.

To the descendants of the Africans who long to know themselves: Although the days of glory may appear to be over, the spiritual heritage is everlasting. You must know with all your heart—It Doesn't Have to Be a Struggle!

May the Ancestors bless you with a clear mind, a peace-filled heart and a powerful African spirit.

OBATALA! Baba Mi, A'dupe.

Egun Ye.

(Translation: The Father of Creation,
My Father, I Salute You. Iyanla)

I will be found by you and I will bring you back from your captivity; I will gather you from all the nations and from all the places where I have driven you; And, I will bring you to the place from which I caused you to be carried away captive.

—Jeremiah 29:10–14

THE HEALING HAS BEGUN

It began when you picked up this book. The goal of these offerings is to assist the children of the earth in the redevelopment of their minds, bodies and spirits. Who are the children of the earth? The children of a darker hue. For they are the ones born of the first Father and Mother. They are the ones who learned, through trial and error, how to bring forth the abundant richness of the earth. They are the ones who have the secret of the beginning and the end buried deep in their souls. These offerings are tools to be used to dig up the secrets so that they can be put to use.

There are a few minor requirements to which one should adhere in order to realize the full value of these offerings. First, you must be open, ready and willing to receive the information. Some of it will be new to you. Most of it you have heard at some time, in some way. The difference is that now you are willing to see, hear and use the information to accomplish a goal: stress-free, peace-filled living. You must be willing to accept that stress is the result of unfinished business. Unfinished business means that there are details which have not been taken care of. Those details are the basic foundation of what you do. What you do is live, and life must begin within. That is the second requirement. The third and final requirement is the willingness to reevaluate, reprogram and rechannel your thinking. Stress will not go away until you decide it no longer has a place in your Life. Obstacles and challenges will not stop until your perception of them changes. Difficulties and disappointments may not cease, yet you can see them in a different light, with a new sense of knowing; everything in life is purposeful.

There are four basic areas that create stress and imbalance for people of color: our relationship with ourselves, our relationship with the world, our relationship with each other and our relationship with money. Consequently, this book has been divided into those four sections. Each will provide you with offerings to consider and hopefully put to use in restructuring your approach and perceptions. It does not matter who you are or where you are in any of those areas. You can make changes, realize improvement and eliminate stress in all of your relationships.

Take time to read a statement daily. Write or repeat the affirmation so that it will make an imprint on your mind. Forty is the number of building foundations. You might want to try repeating the affirmation forty times throughout the day. If you forget, four times will do as the number four represents the cardinal elements (air, water, fire, earth) and the cardinal directions (north, south, east, west). If you can't do that, reading a page a day will still have an effect, there is something for everyone.

Remember also, "As a man soweth in his heart, so shall he reap." What you put into the process of freeing your mind and life from stress, you will get out of it. Change is not easy. Yet it doesn't have to be difficult. A very dear astrologer friend of mine, Basil Farrington, once gave me a very good anaylsis of making change. I share it with you in the hope that it will assist you:

Buried deep in the earth are precious diamonds. In order to get to them, however, we must dig and dig deep. Once we get to the foundation rock, we must apply pressure to shape and mold the diamond. It is not the digging, it is the pressure that makes diamonds. Softness is what marshmallows are made of. Soft, sweet, easy to crumble under pressure and no good for anybody. You are being challenged to decide what you want to be—a diamond or a marshmallow—wait, I think I see a sparkle in your eye! The pressure is on, the healing has begun! May the glow from the sparkle in your eye bring light to all the world.

I SALUTE YOU
AND HONOR YOUR GREATNESS
Iyanla

Self

There is nothing in the world more powerful than the spirit. This spirit is our true Self. It knows exactly what we must learn to do in life, how we will learn to do it and whether or not we are willing to pay attention to what the Self is teaching us. Our real Self is whole and complete. Wise and just. Unlimited and ever present. When we tap into the power, knowledge and wisdom of Self we can fulfill our purpose in life with grace and ease. When we give up our Self to the demands and expectations of others, we become confused, lost and broken in spirit. Our job in life, when we choose to accept it, is to allow the spirit within us to be the Self that becomes a gift to the world.

January 1

There is a power greater than myself who loves me
exactly as I Am.

The stress began the day you learned you were expected to please other people. Parents wanted you to stay
clean and be quiet. Neighbors wanted you to be respectful
and helpful. Teachers wanted you to be attentive and alert.
Friends wanted you to share and hang out. Whenever you
failed to do exactly what someone expected of you, you
weren't good, or good enough. You were bad, weak or
dumb. Unfortunately, you began to believe it. Giving in to
the demands, day by day, you lost a little more of yourself
and your understanding of the truth. The truth is you are
fine, just the way you are! Perfect in your imperfection!
You are divine! Growing brighter and more brilliant each
day, you can accept the truth of who you are. The next
time you want to know who you are, what you are or if
something is the right thing to do, don't ask your neigh-
bor—ask the power within . . . and pay attention to the response!

The divine power within knows
exactly who I Am!

Our hearts are the wrapping which preserve God's
word, we need no more.
— The Koran, Sura 4:155

*W*hen was the last time you sat down to have a heart to
heart with yourself? Have you really examined your heart
lately? Are you harboring childhood wounds? Are you
still nursing a broken heart? Are you frightened? Angry?
Guilty or ashamed? Is there someone you need to apologize to? Who have you forgiven lately? If God were to
speak through your heart today, what would you hear? In
the everyday quest to get through life, we sometimes forget we really do have all we need. It's tucked away safely
inside of us. It contributes to our thoughts and motivates
our actions. If we clear it out it will actually speak to us
and tell us exactly what to do. When was the last time you
had a heart to heart with yourself?

With a pure heart, I am balanced in life.

Don't be afraid to look at your faults.
— Yoruba proverb

*E*ven though we know there is always room for improvement, we tend to shy away from criticism. Our egos tell us we are being attacked and quite naturally we want to strike back. In order to be whole, healthy beings, we need to know all there is to know about ourselves. Sometimes that information must come from others. This may mean admitting that we are not always right and knowing it is okay to make a mistake. A mistake, an error, a poor choice or bad decision does not equal "there is something wrong with me." It means you are on your way to being better. We do not make mistakes on the basis of race or color. We make them because we are human. When we acknowledge our errors and face up to our shortcomings, no one can use them against us.

I Am not afraid to admit when I am wrong.

Take a day to heal from the lies you've told yourself
and the ones that have been told to you.
—Maya Angelou

*T*here comes a time when we have to pause to listen to what we are telling ourselves—"I'm so stupid," "I'm broke," "I don't know how," "I can't take it anymore. . . ." Yet in the midst of our dishonest chatter we are making great strides, accomplishing many tasks, overcoming seemingly insurmountable odds. We can't see it because we keep lying to ourselves. We lie because we've been lied to—"You're no good," "You can't do it," "You'll never make it," "How do you think you're gonna do that? . . ." We can't think because there are so many lies running loose in our minds. The only way to eradicate a lie is with the truth. We must not only speak the truth, we must think in truth. The truth is, we start from a place where success is born, in the mind's eye of the Most High. The truth is that no one has ever made a true deal with the Master and lost.

The truth springs forth from my mind.

STOP!

*M*ost of us know exactly what it is that creates the pain, confusion, stagnation and disruption in our lives. Whether it is a habit, behavior, relationship or fear, we know. Unfortunately, we seem powerless to stop whatever it is. Sometimes we believe we don't have the discipline or willpower to stop. The behavior becomes so habitual we do it without thinking. Other times we know exactly what it is and what we do, but we simply keep doing it anyway. We are the only ones responsible for what goes on in our lives. We can make excuses and blame others, but we are responsible to and for ourselves. When we find something or someone creating in our lives that which we do not want, we must muster the courage and strength to stop it.

Today I use my power to stop what is no longer good to me.

You've got to get the mind cleared out before
you put the truth in it.
— Minister Louis Farrakhan

*E*veryone has something they are ashamed of, afraid of
or that they feel guilty about. Each of us in our own way
will devise a neat little method of handling it. Some of us
deny. Some of us blame. Some of us do a combination of
both. Undoubtedly the day will come when we will be
forced to examine that which we have tucked away. We
can willingly begin the process of examination by telling
the truth to ourselves about ourselves. We all have the
right to make mistakes. Our fault is being righteous about
it. When we fail to admit our faults, the faults become
what everyone can see. When we refuse to admit what we
have done in the past, we block our path to the future. No
matter how terrible we think we are, how bad we believe
we have been, how low we think we have fallen, we can
clean out our minds and begin again.

The only way out is truth.

Do not wish to be anything but what you are,
and to be that perfectly.
—St. Francis De Sales

A minister friend of mine once told me, "On the seventh day God rested." He said, "It is good and very good." Then we come along and try to improve on perfection. For people of color, the most damaging habit we have is trying to be who and what we are not. We expend so much energy trying to fix who we are, we rarely get to really know ourselves. If we truly realized how precious the gift of life is, we would not waste a moment trying to improve it. If we really understood how precious we are to the gift of life, we would not waste time trying to fix ourselves. It's not about what we look like or what we have. It's not about fixing our face, body or lives. It's about taking what we have and doing as much as we can with it. It's about learning and growing. When we are willing to learn what we don't know and use our experiences, our perfection will begin to show.

I accept me as I Am.

Know thy ideal and live for that. For each soul
must give an account for its own self.
— Paramhansa Yogananda

*E*verything that happens to us, and every choice we make, is a reflection of what we believe about ourselves. We cannot outperform our level of self-esteem. We cannot draw to ourselves more than we believe we are worth. The things we believe and say about ourselves come back to us in many ways. Self-motivation comes from self-knowledge. We must inspire ourselves by believing we have the power to accomplish everything we set out to do. We must put faith in our ability to use mind and spirit and picture our lives the way we want them to be. We must use inner strength and the power of our being to tear down the walls, break through the barriers and move through the obstacles with ease. Our bodies have been freed. Now we must train our minds to believe it.

I Am free, hallelujah, I Am free!

You may not know how to raise your self-esteem,
but you definitely know how to stop lowering it.
—Awo Osun Kunle

Self-esteem is a sense of value and worth that comes from a positive self-image. Self-esteem begins with you and extends to all that you do. With the belief that your best is always good enough, no one but you can destroy your self-esteem. You destroy your esteem when you do not keep your word. When you do not honor the agreements and commitments you make. If you say "yes" when you really mean "no." When you don't follow your first thought. It does not matter what your environment may be. It is of little consequence what your past has been. It is not your concern what others may be saying or doing. It is only in your mind that you build and destroy your self-esteem.

I Am as great as I think I Am.

If thy right eye offends thee, pluck it out . . .
—Matthew 5:29

*T*he only way to eliminate stress and pain is to stop doing the things that create it. It is easy to see what others do to us while we forget the drama we create for ourselves. How? Take your pick: The need to be right. Lack of life purpose. How we think others see us. Trying to fix the world. Dishonesty with self and others. Accepting someone else's truth. Seeking material wealth over spiritual values. Doing it alone. My way is the right way. Fear of the future. Negative thought patterns. Trying to prove yourself to others. Anger over the past. Telling other people what to do. It all boils down to "not knowing who we are."

When I know me,
I stop doing what's not good for me.

When you strengthen your self-esteem,
there is no room for jealousy.
—Dr. Harold Bloomfield

*J*ealousy is the surest way to get rid of the very person you are afraid of losing. When you say I love you, it means "I want the very best for you whether or not I am included." You must acknowledge any feelings of jealousy to understand what they are. Jealousy is a signpost of the longings in your subconscious mind. It reminds you that what you are longing for is also longing for you. There are only two emotions, love and fear. When jealousy comes up, stop and recognize that it is actually fear raising its ugly head. Fear of losing someone or something, fear that there is not enough. If you allow yourself to be jealous, you cannot love. It is important to acknowledge all your feelings and not beat yourself up for having them. Your feelings are not good or bad, they just are. Jealousy is simply reminding you that you are worthy of the best. When you remember who you are, the jealousy will dissolve and you will be ready to receive what you want.

I honor my feelings no matter what they are.

There's absolutely no way to save people from
the things in their eyes. They must gather
the courage to do it for themselves.
— Alvin Lester Ben-Moring

*B*efore we were indoctrinated to the rules of the world, with all its do's and don'ts, we were actually very receptive. We were willing to try new things, go into forbidden places and take risks without hesitation. We did not believe in unhappiness, defeat, rejection or lack. We asked for what we wanted and were willing to demand that it be provided. We thought the world existed to respond to our needs. It might do us well to revert to the ways of childhood if we want to bring some good into our lives. It's not the temper tantrums or childish outbursts we want. It is the openness and freedom from limitation we need. We have been taught to accept fear, lack, sorrow and restriction as a part of everyday life. We are afraid to make demands of life because we believe we can't have what we want. We no longer feel free to express what we feel, when we feel it. Now, we want to be everyone's friend. If only we could think like a child again, there's a good chance we would find the freedom we gave up to become adults.

Today, I Am a child again.

Heaven is where you'll be when you are
okay right where you are.

—Sun Ra

*P*retend for a moment that you are a mink—beautiful,
valuable, precious because of the skin that covers you.
Suddenly your homeland is invaded by hunters, with bats.
The hunters seem kind, yet you approach them cautiously.
They pet the younglings who are innocent, less cautious.
As you approach your young, the hunters attack. They
beat you. You are dazed, struggling for composure. The
hunters steal your skin, your heritage, the very essence of
your being. They leave you to die, but you survive. Your
fur grows back. Stronger. More beautiful than before.
Somehow it doesn't make sense. The very thing that
makes you who and what you are is the source of pain.
Confused, distrustful, you hide yourself or camouflage
your fur, your essence. Silently you begin to curse your
fur, because the hunters return again and again. You begin
to understand you will never get away from being what
you are. As long as you have fur, you will be hunted. The
issue is: Will you curse your fur, give up and die? Or just
continue to be a proud but cautious mink?

I will not hide who or what I Am.

Successful people succeed because they learn
from their failures.

—Bettina Flores

*T*he most difficult things to face in life are the things
you do not like about yourself. Not your ears, legs, hair or
those habits and abilities you feel are not up to par. It is
the ugly little things you know about yourself that need a
good long look. You recognize it when you see it in others,
but you make excuses for yourself. You may go to any
length to cover a shortcoming, while you quickly point out
the ills of another. Since the very thing you want to hide is
the thing that shows itself, you need to be able to say, "I
know that and I'm working on it!" It takes a loving heart,
a willing mind and a sensitive spirit to get to the core of
the self. But when you do, you can root out the seeds of
ugliness.

*I acknowledge, accept and embrace
everything about me.*

We [must] realize that our future lies chiefly
in our own hands.
— Paul Robeson

*I*f you can blame anyone for any condition in your life, then you, not they, are digging your grave. Your chief adversary comes to teach you a lesson. Your most difficult challenge strengthens your survival skills. Your greatest fear deepens your faith. Your weakest ability beckons you to grow. Anyone and anything can challenge you. It will not overtake you until you surrender. Only you can determine what you do and how you respond in a situation. It is your responsibility to make a decision about what is important to you; choose what you want and how you are going to get it. Once you accomplish that, it is your responsibility to move forward until you get it.

I Am taking a stand for me.

Sitting in a sacred place means you must sit alone.
— Marilyn "Omi Funke" Torres

*T*here are times when we each have sacred blessings to learn. These are the lessons that will push us to the limit of our greatness. At these times, it may seem that others are abandoning, rejecting or criticizing us without just cause. They are not. No matter how hard we try, we can't seem to do, say or be what others expect of us. We can't. The harder we try to pull others to us, the farther they move away. The more we try to fix things, the worse they seem to get. What we must do at these very sacred times is pull back, withdraw and prepare to grow. Our lessons are very sacred. They are the basic ingredient of our greatness. To accept them we must be open. To receive them we must be willing. To understand them we must be alone.

I Am sitting in a sacred place.

In the solitude of your mind are the answers
to all your questions about life.
You must take the time to ask and listen.
—Bawa Mahaiyaddeen

*T*here are times when we all feel as if we need to be alone. We just want to get away from everyone and everything and be alone. Sometimes we may feel guilty or selfish for thinking this way, but it is perfectly normal. To be alone is the best thing we can do for ourselves. To be alone means to be all one with the spirit within. When we are alone, we have an opportunity to get in touch with, to talk to and be guided by our power source. Spirit. To be alone means going to the essence of your being. To ask questions within and get clear, concise answers. To be alone means taking the time to give to yourself a small portion of what we have been giving of ourselves for so long. It is like drinking from the fountain of restoration to bring back your physical, mental and spiritual health. So go ahead. Tell them all and don't feel bad about saying it. "I want to be alone."

Today I Am all one with the spirit within.

January 18

> I have never been contained except that
> I made the prison.
>
> —Mari Evans

When you concern yourself with doing only what others "think" you can do, you lay the floor of your prison. When you conform your activities based on what others might say, you put the bars around your prison. When you allow what others have done or are doing to determine what you can do, you build the roof of your prison. When you allow fear, competition or greed to guide your actions, you lock yourself up and throw away the key. It is our concern over what others say, do and think about us that imprisons our mind, body and spirit.

*What other people think about me
is not my concern.*

In our deepest hour of need the Creator asks
for no credentials.

— Eulogy of Horace Harris

*T*here are times when we feel bad about ourselves, what we've done and what we are facing. In these moments we may even believe we deserve to be punished, because we are "bad" or have done bad things. There are times when we feel so low, we convince ourselves that we don't matter and neither does anything or anyone else. That is when we usually start to think about God. Is there such a thing? Does God really care? Maybe if we had gone to God before, we wouldn't be where we are now. No matter. We're here, so let's go. This is a prime opportunity to make a new start, begin again and move on. The key is to remember that no matter where we've been, what we've done or how awful we feel right now, the One we may be running from knows exactly where we are. He has placed a light of peace in our hearts. A prayer will flip the switch.

I look within for all the answers I need.

You must learn how to make it
on the broken pieces.
—Rev. Louise Williams-Bishop

*R*ipped from their land; stripped of their culture, religion, name; beaten for rebelling and blamed for their state of existence, the descendants of the Africans have a right to feel broken. Being broken does not mean you are unequipped. There are enough pieces left for you to grab on to, hold on to and paddle your way to shore. Your life is the piece that equips you to have a goal. Your goal is the piece that will equip you with confidence. Your confidence is the piece that will give you persistence. Your persistence is the piece that will ensure your success. There are pieces from your parents, friends, even foes. There are pieces of books, songs and experience. More important, there are the pieces that well up from deep inside your being that will guide you surely and safely. Put them all together and hold on.

*My pieces may be broken but
I am going on anyhow.*
—Rev. Louise Williams-Bishop

You are as much as you are right now.
— Yoruba proverb

We have such poor images of ourselves that we have difficulty understanding the good others see in us. When someone gives us a compliment, we are quick to point out what is wrong. When someone supports or encourages us, we remind them of our failures. We play ourselves down to such a degree that others begin to question the faith they have placed in us. This vicious cycle can only lower our already low self-esteem. Today is a good time to rethink our thoughts about ourselves. We can accept the compliments we receive when we give them to ourselves first. We can build our confidence by celebrating our small victories and successes. We can support the faith and trust others have in us by supporting and having faith in ourselves. It all begins with our willingness to acknowledge that we are really fine, just the way we are.

I really am okay with me.

God isn't alarmed when we hit rock bottom.
He made the rock.

—Baptist Minister

*T*here are times in our lives when we feel there is no way up or out. Illness. Poverty. Confusion. Loneliness. Desperation. They take us to the place called "rock bottom." In these times you may feel weak and vulnerable, and it is easy to lose faith in your ability to go on. It is exactly in these times that you must turn to the infinite power within yourself. You must know that the answer is exactly where you are. The strength you need, the answer you want, the solution that will turn the situation around is you. If you can put aside the anger, fear, weakness and desperation for just a minute you will remember the "other times" you were at the bottom and how in a moment, miraculously, you were lifted up.

There is no spot where God is not.

Ask, and it shall be given you . . .
—Matthew 7:7

We all get to a point where we feel confused and indecisive. We can't seem to figure out what we want or what to do. We want everything, but nothing brings satisfaction. Our spirit is restless because the mind is racing. It may not be that we don't know, it is probably that we are afraid to ask. We may feel as if we are running to something, but actually we are running away. In those times we need to sit down, get still and evaluate just what it is we want. We must do this quietly, honestly and often, if necessary. We are human beings, blessed with the power of reason. We have, at all times, the right and the power to figure out what we want. Once that's done, we must have the courage to ask for it. If we let the color of our skin, the gender we express or the ways of the world limit us, we will forever be denied. We owe it to ourselves to choose a way and ask for it. Once we ask, we can rest.

Today I plan to choose and ask with an open mind.

For no man can be blessed without the acceptance
of his own head.

—Yoruba proverb

*T*he wise Africans knew and understood the power of
the mind. People can only be as good as their thoughts, as
successful as mental patterns, as progressive as their ideas.
Africans did not rely on books, relative theories or postu-
lative quotations. They listened to their thoughts, prayed
for divine guidance, followed the intuitive urging. Education, money, fame and notoriety were considered as useful
as dirty dishwater without a clear, firm, focused mind.
Their process was simple. They developed a strong faith
and connection to the Creator. A healthy love and respect
for their ancestors and parents. A commitment and dedication to the traditions of their family. And a trusting relationship to the spirit of their own head. Trust your head
and your first thought regardless of what others may say.
Your head takes you to the places you want to go.

I bless the spirit of my head.

Check out your own B.S.
— Jewel Diamond-Taylor

B.S. refers to Belief System — those things you hold to be true about yourself and others. Your B.S. is a product of your experiences and perceptions. Those things you have come to believe are true. Those things buried in the back of your mind. But are they really buried? *No!* Your belief system determines your environment, your abilities and the way you approach life's experiences. What do you really believe about yourself? What do you believe about your ability to have, to be and to do all the things you hold dear in your heart? If you really want to know what you believe, take a look at the people, conditions and situations in your immediate environment. They are the reflection of your own B.S.

I Am a true believer in the best about me.

It takes a deep commitment to change and an even
deeper commitment to grow.
—Ralph Ellison

When you know you are thinking, saying or doing
things that are unhealthy or unproductive, you must do
more than know. There must be a genuine, loving support
for the "self" to make a change. Change does not mean replacing one bad habit for another. It does not mean beating up on yourself or feeling guilty or ashamed. Change
means voluntarily removing yourself from the people and
environment that support you in remaining unhealthy.
Change means identifying what you are doing, recognizing when you are doing it and gently guiding yourself to
do something else. Change means not making excuses for
yourself, but doing exactly what you say you will do.
When you support yourself in making needed changes,
you are supporting your own growth. Growth is the commitment to being, doing and having the best.

I Am growing by thoughts, words and deeds.

There are two things over which you have complete dominion, authority and control—your mind and your mouth.

—Molefi Asante

*Y*our mind is an instrument. A precious gift to be valued and cared for. You are not always in control of what goes into your mind, but only you can determine what stays there. If you allow negativity to pervade in your mind, you will produce that negativity with your mouth. Your mouth is the mechanism that reveals how well you care for your mind. The conditions in your life stem from the most dominant thoughts of which you speak. Nothing has a hold on your mind that you cannot break free of. Since your mind will respond to what is said to you, speak to the conditions in your life. When they are wanted, give thanks. When they are unwanted, demand they change.

I Am in control of my mind and mouth.

You've got the right one, baby! Uh-huh!
—as performed by Ray Charles

*Y*ou are the only one who can do it like you do it. You are the best. You have what it takes. You've got juice. You've got the power. You and only you have what you have, and nobody can take that away from you. You come from the best, the beginning, the source. You are destined to be great. You inherited a legacy of success from those who came before you. They knew you could do it, too! You are the light in life. You light up the world. You make life worth living. You can't lose with the stuff you use. You are the beginning and the end of the phenomena called you. You are the one who makes the bed. You call the shots. You stand heads above the crowd. They can't hold a candle to you. When you put your mind to something, you get it done. So what are you waiting for?

I Am the you that can do it.

If you don't sell your head, no one will buy it.
—Yoruba proverb

We are capable of directing and determining the outcome of any and every situation we face through the power of thought. Yet since many of us do not realize our true power, we cannot realize the truth of the statement: "No one can do anything or make you do anything unless you let them." The key is to be honest with yourself and others at all times, keep your thoughts focused on the best possible outcome for everyone involved and never allow yourself to be pushed where you don't choose to be. If someone called you a grape, you probably wouldn't respond. But if that same person refers to you as a coon or spade, you would most likely hold them responsible for your reaction. No one but you can ever be held accountable for what you do. How you respond in any given situation is purely a reflection of what you think—what is in your head. When someone does or says something you believe is offensive, do yourself a favor—don't sell your head.

It's what's inside my head that counts.

Ford got a better idea, you can get one too.
—Linda Green Beatty

The things our parents tell us, the things we read in books, the things we hear and overhear create the foundation of our thoughts. These thoughts grow into ideas. For many people of color, the ideas they have about themselves are not good. There is the idea that it is hard for Black people to make it. This is supported by the idea that Black people don't try. There is the idea that other people are preferred over Black people. This gives birth to the idea that Black people are not good enough. There is the idea that Black men aren't respected. This comes from the idea that Black women have abandoned Black men. The idea is that because there is so much conflict between Black men and Black women, Black children are lost. The thing we seem to forget is that an idea will die unless it is acted upon. Everytime we entertain the truth of false ideas we give it the right to live. If an idea is not of your making or liking, you can choose to have a better one.

I believe in my right to have unlimited goodness in my life.

The mind is and always will be our primary
business.

—Dr. Benjamin Mays

*T*here are times when it is difficult to make sense of the experiences we have in life. How are we to get ahead without money? How are we to overcome intangible obstacles? How are we to move through the challenges, difficulties and limitations we face at every turn? It may seem that no matter how hard you try, something or someone is there to block you. In those times remember the words of Dr. Benjamin Mays:

> *It is not your environment;*
> *It is not your history;*
> *It is not your education or ability;*
> *It is the quality of your mind that predicts your future.*

I take the time to develop my own mind.

February 1

Even if you're on the right track, you'll get run over
if you just sit there.

— Will Rogers

A positive, healthy sense of self-value and -worth is
the foundation of our happiness and success. When we
know who we are and believe it, our greatest dreams are
possible. When we doubt ourselves, question our worth,
and undermine our self-value, our greatest victory will be
worthless. Affirm "I am my greatest hero." That is really
where it starts. We must believe in who we are and what
we do. We must look up to and trust ourselves to make it
through the difficulties knowing that we can. Only we can
truly appreciate and celebrate our own success. We are
equipped and capable of getting to where we want to be.
If we have any doubts, we can always hold our own hand.

*I now create a positive pattern of self-worth
because I believe I Am the best.*

If you plant turnips you will not harvest grapes.
—Akan proverb

When we pass a garden and see everything in full bloom, we don't always think about the seeds that were planted long before we got there. We simply enjoy the beauty of the harvest. Our minds work the very same way. It is the law of expression that says we must ultimately express in form those thoughts, emotions and impulses we store in the subconscious mind. That part of us does not think. It does not reason, balance, judge or reject. It is the fertile ground that accepts any and everything we plant. Good or evil, constructive or destructive, our lives will bear the fruit of the seeds we plant in our minds. If we have no faith, purpose or belief in ourselves, we cannot blame the world. We plant the roses or weeds we see in the garden. We can imagine good big things as well as troubling little things, our minds will accept either one. If we want to lay back and sniff the lilies in our valley, we must tend our seeds of thought with constant care.

I reap a good harvest from the soil of my mind.

The most sacred place isn't the church, the mosque
or the temple, it's the temple of the body.
That's where spirit lives.

— Susan Taylor

Take a moment to check in on your body. Deeply inhale
and exhale. Let your mind flow through your body. Check
in on your feet, legs, hips. Let your mind roam your ab-
domen, your chest, your back. Scan your neck, shoulders,
arms. What are you feeling? Fear, exhaustion, tension,
anxiety, anger, guilt, shame? Inhale and exhale. Where are
you feeling it? Legs? Back? Neck? Chest? Wherever it is,
whatever it is, you are the only mechanic who can fine-
tune your body. With a simple breath you can release the
stress and replace it with what you need. Turn anxiety into
peace, anger into joy, tension into love, fear into faith,
guilt into trust. Take a moment right now and give yourself a tune-up.

When I am in tune with my body,
I relax and release the stress.

May I assume whatever form I want in whatever
space my spirit wishes to be.
— *The Book of Coming Forth by Day,*
translated by Dr. Maulana Karenga

*T*he ancients knew the connection between man and
the Divine. They knew that buried beneath the personality, perceptions and self-imposed limitations there lies a
spirit of unlimited possibility. They knew that you choose
with your thoughts the shape and form of your life. You
create with your words the conditions that you will face.
You limit with your fear the coming forth of your desires.
You destroy with your blame the direction of your destiny.
The ancient ones knew that only with diligent maintenance of the mind and emotions would man master his
fate. Because the blood of the ancient ones runs through
your veins, you have the same knowledge. You have the
ability to be what you want in the place you may choose.
Simply follow the divine prescription for unfettered success, "Begin within."

I Am the beginning and my end.

Nothing can dim the light which shines from within.
— Maya Angelou

$\mathcal{E}$ach of us brings to the world unique talents, gifts and abilities. Even if you don't know what it is, or value what you do, someone, somewhere, will benefit from your presence. No one can do what you do exactly the way you do it. It is this uniqueness that makes you valuable to the world. We are each as unique and valuable as the other. It was designed that way. A gift from God. Gifts are not given on the basis of race or gender. As a matter of truth, gifts come in many shapes, sizes and colors. When you do what you do, exactly the way you do it, you are sharing God's gifts, bestowed for the good of the world.

I have something valuable to give the world.

Nobody knows the mysteries which lie at the
bottom of the ocean.
— Yoruba proverb

*Y*our body is 96 percent water. Like the ocean, you are
a mystery of buried treasures. The deeper you are willing
to go, the greater are the treasures you will find. Your
mind is the only equipment you need. The sharper your
mind, the greater the depths that will be revealed to you.
Never allow anyone or anything to limit your mind because of your race, color or gender expression, since your
mind feeds your emotions. The emotions of your heart will
keep your dreams afloat. If you can feel it, the world must
reveal it. When you take time to breathe consciously, stilling the motion of the mind, you can take a plunge into the
deepest resources of your soul. Take a plunge within yourself to find the joy, strength, peace, freedom and love you
may be seeking on the shores of life.

*I look within the ocean of self to find
the treasures of life.*

If you have no confidence in self, you are twice defeated in the race of life. With confidence, you have won even before you have started.

—Marcus Garvey

A history of oppression, denial, injustice and abuse has been the greatest detriment to people of color. We have listened so long to what we cannot do that we have very little confidence in what we can do. It is this lack of confidence, not racism, hatred, lack of education or social injustice that creates the greatest deterrent to our progress. One of the best-kept secrets in life is when children of God make up their minds, when they bring their minds into harmony with the desire in their hearts, when they pray for and follow intuitive guidance; then no one and nothing can stop them—no matter what color they may be. Confidence and a made-up mind are the stuff kings and queens are made of.

I Am confident and
possess all I need to succeed.

Luck is what happens when preparation
meets opportunity.

— Unknown

*F*ear, lack of confidence and low self-esteem tends to
make us jump to conclusions. If what we are facing is near
to our hearts, we have a tendency to expect the worst. We
miss so much, including opportunities to change, when we
jump to the end from the middle. We forget our focus and
the goal when we poise ourselves for failure. The ancient
Africans knew that no matter what was going to happen, it
would not happen until it happened. Therefore, they were
prepared for all possibilities, the good and the bad. Do not
jump to conclusions, you could be wrong. Do not pull out
in the middle, that is a total waste of time. Keep your faith,
trust and stay focused, put your best foot out anyway. The
ancient ones had faith and trusted, knowing the end is only
a reflection of the beginning.

The end is not here yet.

I am sick and tired of being sick and tired.

—Fannie Lou Hamer

*M*any of us believe that unless we are struggling, we are not doing it right. We struggle with thoughts, feelings, even other people. We struggle with money problems, family problems and personal problems. Many of us have said, "I am tired of struggling!" Well, guess what? When you make the decision to stop struggling, you will stop. When you stop struggling, things get better. Struggle goes against the flow. It creates exhaustion in the mind and body. When you are exhausted you get sick. If you are sick, you must make a decision and commitment to do everything in your power to get better. The power is in the commitment never to do what makes you sick. The key is the decision never to tire of doing what is best, good and right for you.

I give no thing power over me.

There must be inner healing for the broken vessels.
— Rev. Linda Hollies

$\mathcal{S}$he spent two days making her outfit, spent her last $50 on a new pair of shoes. She had her hair and nails done, spent forty-five minutes putting on her makeup. When she got there, she spent the entire evening sitting in the corner, half smiling, half crying. On the outside she looked beautiful. On the inside she felt worthless. So many of us invest a fortune making ourselves look good to the world, yet on the inside we are falling apart. We manage to muddle through life saying and doing the right things, but when we're alone we cry silent and desperate tears. It is time to pause and heal the inside. It is time to heal the hurts, mend the fences, dig up the hatchets and throw them away. It is time to heal the doubts, answer the questions and release the fears. It is time to invest some time to what is going on inside. When we can do that, the outside will shine.

*I Am investing my time in
something that matters.*

When there's anger in your head, rage in your heart,
that's the time you can't forget to boogie!
— BarbaraO

*M*any people of color are extremely diverse, wonder-fully creative and desperately depressed. For some reason, all we know, are capable of doing and desire to accomplish never gets done. We seem to be held down by our frustra-tions, challenges and failures. This in turn makes us so angry we could scream. What we fail to realize is that anger is what stops us in the first place. It's not the other way around. Angry people are stagnant. Angry people are frustrated. Angry people see challenges as obstacles. Angry people fail before they start so they usually never try. Angry people tell themselves, "I'm not angry, I'm Black. I'm not angry, I'm poor. I'm not angry, I'm just tired." Yet buried beneath the poverty and fatigue is the black hole of anger that must be healed. Anger, not de-pression. Anger, not alcoholism. Anger, not hypertension. Anger, not cancer. Anger, not strokes is what holds us back, so we might as well scream and let a little of the anger out.

I Am willing to recognize and
address anger when I experience it.

Depression is anger that you turn on yourself.
— Dr. Craig K. Polite

*T*here is a collective pain among people of color that has been denied, mislabeled or unacknowledged. The pain of our collective past, the pain of our parents, the pain we experienced as children, the pain we create for one another. Regardless of the source or the age of the wounds, our pain is the source of our anger. Yet we are taught it is not "nice" to be angry. We are discouraged from voicing or acting out on what we feel. We come up with cute little names for the things we do to deny that we are angry. When we fail to acknowledge anger, it quickly becomes depression and the weight makes it difficult to move forward. It robs us of our dreams. It steals precious hours, days and years. Depression may be labeled laziness, confusion, ignorance or just the way we are. Very often these labels make us angry. The only way to end the cycle and get off the roller coaster of denied emotions is to admit that we are angry and go within to find the remedy.

I Am angry and I Am still okay.

Don't worry, be happy.
— Bobby McFerrin

*W*orry is the vampire that drains life of its force. Worry stagnates the mind, creates an imbalance in the immune system; weakens the throat, your power and authority center; impairs the ability to see beyond the thing being worried about. We worry about things we cannot control. We worry about the past and the future. We worry about those things we cannot do or have not done and how they will affect what we are doing right now. We worry about what we do not have, cannot get and things we have lost. Worry creates confusion, disorder and helplessness. Then we worry because we cannot figure things out. We must eliminate the tendency to worry without worrying if it will work out. Take the situation creating the worry, briefly and concisely write it down. Place the paper on which you have written in a window, facing the sun. Make a commitment to yourself to let it go and move on. Everyone knows that when sunlight hits a vampire, it first shrivels up and then it is gone.

I Am worry free.

Before you run, check to see if the bulldog has teeth.
— Les Brown

*F*ear is a very natural and normal response to the challenges we face in life. Fear tells us there is something we must be cautious about. Fear puts us on alert and tells us there is something we must be prepared for. Fear means something we know nothing about is about to come upon us. Fear of change, the unknown, rejection, failure and success are like the barking of a ferocious bulldog. For people of color, the fear of being bitten, again, immobilizes us. A history that has not honored our sense of worth and value supports the fear. The best thing we can do to fear is confront it. We must know the validity of the things we fear. We must believe we can conquer them. The next time the bulldog of fear is upon you, stare it down, open its mouth and check to see if the thing has teeth.

I give no power to fear.

A delay is not a denial.
— Rev. James Cleveland

*P*atience is a virtue many do not possess. We have very little difficulty identifying what we want and need. The difficulty comes in waiting for it to manifest. We become nervous, doubtful, even fearful when we don't see our good coming as quickly as we think it should. Sometimes we even allow ourselves to believe someone or something can hold us back or stop our good from coming. We worry, we complain and sometimes we give up hope. We cannot see how we get in our own way. We forget about universal timing and divine order. We may not realize how our negative thoughts, doubts and fears uproot the positive seeds we plant. We just don't understand that we would not have the desire unless the supply were ready to come forward. We must learn the virtue of patience because every time we open the oven door, we run the risk of making a good cake fall.

I have all the time in the universe.

Keep thy heart with all diligence; for out of it
are the issues of life.

—Proverbs 4:23, 24

*Q*ueen Maat is the gatekeeper of the heart. It is said that before man can pass on to eternal peace, his heart must be balanced on the scale of Maat. On one side she will place your heart, the cause behind all of your actions. On the other side, she will place her feather, which contains all the issues of life. If your heart tips the scale, you are banished from a peaceful rest and your spirit must continue working to cleanse itself. What are you harboring in your heart? Hate, anger, fear, judgment, shame or guilt will tilt the scale against you. The feather of Maat contains truth, honor, justice, harmony and love, which the ancients believed were the only requirements for a long, prosperous and peace-filled life. To pass through the gate of Maat you must seek and speak the truth, harboring no ill thoughts or feelings, you must honor the ways of those who came before you, you must deal justly with honesty in all situations, be harmonious in all that you do, seeking no quarrel with anyone and extending only love to others.

My heart is as light as a feather.

I ain't gonna study war no more . . .
—African-American spiritual

*L*et us insist on peace today turning our minds away from war. There is war in our hearts, minds, body organs and words because of the fast pace in which we live. Yet just for today, we will lay down our weapons, insisting that peace be the light and the way. Let us know today that we are spiritual beings, programmed for peace and love. Let us teach by example, demonstrating peace in everything we say and do. Let us know that it does not matter what others say or do. We will think in peace, speak in peace, knowing in our hearts that like will draw like. Let us know we are bound to become that which we study, so let us study peace and love and truth. If we commit ourselves to just one day of peace it is bound to feel so good, we will want to do it again.

I Am a peaceful warrior.

Don't let anyone steal your spirit.

—Sinbad

*T*here are times when we find ourselves at odds with someone. It may seem that our only choices are to get caught up in the situation or walk away. The ego tells us we must prove we are right. If we walk away, the other person will win. The ego keeps us from recognizing there is another choice. Whatever situation confronts us, we must recognize our right to be at peace. The need to be right and meet discord head on begins within. It is a need that stems from feelings of powerlessness, unworthiness and a lack of love. It shows up in life as arguments and confrontation. When we have peace in our hearts and minds, we draw peace into our lives. When discord and disharmony present themselves, we can stand firm. When we let go of the need to prove to ourselves, nothing and no one can disturb the quiet and peace of our minds.

I Am rightfully peaceful.

Where you will sit when you are old shows
where you stood in youth.
— Yoruba proverb

*W*e can become so consumed with trying to make it that we never do. Unfortunately, before we know it, we are seated by age, hardened by experiences, having never realized the full value of life. We want so much. We try to do so much, it seems as if nothing ever gets done. The ancient Africans knew that quality not quantity makes life precious. It is our individual responsibility to set the standards for quality in our lives. Do we have peace in our lives? Do we have a source of happiness in our lives? Are we living up to the standards we set for ourselves? Have we set standards? Are we committed to following our heart's desire? Are we making our dreams come true? We must decide for ourselves what we want for ourselves while the sunshine of youth is upon us. It is quality, not quantity, that brings wisdom with age.

I will let the sun of life shine on me.

You can look ahead, you can look behind, what is
written cannot be changed.
—The Oracles of Ifa

*W*e cannot change the color of our skin. What we can
change is how we feel about it. We cannot change a pain-
filled past. What we can do is change how it affects us. We
cannot change how others may feel about who we are and
where we've been. What we can change is how we see it,
how we use it and how others use it to our benefit or detriment. The past has already been written, but we have the
power to write the future, based on who we are and what
we do now. Only we can write a future based on self-sup-
port and respect. We can write a future based on how
much we have grown. We can write a future full of
strength, peace, wealth and love. All we have to do is what
is right now.

I Am choosing my future by what I do now.

Those whom the Gods would destroy,
they first call "promising."

—Jan Carew

*T*he road of life is strewn with the bodies of promising people. People who show promise, yet lack the confidence to act. People who make promises they are unable to keep. People who promise to do tomorrow what they could do today. Promising young stars, athletes, entrepreneurs who wait for promises to come true. Promise without a goal and a plan is like a barren cow. You know what she could do if she could do it, but she can't. Turn your promise into a plan. Make no promise for tomorrow if you are able to keep it today. And if someone calls you promising, know that you are not doing enough today.

My life needs a plan, not a promise.

Deal with yourself as an individual worthy
of respect and make everyone else
deal with you the same way.

— Nikki Giovanni

*M*any of us live from day to day without a real sense of purpose. We know we want more out of life, but we can't seem to put a finger on exactly what it is. We believe our fate is due to a lack of career, money or the freedom to do what we want. Actually, what we may be longing for is a personal mission. When you have a mission, you have a core passion that gives you vision. With the vision of your mission, you move gracefully through your goals. When you have a mission, you wholeheartedly embrace a task and you remain focused until the task is done. When you have a mission, you feel valued, worthy and respectable. You manage to keep your head up and others notice you. What is your mission? Is it teaching, healing, painting, driving? Perhaps it is building snowmen, counting pea pods or keeping others on their mission. Respect your life enough to pursue a meaningful mission. Respect yourself enough to give yourself something to do.

I Am mission-minded and focused on a goal.

The one thing grander than the sea is the sky.
The one thing greater than the sky is the
spirit of the human being.

— Anonymous

*T*he reason we can't get clear is because we have so many things cluttering our minds and lives. We have so much mental chatter we can't hear ourselves think. We have so much emotional baggage we can't feel what's good, what's bad, what's right or what's wrong. We want so much, so fast, that we can't get clear about what to do first. The first thing we have to do is get clear about the one thing we want. We must describe it, identify it, see it in our possession. Don't stop to worry about how, that will create more clutter. Just want it and see it the way you want it. Once you do that, eliminate everything that is not getting you to what you want. Eliminate it from thought, word and deed. Eliminate people if necessary. Stop doing things that will not get you what you want. When you are comfortable with the energy you have put into your first want, move on to the next one. The trick is to want one thing at a time. Focus on it. Concentrate on it and then let it go.

I Am clear about what I want.
I can see through to it.

You must never be stupid enough to say,
or smart enough to admit, you "know" what
someone else is talking about. The moment
you do your learning stops.

— Awo Osun Kunle

*T*he ego encourages you to constantly prove yourself and what you already know. When you are in the presence of someone you feel the need to impress, the ego's automatic response is "I know." When you are in the presence of someone your ego thinks is smarter, richer, more experienced than you, your ego tells you, "I know what they are thinking about me." When you are in the presence of someone your ego believes is not as smart, rich or experienced as you, "I know" is the way to cut them off. The moment you say "I know," you are demonstrating that you don't know. You can learn something valuable from everyone, in every situation.

I Am open and willing to learn.

Speak your truth and speak it quick!
—Michael Cornelius

Saying what you really think, feel or believe is often difficult. Usually you don't want to hurt other people's feelings. Even when they infuriate you, you don't want to make someone mad. The real truth of the matter is, somewhere deep down inside, you don't believe your feelings are "right" or that you have the "right" to feel the way you do. When you hold on to feelings you become angry, fearful and confused. When you don't say what is on your mind you will be prone to gossip, rebel or commit acts of betrayal against yourself and others. The only way to free yourself from the stress of not saying what you think is to speak your truth with love, clarity and conviction. And to speak it quickly with a conscious tongue.

I speak my truth from my heart.

You've been tricked! You've been had!
Hoodwinked! Bamboozled!
— El-Hajj Malik El-Shabazz (Malcolm X)

Somebody sure pulled a fast one on you! Somebody, somewhere tricked you into believing there were certain things you could not do because of who you were. Someone else told you that only certain people could do or be the very thing you wanted to be. And you were not one of those people. With a sleight-of-hand manipulation of facts, someone made you think you didn't have what it takes, so they took it. Somebody told you that you were slow, or lazy; not good enough; or crazy. And you believed that? They tricked you into believing what they wanted you to believe. They knew who you were and they knew you had no idea. They pulled the wool over your eyes. Ran a game on you and you fell for it! The truth is they downright, open-mouthed, bare-faced told you a lie! Now what are you going to do?

I am not falling for the same old tricks again.

The tongue of a man is his sword.
— *The Husia*, translated by Dr. Maulana Karenga

$\mathcal{W}$ars do not begin when one force is aggressive toward another. They begin when one force speaks aggression toward another. No act of aggression begins without a word. The word ignites the warrior mechanism in the mind and body. When we hear aggressive words, we are compelled to respond. When we speak aggressive words, we are advanced upon. A wise soldier knows never to draw his sword unless he is ready, able and willing to do battle. A fool draws his sword aimlessly and is prone to cut himself to death.

My tongue is my sword of power. I use it wisely.

You don't always have to have something to say.
—Sammy Davis, Jr.

*E*very time we open our mouths we release a powerful energy. If we could learn to hold on to that energy, it could be used to nurture our dreams, heal our bodies and fuel our minds. But we always have so much to say. Talking can take us off the track, knock us off our center and kill off our dreams when we speak mindlessly. Talking is something we must learn to use, not something we must always do. There is a power in silence that energizes the mind, body and soul. Think of the sun, moon and stars. They all appear silent and never fail at their job. There is wisdom in silence. Think of the mountains and trees. They never have anything to say, yet it takes great effort to bring them down. There is love in silence. Think of the womb. Perfect timing, order and completion accomplished in total silence. Silence is an art, a tool of the wise. When we perfect the art of silence, chances are we will get a lot more done.

Today I will practice the art of silence.

The dog is sometimes smarter than the owner.
— Yoruba proverb

*T*he tongue has no mind of its own. Like a dog, the tongue follows where the owner leads. If the owner leads the dog into harm's way, the dog will not question the direction or intent. The same is true for the tongue. Unlike the dog, however, the tongue has a power the owner may not always be aware of. The tongue can create. The intent of the mind creates a force for the tongue. The power of this force will materialize as a physical condition or an emotional state for the owner. The tongue knows, even when the owner forgets, what you say is what you get — whether you want it or not.

I speak with a conscious tongue.

It is impossible to pretend that you are not heir to,
and therefore, however inadequately or unwillingly,
responsible to, and for, the time and
place that give you life.

—James Baldwin

We each come into this life to learn, relearn or unlearn
something we need to know. As difficult as it may be to accept, we choose the exact circumstances into which we are
born. Whether it is poverty, abandonment, abuse, rejection or disease, our deepest self knows the lessons we must
learn. Our mind chooses the path. Life's lessons are few:
peace, freedom, strength, justice, faith and love. All the
answers you need are buried within you. For just a moment let go of the anger, fear, guilt, shame and blame.
Focus all of your attention on the center of your being and
ask yourself, "What is it that I must learn?" The longer
you ask, the more sincere you are to know, the faster your
answers will come.

I Am willing to take full responsibility for me.

Lord, make me so uncomfortable that
I will do the very thing I fear.

—Ruby Dee

*W*hen it is time for us to grow we get restless. When it is time for us to move forward we get tense. When the time comes for us to let go of the things we know are holding us back, all hell breaks loose. Unfortunately, we sometimes misunderstand what we are feeling and use it as a reason to stay where we are. Nothing forces us to move faster than pain. Restlessness is pain. Tension is pain. Hell breaking loose is a sign that pain is on the way. When we are in pain we must do something to make ourselves feel better. And if the old remedy does not work, we must try something new. Too many times we have cut ourselves down to fit into the situation. Fixing ourselves to stay where we are is the very source of our pain. If we allow ourselves to live with a constant, dull ache, it means we are not getting the message. But you can be sure all dull aches eventually turn into a throbbing pain.

Pain tells me there is something wrong.

How I wish I could pigeon-hole myself and neatly
fix a label on! But self-knowledge comes too late!
By the time I've known myself I am no longer
what I was.

— Mabel Segun

*Y*ou are growing and learning every moment of every
day. Regardless of what you have been told, you can and
do change with every new experience. Each experience
enhances your capabilities by giving you something new
to draw upon. Every new capability you discover and develop leads to a new opportunity. As long as you have the
capability and an opportunity, there is a new possibility
for you to grow and learn something new. Dare not to
limit yourself to only knowing or doing one thing. Take a
chance by putting all you know to use. Accept all invitations to do a new thing and when you do it, celebrate.
Move toward your wildest dream, take the labels off your
mind and step boldly into your greatness.

With every new step I create a new me.

One's work may be finished someday
but one's education, never.
— Alexandre Dumas, the Elder

Unless you make every waking a learning process, you are wasting a major portion of your life. You can learn from people you do not like as well as from those you love. You can learn from the elders and the youth. You can learn more about the things you know about and fine-tune the things you are good at. You can learn by observing, listening and serving. You can learn by assisting, completing and forgiving. Never withdraw from the education process by picking and choosing from who you can learn. Keep your mind open, your ears attuned and your willingness to learn in the humble state of a student.

I Am learning a little more every day.

The determination to outwit one's situation means
that one has no models, only object lessons.
—James Baldwin

*I*f you are facing a challenge in your life, before asking
someone else what to do, remember what you did the last
time. Nothing is new in life. Everything has been said or
done by you. It may look different. There may be new
people involved. It may even feel different, but it's not.
The key is to recognize the lesson. Ask yourself, "What
am I learning in this situation?" Is it patience? Peace?
Forgiveness? Independence? What am I feeling now?
Have I felt it before? What did I do then? Remember, no
one can learn your lessons but you. And the best teacher
you will ever have is experience.

*I Am divinely guided at all times and
I know exactly what to do.*

Education is your passport to the future,
for tomorrow belongs to the people
who prepare for it today.
— El-Hajj Malik El-Shabazz (Malcolm X)

*E*ducation is not limited to the classroom. It takes place in the kitchen, on the corner, as you ride or walk to any destination, when you listen or speak to others and in the silence of your bedroom. Education springs forth from books, songs, children, elders, women, men. It rises from victory, tragedy, joy and suffering. Education does not take place when you learn something you did not know before. Education is your ability to use what you have learned to be better today than you were yesterday. No matter how much you know or how you learn it, the ultimate goal of education is to give "you" greater insight to "yourself."

I Am educating the world about me.

March 7

You must live within your sacred truth.

—Hausa proverb

So much of our time, energy and attention is wasted trying to convince other people how wrong they are about us. We want them to know we are not ignorant, lazy heathens. We want them to retract the untruth that has been told. We try to convince them that we have a valid history, a rich culture and that our ancestors have made valuable contributions to the development of the world. We spend so much time trying to show them who we are not, we lose sight of who we really are. It is not our responsibility to prove to people who we are. Our job and responsibility is to "be." What you do is proof of who you are; manifestation is realization. People have a right to think whatever they choose to think. Just because they think it does not make it right.

I Am who I Am.

Sometimes the strong die, too!

—Louis Gossett, Jr.

*A*re you one of those people who is always there when somebody needs you? You know just what to say, exactly what to do to turn the worst situation into a conquerable challenge. Everybody calls on you. Everybody needs you. You are, after all, strong enough, smart enough, tough enough to make it through anything and everything. Well, who do the strong go to? Who do the strong lean on? Where do the strong go when they are not feeling very strong? When you set yourself up to be an anchor for everybody else, you jump ship on yourself! The need to be needed, the illusion that without us things would not get done, is actually the way we escape ourselves. The strong have needs. The strong have weaknesses! Sometimes those needs are so deep and painful that, rather than face them, the strong run away. When the strong take the weight of the world on their shoulders, they eventually break down. The question is, Who will be there for the strong?

*I take time for me, to do for me the same things
I do for others.*

If we stand tall it is because we stand on the backs of those who came before us.

— Yoruba proverb

As painful as it may be to accept, our ancestors were required to die as part of the evolution of the race. They died in order that our genius could be spread throughout the world. They died so that their energy would be shifted into the invisible, untouchable force that sustains life today. They died in order that we could stand in a new place, do new things and create a new order. We must stand tall knowing the power, strength and wisdom of the ancestors is as close as a breath. All that we ever need to be, to do, to know, to have is available. All we need do is take a stand.

I Am standing on a solid foundation.

Instead of wallowing in my misery,
I just made some changes.
—Stephanie Mills

*Y*ou can do something the same way for so long that you begin to do it without thinking. When you are not thinking about what you are doing, you may not recognize its harmful effects. Very often, the habit of doing a certain thing in a certain way robs you of new experiences. In order to learn to grow and be happy, you must always seek the new. Take a new route to work today. Eat lunch in a new environment. Speak to someone before they speak to you, or let them speak first. Try the radio instead of television. Bathe in the morning instead of at night. Be conscious of what you do, how you do it and be open to happy new experiences.

Today I Am willing to do it differently.

There are three kinds of people in the world: those who make things happen, those who watch things happen, those who wonder what happened.

—Unknown

I was thinking about it but . . . I was going to but . . . I want to but . . . I wish I could but. . . .These are the excuses we give for sitting on our butts. We tell ourselves we are waiting for something to happen. We tell ourselves something is missing. We tell other people we will do it, whatever it may be, but we never do. If you think what you need is not there, find it. If you cannot find it, make it. If you cannot make it, find someone who can. If you do not have the money to pay them to make it, get it done on credit. If you have no one to borrow from, ask someone else to borrow it for you. If you do not have credit, get some. If you cannot get credit, go out and do something that someone will pay you for so you can pay for what you need. There are no "buts" so big they cannot be moved. Once you move the "butt," everything else will follow.

I would sit here, but I have something to do.

The spirit indeed is willing, but the flesh is weak.
—Matthew 26:41

*T*here are many times in life when we want to do, know we should do, may even know what or how to do, but we don't. At these times we are relying on the body. We must realize that the body cannot move without the spirit. Spirit is the force behind all motion. No matter what situations we face in this world, spirit is always with us. That presence is always guiding, protecting, loving us—to ensure that we do the best. The love of spirit will inspire us and never abandon our needs. Spirit brings divine knowing and order so that we can express strength, peace and power in every situation. When we are fearful or feeling alone, we can turn within and affirm the love of spirit. We need never to rely on the physical body alone, for we are always in the mighty presence of spirit. Closer than breath, nearer than arms and feet, spirit will move the body when we ask and obey.

The guiding love of the spirit within conquers all without.

A man who stands for nothing will fall for anything.
—El-Hajj Malik El-Shabazz (Malcolm X)

*I*f you had to tell someone in ten words or less what you stand for in life, what would you say? It might be noble to speak of the liberation for all people of color, but what do you stand for? Perhaps you would take up the cause of starving or abused children, but what do you stand for? The freedom of political prisoners? Decent housing? Equitable distribution of food and natural resources? An end to all wars and warlike aggression? Or perhaps it's education? It is good, honorable and very noble to have a cause, but before you can do that, you must be able to stand on your own two feet. More battles are lost in this life to weary soldiers than are lost for lack of cause. What do you stand for? How about peace of mind, radiant health, truth and honesty, viable use of your God-given talents, gifts and abilities, or maybe just plain old love. When you are standing on well-cared-for and rested feet, you will be victorious in any cause.

I stand on the principle of me first.

God is as dependent on you as you are on Him.
— Mahalia Jackson

*O*ne good way to know whether something is working is to actually see it work. No matter what your philosophy, regardless how much you believe it, if it does not produce, it is worthless. God is the same way. We can talk about Him, sing about Him, pray to Him, for Him and about Him, but if His glory is not produced in our lives, what are we really saying? The only way for God to be seen is through our lives. Our lives must reflect all the things we say God is. We are His hands, feet, eyes and voice. Our lives reflect who and what God is. Are we living a happy life? Are we thinking peaceful thoughts? The only way for God to demonstrate who He is, is for us to do it for Him. We must demonstrate what we know about God in the way we think, talk, walk and live. God is peace. God is strength. God is mercy. God is forgiving. God is all knowing, all powerful, abundant, radiant life. God is love. To know God is to be like Him. All else is a figment of your imagination.

If I want to know who God is, I look at me.

Truth is more than a mental exercise.
—Thurgood Marshall

The human mind is always searching for truth. The mind guides us through books. It interprets our experiences. It limits us based on our exposure. The mind searches to find truth, not realizing that truth was never lost. Unfortunately, truth cannot reveal itself in a mind that is busy with personal chatter. That chatter refers to what you think we need or want and what you say. Unlike truth, your mental chatter may have nothing to do with what is real. The only way to find truth is to go deep within the self and to live from that consciousness and understanding. The truth is the reality of who you are from the inside out, and that is something we rarely think about. Truth is the joy of living, of being, of having a connection to everyone and everything, without thought or malice or condemnation of any part of you. Truth is the spirit of life.

I live in the light of truth.

If your spiritual philosophy is not moving you to the
state of peace, health, wealth and love your spirit
desires . . . you need a new spiritual philosophy.
—Sun Bear

What is your spiritual philosophy? Your life philosophy? Is it leading you to the places you want to go? Is it
moving you through the challenges and obstacles you
face? Is your spiritual philosophy yours? Or is it one that
was passed on to you? Is your philosophy creating the op-
timum conditions in your life? Your spiritual philosophy is
the way you approach life. It is the foundation upon which
you can stand at any time, in any situation, without fear of
falling or failing. If your spiritual philosophy leaves any
room for fear, lack, hate, intolerance, anger, pain or
shame, it may be time for a change.

I Am open and willing to change.

Although the face of God is before all people,
the fool cannot find it.
— *The Husia,* translated by Dr. Maulana Karenga

The Creator asks very little of you. He asks that you seek the truth and speak it when you find it. He asks that you treat your brother as you would be treated, forgiving what you need to be forgiven of. He asks that you honor your parents, discipline and value your children, trust and honor yourself as an expression of Him. When you look to anyone or anything as your road to God, you are on your way to being lost. "Seek ye first the kingdom and all things shall be added." The kingdom is your heart, free of hate, greed and lust. To find it, you must surrender your willfulness and listen to the quiet voice within.

I Am One with God.

Spiritual growth results from absorbing and
digesting truth and putting it to practice in daily life.
—White Eagle

When there is trouble or trauma, we have a tendency to become real spiritual. We pray, we say we believe and usually we collect the miracle we expect. Then we go back to being our normal human self, doing the same human things that got us into trouble in the first place. What we don't understand is that our issues in life are determined by our consciousness about life. It is only in our moments of despair that we surrender our humanness. We go to that higher force, higher consciousness that is within us all the time. It is quite possible for us to live from that higher place at all times. We would save ourselves a great deal of grief if we lived from the truth that we, as humans, can't do it. Yet through our higher consciousness we are the conduit. The higher consciousness moves us through racism, sexism, disease, poverty, fear and confusion. So why not make that a permanent residence.

I live, move and have by being
in a higher authority.

TRUTH

*A*re you living your truth? Is it based on your belief, in the deepest part of your heart? It is that thing you want to be, to do and have about which you rarely speak to anyone. It is that sacred place in your spirit that lets you know no matter what that you are really okay. Are you living your truth? Are you doing what brings you peace and joy? Are you smiling to yourself in the face of adversity, believing you are a divine creation of a loving Father and Mother? Are you beautiful and strong? Powerful and humble? Understanding and merciful? Intelligent and faithful? Protected and prayerful? Is your truth plainly clear and simplistic? Does it bring you the understanding that all is well without when all is well within? Are you living your truth all day, every day, when others tell you it is impossible, impractical, irrelevant and dumb? Is the truth of your being an expression of God? If not, are you really living?

Today I surrender to my truth
and live in its being.

March 20

Strategy is better than strength.
— Hausa proverb

On the busiest road leading to the village an old wise man sat watching a young man struggling to move logs. The young man sweated, panted and moaned. He called out to the old man, "Hey, aren't you going to help me get this work done?" The old man smiled and said "Yes" and continued to sit. A man passed by and greeted the old man with a smile. The old man asked, "As a favor to an old man, would you move a log?" The man complied, as did the second, the third and so on until all the logs were cleared from the old man's field. The young man saw this and rebuked the old man for being lazy. The wise man smiled and replied, "If you are in the right place, at the right time, using your assets, the work will get done."

I Am open to receive all help that comes to me.

I cry out with my whole heart.

—Psalm 119:145

Water purifies. Water nurtures. Water is the healing force of the universe. Water cleanses. Water corrodes. Water refreshes. It is the conduit of growth, protection and maintenance. Crying produces salt water. It purges, protects and expands the spirit. Crying is a release, a cleansing, an expression. However, we must learn to cry with an agenda. Are you crying to release, to purify, to cleanse? Are you angry, frightened, worried or elated? We may cry because of a particular situation, but there is underlying emotion we really need to express. When done properly crying brings clarity and healing to the body and spirit. It can be a refreshing experience, so do it as often as you like. The moment the tears start to flow, just write down your agenda.

When I cry with an agenda, my needs are met.

God makes three requests of his children:
Do the best you can, where you are,
with what you have, now.
— African-American folklore

There are no guarantees in life, but it is a sure thing that you will get back what you give. If you give 100 percent of your attention, energy and time to a thing, you will get exactly that back. Spending your time and attention focused on what you cannot do and do not have assures that more of the same will come. When you concentrate on lack, weakness, fault and blame, it is sure to become a reality. Nobody has everything, but everybody has something. Use what you have right now! Use it wisely, freely, with love. Wherever you are, use your time, energy and talents to do the best you can right now. Give no thought to what is missing. Spend no time wishing it were better. Make *sure* you give all that you have to make sure you will get all that you need.

I am giving my all right now.

When you stand with the blessings of your mother
and God, it matters not who stands against you.
— Yoruba proverb

*I*t is the African way to ask for the blessings of God in
everything you do. No child of African descent would attempt an undertaking without the blessings of his or her
mother. God and your mother work hand in hand. They
created you. They nurtured you. They are your first and
eternal teachers. Once God blesses you with the idea and
gives you the strength to carry it through, your mother
cannot help but want the best for you. If you cannot ask
your mother face-to-face, cry out for the blessings of her
spirit. When even that is not possible, stand firm and draw
your strength from the Mother Earth who will support
your good steps without question.

I Am blessed with the strength of God
and my mother.

It ain't that I don't believe in God,
I just don't trust his judgment.

— Terry McMillan, from *Mama*

*T*here are fifty-one ways to get help from God: (1) Ask for it; (2) Believe; (3) Recognize Help when it comes; (4) Listen; (5) Obey; (6) Love; (7) Praise; (8) Forgive; (9) Be Real; (10) Seek Truth; (11) Face Yourself; (12) Be Honest; (13) Order; (14) Understanding; (15) Silence; (16) Simplicity; (17) Purify; (18) Know; (19) Grace; (20) Joy; (21) Peace; (22) Trust; (23) Natural Law; (24) Balance; (25) Harmony; (26) Self-sufficiency; (27) Dream; (28) Self-discovery; (29) Right Thinking; (30) Right Action; (31) Right Reaction; (32) Breathe; (33) Shut Up; (34) Be Still; (35) Feel; (36) Live Now; (37) Friends; (38) Parents; (39) Children; (40) Openness; (41) Realization; (42) Relaxation; (43) Laugh; (44) Patience; (45) Give; (46) Cry; (47) Create; (48) Judge Not; (49) Oneness; (50) Faith; (51) Surrender. Living in and with the ways of God places you in alignment with the substance of God.

Help is on the way!

It is always there.

Whenever we need an answer it is there. No matter what the situation, our higher self knows exactly what is best for us. It is not a political, social or intellectual self; it is the core of our being. No matter how long it's been since we consciously communicated with it, the power within us remains steady. Two o'clock on a Saturday morning, it's there. Winter, summer, spring or fall, we've got the power. At the break of day or nightfall, we are guided and protected. There is within a source of light that does not keep a schedule, nine to five, Monday to Friday. It works overtime all the time. It doesn't matter whether we went to church last Sunday or if we haven't been since whenever, if ever. The spirit within is there for us, always. We just have to acknowledge it, praise it, thank it and know everything is all right now.

*The spirit is the one and
only active power in my life.*

God is always capable of making
something out of nothing.
—Minister Louis Farrakhan

"The earth was without form, and void . . ." (Genesis 1:2); today it is a multinational conglomerate. Remember when there was a void in your life, seemed to be no way up or out, and then suddenly a way was cleared. What about when you were down to your last dime and didn't know where the next one was coming from; it came from somewhere. When you were at your wits end, the wolves were on your heels and you had reached the end of your rope, somehow you rose above it and lived to talk, even to laugh about it. You may think you did it on your own, by yourself, without help from anyone, but you didn't realize where the help was coming from. So the next time you find yourself in need, ask, who can make something out of nothing?

I know who can fulfill my needs.

If you always do what you always did, you will always get what you always got.
— Jackie "Moms" Mabley

Can you imagine not doing what you're doing in your life right now, but doing something completely different? Something exciting, fun, even risky, like quitting your job and traveling around the world. Or working part-time and going to school full time to study scuba diving or basket weaving. Or owning your own home, business, plane or boat. If you can imagine it, why aren't you doing it? I'll tell you why. Because the moment you think about it, you think about all the reasons you can't. "How will I pay my bills?" "Who will take care of my family?" "Where will I get money?" "What will people say?" Well, here's another question for you: How do you ever expect to be happy or at peace if you stay where you are? If you don't allow yourself to dream, to dare, to move up, out, forward; how will you ever know what you are really capable of? Look at it this way, what's the worse that can happen? You could end up right where you started, doing exactly what you are doing.

Oh, what the heck, go for it anyway.

Progress means ease, relief, peace, less strife, less struggle and happiness.
—Sufi Hazarat Inayat Khan

*H*ow many times have you heard someone say, "That's just the way I am," or "I can't change." How about, "This is me, take it or leave it!" Oh, how we fight to hold on to what limits us. Don't we realize, if our way worked, it would be working. Can't we see that holding on to what "I am" keeps us from realizing who we are? It is natural to resist change. It is insane to fight against it. For some reason we believe if we have to change, there must be something wrong with the way we are. The issue is not right or wrong. The issue is working or not working. Everything must change. The best can always be better. The fast becomes fastest. The great becomes the greatest. When we make minor adjustments as we see they are needed, we save time and the expense of a major overhaul.

Behold, I do a new thing.

Where the mind goes, the behind follows.
—Randolph Wilkerson

Whatever situation you find your behind in today, your mind put it there. Your thoughts direct the flow of activity into and out of your life. Your mind can make you ill. Your mind will make you well. Your mind can strengthen your relationships. Your mind will chase all friends and suitors away. Your mind makes you wealthy. Your mind will keep you broke. Your scattered thoughts will create confusion. Dark thoughts will cast out creative light. Thoughts of fear bring negative experiences. Thoughts of enemies bring them to your door. At all times, in all situations, if you don't like where you find your bottom, change what's going on at the top.

I plant positive seeds
in the fertile soil of my mind.

After we fry the fat, we see what is left.

—Yoruba proverb

*R*eading it, saying it, preaching or teaching it does not make it work. The only way to do it is to:

1. Begin within, take quiet time alone.
2. Trust your head, follow your first thought.
3. Don't be fooled by appearances.
4. Plan prayerfully; prepare purposefully; proceed positively; pursue persistently.
5. Be willing to be wrong.
6. Be flexible.
7. Do the best you can where you are with what you have.
8. Be prepared.
9. See the invisible; feel the intangible; achieve the impossible.
10. Focus+Courage+Willingness to Work=Miracles.
11. Help somebody else.
12. When in doubt, *pray*.

I've got it now.

You cannot fix what you will not face.
—James Baldwin

The time has come for people of color to admit the role they play in their own condition. We have been disobedient to the laws of nature, the traditions of the ancestors and the will of God. We have allowed ourselves to remain in situations we know are unproductive out of fear, which is a result of our disobedience, violations of tradition and arrogance in the face of the laws of God. We blamed others for the things we do not do for ourselves. We have betrayed one another to acquire personal riches. We have behaved irresponsibly toward ourselves, have been unaccountable for ourselves, disrespectful toward ourselves by being disobedient and abandoning the word of God. What is God's will? Put the Creator first in all that we do. What is God's law? Do unto others as we would have them do unto us. What is God's word? Love thy brother and thy sister as you would love yourself. If we are to regain our stature in the world as a proud and mighty people, we must be obedient in following the traditions of the ancestors and we must adhere to the will, laws and word of God.

Today I Am obedient to the ways of God.

World

If you are making soup, you need many ingredients in order to get just the right taste. When you serve the soup, people will enjoy what you have been able to blend together. In some cases, a particular ingredient may stand out, but it cannot stand alone. Without everything else in the soup, that one ingredient would be insufficient. We are all ingredients in the soup of life. We contribute to the goodness and the flavor of the whole. As we move through the world, we must remember that we are an important ingredient and that what we do in life and with our life is important. We must blend with everything in our environment to get just the right flavor and texture we desire in life. If we try too hard to stand out, or fail to mix well, the flavor of life can be drastically altered.

April 1

As long as you can find someone else to blame for
anything you are doing, you cannot be held
accountable or responsible for your growth or the
lack of it.

—Sun Bear

*P*eople of color must stop blaming everyone else for their
current condition in the world. We cannot forget our history. We cannot forget the past. We know there are forces
that oppose us, but because they oppose us does not mean
they have won. We must stop believing what has been said
to and about us; we must take full responsibility for how
and what we are. Many people of color are afraid to look
at the lessons we must learn from the past. If we do not
learn the lessons, we will continue to repeat the class. We
have a reason to be angry; we have a reason to be afraid;
but there is absolutely no reason for us to remain where
we are. When we want to rise, we will. When we are
ready to grow, we can. The only thing holding us in place
right now are the things "we" do not do.

If I continue to blame them for where I've been,
I can only blame me for where I go.

We have to move beyond the mind-set of
powerlessness.
—Audrey Edwards

*H*ave you ever stopped to wonder why children do not concern themselves with all the problems in the world? They seem totally willing to believe that somehow, some way, everything will be fine, and somehow for them it is. Children do not have philosophical ideals, political positions or principles to uphold. They know what they know, they accept it and they never try to convince you that what they know is real. Children ask for what they want; they refuse to take no for an answer; and they know that if you say no, Grandma usually says yes. Children will try anything once. They will go anywhere that looks safe. They are not hung up on styles or profiles, positions and postures, power or powerlessness. Yet we believe children don't know, can't do, shouldn't have, can't be, won't make it without us. Isn't it a shame that we don't remember as adults that we are always children of God.

Today I Am a child again.

> Quickened together with him,
> having forgiven you all trespasses.
>
> —Colossians 2:13

*B*lack men must forgive Black women for doing what is necessary for the survival of the race. While it may appear that the women have been insensitive to and influenced away from the men, it has really been a matter of doing what was required at any given time. It is the nature of women to nurture and support. If that support looks like working in the big houses of the world, learning how to read and going to school, leaving the men to save the children, it was necessary at the time. Black men have an ancestral memory of anger, resentment, guilt, shame and fear directed toward their grandmothers, mothers and sisters. How can they feel good about their lovers and wives? They must forgive. Black men must forgive Black women for the things they have said and done, for the things they did not say and do. Black men cannot accept Black women with the memory of a wounded ego. They must first forgive. Black men must forgive not for the sake of the women, but to heal their souls.

Today I see all women through
forgiving eyes.

Black women must forgive Black men for
not being there to protect them.

—Suliman Latif

*E*tched into the memory of our being are the very painful memories of the past. What they feel like today are: "Black men are irresponsible." "Black men can't be trusted." "Black men are no good." Are we really talking about Black men today? Or are we remembering those of the past who were powerless to save our grandmothers from the events that have created the painful memories? Whether the memories are from yesteryear, last week or last night, Black women must individually and collectively forgive Black men. We must forgive our grandfathers and brothers, our husbands and sons. If we have anger for one Black man, we have anger toward them all. We must forgive Black men for leaving us; we must forgive them for the excuses they did not make. We must forgive Black men for the things they say; we must forgive them for the things they do not do. Forgiveness is the only way to free ourselves and our masculine complements from the atrocities committed against our mutual souls.

There is a place of forgiveness within me.
Today I lovingly share it with Black men.

You will never know who you are in the world until
you know thyself.
—Dr. John Henry Clarke

We are descendants of the parent race, Africans, trans-
ported to a new land. We are African-Americans, African-
Caribbeans, African-Latinos and Africans natively. Over
the course of the last twenty years we have become eager
to embrace our ancestral roots. That is good. It is not
good, however, that we continue to define our "African-
ness" in concepts foreign to us. We claim the music, dance,
art and clothing. Yet we become uncomfortable about dis-
cussing the so-called dark side of the motherland—rituals,
scarification, wearing leaves and animal skins, root medi-
cine, bones in the nose, animal sacrifice, plates in the lips
and tribalism. We shy away from what we have come to
understand is still unacceptable by other standards. We
must study ourselves, for ourselves. Until that time, it will
remain difficult, confusing and uncomfortable to accept or
reject the place we call "Mother."

From my darkness comes the light.

Intuition is the spiritual faculty that does not
explain, it simply points the way.
— Florence Scovel Shinn

Nia had been prepared to inherit the wise woman's
book. The old woman was the salvation and the backbone
of the entire village. She was wise. She was loved. But she
had become too old to carry out her duties. In return for
twenty-two years of training, Nia was to inherit the old
woman's key to life. The ceremony was long. The people
were many. The responsibility was great. Nia was prepared. She was eager to get started. She believed the book
would reveal the answers to all of life's questions. It required two strong men to carry the book to her chamber.
When they placed it on her table, she quickly waved them
away. The book was solid gold, trimmed with emeralds,
rubies and sapphires. In the middle of the front cover sat a
seven-carat diamond. Nia's heart was pounding. Her
mouth had gone dry. With her eyes closed, she fondled the
cover of the book. The time had come to open it. She was
about to learn life's secret. She opened to the middle of the
book. She looked down at the page. Nia had inherited a
book of mirrors.

The storehouse of abundance
is already mine.

Our greatest problems in life come not so much from the situations we confront as from our doubts about our ability to handle them.

—Susan Taylor

*I*t makes perfectly good sense to get directions when you are traveling to a new place. Culture and heritage are directions that will help you move forward. You have a rich culture and a powerful heritage. Yet we forget that our ancestors built the world, healed the sick and educated the ignorant. Why should we forget the African minds, bodies and spirits of the past who paved the way into today? We must accept and understand that they didn't do it "because" they were Africans; rather, they were Africans and they knew how. Culture is a rock in a hard place, and we know the Africans knew a great deal about rocks. Let us stand on the knowing of our ancestors, remembering the heritage of the people, the traditions of the family and the wisdom and strength they used to make it through the rough days.

I know what the ancestors would do.

Every time I had the good fortune to research into someone's religion I found "God" to be in the image of the people to whom the religion belongs.
— Yosef Ben-Jochannon

Would the Creator, with all the love, power and wisdom of the universe, make us all so different and then deem only one right way to get to His kingdom? I would think not. As an expression of the awesome power of the ultimate creative energy, we the people have been blessed to bring forth various expressions. We call it race, culture, tradition and heritage. In essence, who we are collectively is a unique expression of God. No one knows better than He the beauty we bring to life, and He cannot be wrong. As we lift our minds and hearts to know, to be aware and to understand that we are all expressions of the Most High, we will begin to recognize the beauty of God at our disposal. Our world reflects God's strength as tradition, God's wisdom as culture, God's love as race and ethnicity. Who are we to decide which part of God is the best?

God's strength, wisdom, power and love are being expressed as me.

A strong man masters others. A truly wise man masters himself.
— *The Wisdom of the Taoists*

There are so many scars inside of people of color, it is incredible that we survive. Scars from childhood memories. Scars from dreams deferred. Scars from words, incidents and our judgments of them. We cover the scars with personality, habits and, sometimes, drugs, sex and alcohol. We take our wounded souls into the world and pretend that we are not hurt. Yet every time we are confronted with an event similar to the one that caused the scars, the wounds are reopened. There can be no healing in our external world until we give intensive care and healing to our internal wounds. We may think we do not know what to do. We do. We must first admit that the wounds exist. We must be willing to examine them, touch them and expose them to ourselves. Then we must wrap them in the most potent antiseptic there is — love.

Today I will nurture my wounds with love's light.

April 10

Until you free yourself from the final monster in the jungle of your life, your soul is up for grabs.

—Rona Barrett

Many of us do not realize we have a problem because the way we live is a reflection of what we have lived with. There are men who don't know they are abusive. There are women who do not know they are being abused. There are people who don't know how to take care of themselves. There are people who believe just getting by is fine. There are children who think it is okay that they are not nurtured. There are people who do not know how to ask for what they need. There are people who fall down and never try to get up. There are people who get up by stepping on the people who fell down. Each one of us believes we are fine just the way we are, so we make no effort to get better. If the world and how it works is a reflection of the people who live in it, what will it take for us to realize we have a lot of work to do?

Today I will take a long, hard look at me.

We are the children of those who chose to survive.
— Nana Poussaint in *Daughters of the Dust*

*I*f you have ever doubted your ability to survive, look at who you came from. Don't limit yourself to parents and grandparents, go all the way back to the root. In your family line is the genius of those who were born into a barren land and built the pyramids. In the oasis of your mind is the consciousness of those who charted the stars, kept time by the sun and planted by the moon. In the center of your being is the strength of those who planted the crops, toiled in the fields and banqueted on what others discarded. In the light of your heart is the love of those who bore the children who were sold away only to one day hang from a tree. In the cells of your bloodstream is the memory of those who weathered the voyage, stood on the blocks, found their way through the forest and took their case to the Supreme Court. With all of that going for you, what are you worrying about?

I move in the power of a mighty past.

Rather than face how bad I truly felt about me, I stuffed myself with stuff, puffed myself up with a false sense of power and importance.

— Patti Austin

Many people of color believe they are lacking something. We have been programmed to feel that way. We are taught we lack good looks. We are led to believe we lack intelligence. We are educated in a system that denies our history, culture and traditions. How are we expected to feel complete? We are not! We are, however, expected to look good on the outside. We do. We dress up to hide our inner feelings of inadequacy. We are led to believe that if we have a home, a car, a few jewels and nice clothes we have enough to matter. It doesn't work! In order for people of color to thrive rather than survive, to flourish rather than make it, to stand tall rather than just stand up, we must individually and collectively get rid of the stuff and get to the core—what does it really feel like to be a person of color?

*I Am in touch with my feelings
about who I am.*

We are living in a world where your color matters
more than your character.

—Sister Souljah

*P*eople want you to believe that color doesn't matter. It shouldn't, but it does. We cannot get away from the color question. The question is, who does it matter to? Does it matter to you that you come from a rich tradition of proud people who believe in self-determination? Does it matter to you that your ancestral culture is based on a spirit of support and respect? Does it matter to you that you are genetically coded for genius, thereby rendering you capable of realizing physical, intellectual and spiritual perfection? Does it matter to you that you are the keeper of a legacy of worldwide accomplishments? Does it matter to you that you have the God-given right, by virtue of your color, to glorify, magnify and fortify the legacy that you have inherited as a descendant of the first doctors, chemists, agriculturists, astronomers, astrologers, artisans, teachers and spiritual masters? Or does it matter only to those who tell you what you cannot do because of your color?

I really do matter.

April 14

You must act as if it is impossible to fail.
— Ashanti proverb

*T*he truth is that we start from a position of success. No matter what happens, no matter what the appearance, we are always successful. The truth is that we have lessons to learn through our experiences. What appears as a failure is simply a stepping-stone to realizing success. The truth is that we can do anything we focus our mind to do. What looks like failure teaches us what not to do, what does not work. It sends us back to the drawing board. It forces us to refocus, and redo. All circumstances in the physical world are subject to change. The truth, however, is consistent. It never changes. The truth is that, as long as we are breathing, we are one with God. God never fails. Our job is to act like we know.

Victory is the stuff I am made of.

In a moment of decision, the best thing you can do
is the right thing to do. The worst thing you can
do is nothing.

—Theodore Roosevelt

*W*e always want to do the right thing, but we do the
wrong thing when we do not make a decision about what
to do. Decisions have power. Decisions have force. They
usually take us to the exact place we need to be, exactly
the way we need to get there. It is the wavering back and
forth that is dangerous. It places us at the mercy of events;
we fall prey to the choices people make for us. Since time
and opportunity wait for no one, our lives will not stand
still until we figure out what to do. The rightness of a decision is based on our ability to make the decision. When we
weigh what we want against what we will have to do, a decision can be an effortless event. We must know what we
will and will not do, what we can do and choose not to do;
and decide in harmony with the things we know. The freedom from making a decision can only come after we have
made the decision.

Today I decide to be free from all decisions.

April 16

Your world is as big as you make it.
—Georgia Douglas Johnson

*G*uess what? You are not the worst person in the world! Sure, you've made some bad judgment calls, taken some pretty foolish chances, created some awful situations, but you give yourself too much credit. Others have done far worse. Then there are those people who haven't done anything to anybody—ever. They are quiet. Go unnoticed. They have flawless characters and records. But you know what? They haven't done anything for themselves either. They are probably just as, if not more, miserable and confused as you. Think about it this way: The future will be what you make it today. Whether you are a doer or a nondoer, you must work on your future. If you've made a mess, clean it up. If you are afraid to take a chance, take one anyway. If you've done things that didn't work, do something else. If you have done nothing, do something. What you don't do can create the same regrets as the mistakes you make. In the long run, either you must happen to life, or it will never happen for you.

Step by step, I Am getting better and better.

When the shoe fits, we forget about the feet.
—*The Wisdom of the Taoists*

Many of us look at life as work. We approach it and try to handle it like a job. We complain about it. We blame others when it is not working. We hold someone else responsible when it does not give us what we want. Some of us give up on life. We move from day to day, with no plan, no goals and ultimately no rewards. We fail to understand that if life is work, the better we do it, the better it will pay us. When we perform our tasks to the very best of our ability we receive just rewards for what we do. When we are thorough in our work and put our best into it, we become better at it. When we become too good for where we are, we will be advanced to our rightful place. The things we must realize about life is it cannot be better until we are better. We cannot get more until we are more. The only thing that can stop our advancement in life is our not being ready to move. If life is work, run it like a multimillion-dollar corporation and elect yourself chief executive officer.

The better I Am at life the better it gets.

Life has to be lived, that's all there is to it.
— Eleanor Roosevelt

*L*et's be honest, we don't really want to work at life. Work is hard. Work is tiring. We want to have fun. We want to play! We want to have a good time and have all the things we want. Why not play the game of life? We are the dealers. We hold all the cards. Somewhere along the line, somebody cheated us. They told us we were needy, helpless and dependent. That is baggage. We must put it down in order to deal ourselves a good hand. We must also know the rules. We must play fairly, dealing with everyone the way we want to be dealt with. We must expect to win. If we entertain failure at any point, we lose. When we play, we must be on the lookout for fouls. When we see a foul, we must call it. We don't have to fix it, but we must call it. The final and most important rule is that we must follow all the rules, all the time.

When I play by the rules, I win.

In the province of the mind, what one believes to be
true either is true or becomes true.

—John Lilly

What do you believe about the world. Do you believe it
is big and beautiful? Or that it is dangerously doomed?
Do you believe there are people out there waiting to get
you? What do you think they will do with you when they
get you? Do you believe you can't because they won't let
you? Do you believe you can because nobody can stop
you? Do you believe in choices or in the power of destiny?
Do you believe in evil? Do you believe you are free? Do
you believe that someday, somehow you will be what and
where you want to be? Do you believe that someone else
has more power than you? How much power do you believe you have? What you believe will come true whether
it is good or not so good. What you believe about the
world is exactly what you will experience because that is
what "you" bring into the world.

The world as I see it is a reflection of my thoughts.

The one who asks questions doesn't lose his way.
—Akan proverb

*B*ecause we don't want to seem stupid, uninformed or feel belittled, we don't like to ask questions. For some reason, we think we are supposed to know everything. When we don't, we don't let anyone know. Questions are not a sign of ignorance. They are an indication that you are broadening your scope, sharpening your skills, improving your capabilities. Inquiries indicate humility, the willingness to serve, share and support. Questions keep you on track, define and broaden your boundaries and remove limitations. Questions put you in touch and keep you in touch. Questions create and build resources, both natural and human, which can be very useful when there is no one around to answer your questions. Your ego, the nasty little voice that is overconcerned with what other people think, will tell you not to ask questions. Tell ego to shut up and then ask what you need to know.

Who? What? Where? When? How? Why?

April 21

The cost of liberty is less than
the price of repression.
—W. E. B. DuBois

*R*epression of your will and desire are the cornerstones
of stress. When you believe or are led to believe you are
unable to act upon the greatest desires of the soul, the result is mental and spiritual enslavement. The price you
pay for your enslavement is your self-dignity, self-respect
and self-esteem. To be free, you must acknowledge your
personal liberty as the God-given right it is. You must be
willing to take a stand for yourself. When you stand, you
must be responsible for yourself. Liberty is the God-given
right to declare who you are and to pursue what you want.
If you surrender that right, you repress yourself.

I Am the only one who can limit me.

The bell rings loudest in your own home.

— Yoruba proverb

*A*s you look around the community, society, the world, you probably see many things you would like to change. Injustice, inequality, hatred and poverty probably disturb you. You may be angered by the lack of respect and insensitivity to people and their needs. You want to speak out and sometimes strike out to make the changes happen, but don't forget that God works from the inside out. You must first look within yourself to eliminate the fear, the anger, the imbalance in your life. Then and only then can you move forward to create peacefully and powerfully the changes needed in the world.

The world I want begins within me.

It is far better to be free to govern or misgovern
yourself than to be governed by anybody else.
—Kwame Nkrumah

*W*hen you look at the world, it is very easy to see what
is not being done for you. When your needs are not met,
when your interests are not being served, there is a tendency to complain. If the one entrusted to serve, protect
and guide you promotes his own interests above yours,
you learn to do for yourself. It matters not what experience you lack. Your interests will guide you. Give no concern to what they say you cannot do. Be willing to accept
the challenge. Do not be afraid to question the process.
New systems are born from the questioning of the old.
Take time to retreat to that quiet place within the pit of
your soul and unleash your right to decide what is best
for you.

I Am the source of my own governance.

Men build institutions . . . so that four hundred years later their descendants can say, "That's what he left."

—Na'im Akbar

*F*rederick Douglass warned us many years ago that as long as we are not the direct beneficiaries of the fruits of our labor, we will remain slaves. There is something insidious about a contentment with working "for" someone throughout your life. Silently it says, "You need me." It is imbedded in your consciousness, "You can't do without me." Eventually you believe, "I'm not capable of taking care of myself." Eventually you stop trying. The world needs the kind of institutions men of color can build. Whether it is a business to be managed, a school to be staffed, a publication to be circulated, an organization to be advanced or a service to be carried out, men want more from the world than a gold watch and a fond memory.

I am building more than a nest egg.

April 25

Fewness of words, greatness of deeds.
—Abdul Baha

What are you waiting for? With all you say you want, there is:

A dream for you to follow;
A goal for you to set;
A plan for you to make;
A project for you to begin;
An idea for you to act on;
A possibility for you to explore;
An opportunity for you to grab;
A choice for you to make.

If not, you shouldn't have anything to talk about.

Today I will make it my business
to say less and do more.

April 26

You must realize what is actually going on before
you can effectively deal with it.

— Ralpha

When our fears, weaknesses and views about life are colored by low self-esteem or lack of self-worth, we are restricted. It seems as though we have a road map that leads to nowhere. What we don't always realize is that we have created the road. It is a reflection of what we think about ourselves. We measure the future by the errors of the past. We make agreements with ourselves or others, which we do not keep. We surround ourselves with people and situations that degrade, devalue and limit us. Then we question why we have no confidence. No matter what race we are or what other people think or say about us, the first limitations we must overcome are those we place on ourselves.

New patterns of living are open to me.

I cannot win anything until I am willing
to lose everything.

—Kennedy Schultz

*F*or some reason, we believe struggle is noble. We think it brings special rewards or that the God force is pleased with us when we struggle. Struggling people have so much to do and say about the things they are struggling with that they hardly have time to get anything done. Struggling people know how to struggle well. They know what to wear, where to go and how to behave in a way that will undoubtedly create more struggle. Struggling people impose conditions, restrictions and expectations upon themselves, because it is easier to struggle doing nothing than it is to bring up and use the creative force within. Struggling people love to sacrifice in the name of the struggle. They sacrifice themselves, their families and if you are not careful, they will sacrifice you. God does not ask us to struggle. What we are told is, "Come up to Me all ye that labor and I will give ye rest."

I ain't gonna struggle no more.

You can't solve the problem because
you don't know what it is.

—*A Course in Miracles*

*D*oes it ever seem that as soon as you solve one crisis, another pops up? What about the way you think about the challenges in your life? Do you think it's money, or the lack of it? When you get the money together, the kids or maybe the spouse act up. As soon as they calm down, it's the job or the car or the pipes in the basement. You can spend the better part of your life putting out little brush-fires with your teakettle without ever realizing there is a forest fire burning in your life. By now you should have realized you cannot solve the problems in your life. No matter how hard you try, you cannot do it. Want to know why? It is because you think you are in control when you really aren't. There is a divine source, a powerful force, a perfect order that controls everything. When you recognize it, acknowledge it and surrender to it, you won't have to struggle to solve problems. There won't be any.

The universe will perfect that which concerns me
when I surrender control.

Identification with an organization or a cause is no
substitute for self-realization.
— Swami Rudrananda

*P*eople of color have many causes to battle, confront and
overcome—or so we think. We keep bringing up causes
and creating organizations to address them; however,
most of us take very little time to look at ourselves.
Throughout history there have been a myriad of physical
and spiritual forces that have drained us. Yet when we feel
drained we try to keep busy. We find a cause to work on
or a group to join, taking our drained, imbalanced energy
along. Self-realization requires that we break down everything we identify with in order to understand where we
are and how we feel about being there. We must free ourselves from all encumbrances in order to look within and
discover the mental and spiritual freedom that is our
birthright. When we are free from cause identification and
organizational duty, we will know for sure exactly who we
are and where we should be. Self-realization puts us back
in touch with our first cause, the self.

Anything I hang on to will get in my way.

When you are down and out lift up your head and shout, "I'm outta here!"

—Lynette Harris

I'm outta here! It really is just that simple. There comes a point in life when you get tired of feeling, doing and looking bad. When that time comes, you move on instantly. I'm outta here is an affirmation. A statement of truth. It gives power to your decision to no longer be where you are physically, mentally and emotionally. I'm outta here puts the world on notice that you have a commitment to be better, do better, have more than you have right now. Debt—I'm outta here! Make a budget and payment plan. Stick to it. Illnesses—I'm outta here! Take responsibility, not pills, for what ails you. Find out what you are doing that is not good for you and stop. Lousy job—I'm outta here! Figure out what you like to do, want to do and what you are good at and do it. Struggle—I'm outta here. Do not beat up on yourself. Do not criticize yourself. Above all, do not limit yourself. Pick yourself up. Put yourself on a path and let yourself know—

I'm outta here!

For unto whomsoever much is given,
of him shall much be required.

—Luke 12:48

*H*ave you ever wondered why certain people are expected to do things a little faster or better than everyone else? The simple answer is because they can. Have you ever wondered why you are expected to do the impossible, achieve the unattainable or overcome the insurmountable? Very simply because you can. You know how you can just look at somebody and know they can do it? Well, the exact same thing is true about you. Unfortunately, we are not always aware of just how magnificent we are. The same light others see shining blinds us about ourselves. We become content being like everyone else when something inside tells us we are not. But we plod along being angry or bitter when others expect us to do what they cannot. The key is not to do what others do and say; it is to know we can, believe we can and do what we can to the best of our ability. If we know what to expect from ourselves, we will always live up to our greatest expectation.

I am expecting as much as I can because I can.

May 2

LENT—Let's Eliminate Negative Thinking.
—Earl Nightingale

When you think negatively, you attract negativity. That is the awesome power of the mind. When you confront the world with negative thoughts, you will have experiences to confirm what you are thinking. Thought to experience, that is the process. It is not the other way around. What you believe people and the world are doing to you is actually a reflection of what your thoughts are drawing to you. If you want to free yourself from the harshness of the world, clear harsh thoughts from your mind. Clear anger with forgiveness, confusion with orderly thinking. Clear restriction with an open mind, violence with peaceful thoughts. Clear denial with acceptance, hate with thoughts of love. When you clear what you do not want from the recesses of your mind, it will miraculously disappear from your life.

I will think negativity out of my way.

No man can serve two masters . . . or else he will
hold to the one, and despise the other.

— Matthew 6:24

*Y*ou cannot love while hating, progress while oppressing, come together in disunity, build while tearing down, join while separating, understand while not listening, give while withholding, create while destroying, overcome while in fear. It is simply impossible! People of color must make a choice: Either we accept what we believe others are doing to us, or reject it and do something else. If we love each other as a foundation for our own progress, we do not have to worry about others hating us or our hating them back. If we work with everyone for human good, giving what we can to create what we want, we will not be disturbed by what anyone attempts to keep from us. If we stand on the faith of our ability to survive, it does not matter who is out to destroy us. If we celebrate, support and nurture ourselves, we will not need anyone else to do it for us.

Today I will feel one thing at a time.

You can be so heavenly bound until you
are no earthly good.
— Dr. Oscar Lane

*W*e can find so many reasons to postpone doing and receiving our good:

> "It's not the right time."
> "If it's for me, I'll get it."
> "I'm waiting for a sign."
> "I'll do it later."
> "I'll receive my rewards in heaven."
> "I guess it's not for me."
> "I didn't want it/need it anyway."

These are just a few of the ways we convince ourselves not to follow our dreams. The belief in a hereafter paved with gold is no reason to live in poverty now. "As above, so below" means whatever we can have later, we can have right now. If heaven is a place prepared for kings and queens, we want to do our work on earth so we won't show up looking and acting like paupers.

There is no earthly reason for me
to delay my good.

When the door is closed, you must learn to slide
across the crack of the sill.

— Yoruba proverb

*H*uman beings are creatures of habit. We do what we know, what is comfortable and what we "think" will work. There are, however, those occasions when "our" way is not "the" way to get us to the goal. When your way doesn't work, don't be disheartened. You must be willing to try another way. Don't be discouraged when someone says, "no." Be willing to ask someone else. Always be willing to start at the bottom. Being willing does not mean you will stay there. A closed door does not mean you have been cut off permanently. It is a challenge, an obstacle, a tool to be used. The keys to all doors are within you. If you have faith in yourself, practice and patience will make you a master locksmith.

*I Am willing to do it by any means honorable
and necessary.*

Faith without work cannot be called faith.
— *The New Open Bible*

Faith must inspire action. It alone cannot be verbal. Mental faith is insufficient. Faith is not believing, trying or hoping. It is the knowing by which you do. Faith develops endurance to face the trials without being tempted to stop. Faith produces doers. Those who understand fewness of words, greatness of deeds are a measure of true faith. Faith is obedience to the urgings of the spirit, the porthole through which all things have their being. Faith controls the tongue, soothes the head and stifles the lust to complain. Faith produces patience. Your life is the only true measure of your faith. Your words and actions determine the fullness of your cup. If there is anyone or anything of unworthiness in your life you must ask yourself, "To what am I giving my faith?"

*I put my faith in only those things that
produce good for me.*

TRUST

*H*ave you ever worried whether there would be enough air for you to breathe? How often do you ponder what you would do if the laws of gravity ceased to operate? For some reason, you never worry about the very essential elements you need to stay alive. You just trust they will be there, and they are. You trust that your heart will beat, your blood will flow, your lungs will expand and that you will stay firmly planted on the earth. You trust that every organ within you will do exactly as it should. You trust that your body will support you. Why not extend that trust to every area of your life. Trust that the universe and Creator will provide everything that you need without any effort on your part. All you ever need do is ask and trust.

As I trust, my needs are met.

You must eat the elephant one bite at a time.

— Twi proverb

You cannot get to the end from the middle. You won't find the beginning at the end. No matter what we are doing, there is a process. Whether the situation is positive or negative, we must go through the process. When we rush ahead we miss important steps. If we become impatient, we can overlook details. We must be willing to move step by step, inch by inch to get to the end. There is no way to rush the process. When we are excited, we want to see how a situation will end. When the situation is unpleasant, we want it to end quickly. Whether anxiety or fear, the anticipation of benefits or pain, no matter what we do, we must be willing to do it one step at a time.

An inch is a cinch, a yard is hard.

That my joy might remain in you,
and that your joy might be full.

—John 15:11

Waiting for a particular turn of events is a good way to lead yourself into disappointment. Depending on anyone to make you happy, make you feel good or lift your spirit is a sure way to place yourself in isolation. When your joy is dependent on people and conditions, it is restricted. Joy must spring forth from you before it can surround you. Joy must be the way you walk and the way you speak to those who come into your realm. Joy is knowing you are doing what you can, the best you can, and you are feeling good about it. Joy is knowing time is on your side and wherever you are, you are the joy. Joy is taking a moment to say thank you, a day to do for self and an energy of sharing what you have. Joy is not what happens to you; it is what comes through you when you are conscious of the blessing you are.

I Am the source of joy.

Grandma's hands used to issue out a warning,
baby don't you run so fast, there might be
snakes in that grass . . .

— Bill Withers

*W*e cannot rush the sunrise or pay to bring on the full moon. Winter knows exactly when to turn into spring, and nothing can coax the grass to come up before it's ready. As we move through life, we must accept that everything will happen when it is supposed to happen. Accepting that will teach us patience. Days and nights whiz by. Frenzied minds, pressured people come and go. Worry, anxiety and fear do not concern the laws of nature. Nature knows that destiny takes its time. The key to patience is trusting the inner presence that knows exactly what you need. That inner presence allows everything to unfold divinely at just the right time. Be patient and trust you will get exactly what you want, especially if the "great" grandmothers have anything to say about it.

I wait patiently on my good.

Spirit works on a full-time basis.

*L*ife requires that we spend parts of our time doing certain things. We work sometimes, go to school at times; we are children or parents and friends part-time. The one area of life that cannot be addressed on a part-time basis is the spiritual life. To be a part-time Christian, Buddhist, Muslim or anything else results in "a house divided against itself," which cannot stand. The spiritual house is the mind, and it requires constant care. Spiritual conviction is the manner in which the house is run. When you have a spiritual conviction, it will serve you in all situations, all day, every day, in every way. The same spirit that guides your family life must also run your social life. If you turn to spirit for financial guidance, you must also ask for professional guidance. If you let spirit pick your friends, you must trust it to pick your mate. Part-time spirituality creates inner turmoil, indecision, confusion and stagnation. Once we let spirit take over full time, we will find life is more enjoyable and peaceful than we ever thought possible.

I let go and let spirit guide me
every day in every way.

Pride that you express to others is ego. Pride that
you express silently to yourself is real pride.
—Stuart Wilde

*W*hen you are proud of yourself, you show it, you feel it
and you know it. It shines in your eyes, the way you speak
and the way you carry your very being. You are proud because you could and you did, you can and you will, you
cannot but you know it, and it is still okay. When you are
proud you do, give and share rather than take, talk and
promise. Pride is peaceful service, joy-filled sharing, inner
knowing that there is more to come. Pride does not argue
to be right, push to get ahead, step over others to get there
and forget them once it does. Pride is gentle, calm and balanced. It is not boastful, frightened or hurried. Pride is
pleasant. Pride is grateful. Pride is peaceful, patient and
poised. Pride is secure. Pride is mastery, but most of all,
pride is silent.

*I am gently, calmly, silently proud of me
and what I Am.*

I am not a special person. I am a regular person who
does special things.

—Sarah Vaughan

*M*ost of us want to be singled out, patted on the back
and rewarded for what we do. It may never happen; however, that does not mean what we do is not valuable or
worthy of recognition. No one is special in God's eyes. We
are all provided with the ability to do. What we have not
been taught is to do good just for the sake of doing it,
without pursuing rewards or recognition. When you do
what you can for the sake of doing it, the reward is an improvement of the skills. When you use what you know to
do what you can and someone else benefits, that is recognition. We all have a need to be appreciated for the contributions we make to the world. We must learn to recognize
our own value before the world can respond to our needs.
Some of us will plant the seed and never see the plant.
Some of us will harvest the crop without knowing the
planter. Some of us will eat the plant, paying someone else
to prepare it. When the process is complete we will all be
rewarded, recognizing how special the process has been
to all.

I do my part.
I Am rewarded when others do theirs.

The ego needs recognition.
The spirit does not need to thank itself.
— Stuart Wilde

*T*he ego wants to be noticed. It needs stroking, pumping up and limelight. The ego needs to compete just to prove it is better. It senses danger around every corner, difficulty in every challenge and trouble coming through everyone. The ego can never be enough, do enough or have enough. The goal of the ego is to be well liked and authorized because, for some reason, it does not feel qualified. The spirit is qualified by light. The light of truth, peace, joy and love. It does not seek to condemn, condone or compromise what it is. It simply knows and is it. The spirit does what it can and moves on to something else. It does not ask for an award or wait for rewards, it is just spirit being spirit. One of the difficult problems in the world is the competition of egos. They want to be noticed and applauded so they compete and dominate. When we truly understand that we are spiritual beings, we will no longer have a need for recognition. We will do what we can because we can do it by virtue of the light of spirit.

Today I will go unnoticed.

With your hands you make your success, with your
hands you destroy success.

—Yoruba proverb

*T*he key to success is not what you do, it is how you feel
about what you are doing. It is possible to take a simple
idea and create a huge success. We think people who accomplish this work hard or have others to support them.
We believe they are smarter, richer or in some way more
endowed than we are. What we cannot see and do not
measure is people's attitudes about what they do. Success
begins with a positive attitude; it is the most valuable asset
we may own. The people at the top did not fall there. They
were willing to do whatever it took, taking the ups and the
downs, asking for what they really wanted and staying focused until they got it. Success is not bought or inherited.
It is a product of what we put out. Success begins with a
good feeling about where we are and a positive attitude
about where we want to be.

*My success is worth the effort of a positive mind
and a genuine smile.*

When you don't have a grip on life, it will definitely get a grip on you.

—Jewel Diamond-Taylor

*L*ife is:

> *A mystery, Unfold it.*
> *A journey, Walk it.*
> *Painful, Endure it.*
> *Beautiful, See it.*
> *A joke, Laugh at it.*
> *A song, Sing it.*
> *A flower, Smell it.*
> *Wonderful, Enjoy it.*
> *A candle, Light it.*
> *Precious, Don't waste it.*
> *A gift, Open it.*
> *Love, Give it.*
> *Unlimited, Go for it.*
> *Light, Shine in it.*

I Am all that life is.

Ain't gonna let nobody turn me around . . .
—African-American spiritual

Some mornings we wake up feeling good, ready to go out and take on the world and "be" a great day. But on other days we wake up to a grayness that makes the whole world seem depressing. On those dark days we need to remember: "Every day is a blessing to behold." We must realize that the attitude with which we greet the day says a great deal about what the day will be like. We make our days pleasant or miserable. If we insist on being miserable, irritable and nasty, more than likely the day will give us exactly what we give it. When we start the day with a spirit of joy, openness, peace and love, we put the universe on alert, we want more of the same. A day is too valuable to waste on misery and unhappiness. Even misery cannot stand up to a happy face and heart.

Today is a great day full of great people and events.

> Examine the labels you apply to yourself.
> Every label is a boundary or limit you
> will not let yourself cross.
>
> —Dwayne Dyer

*Y*ou are first of all a human. That gives you a certain amount of power. You are not limited in how you express your humanness; you are limited by the labels you choose to describe it. Men do this, Women do that . . . Blacks like one thing, Asians like the other . . . Native Americans are proud, Latinos are rowdy. These views and labels limit the self and set up expectations from others. You are never too old or too young, rich or poor, too much of a man or woman to think. You can be anything and everything you think you can be when you don't think yourself into a book. You must keep reminding yourself that you are more than a body. You are more than an image. You are more than the things you have told yourself about your-self. You are a spirit expressing as a human being. And that, my dear, is unlimited.

I Am a no-name brand of human being.

Help your friends with the things that you know,
for you know these things by Grace.
— *The Maxims of Ptahhotpe*

*A*t a time when unity is so desperately needed it is significantly lacking. Misunderstandings about basic philosophical differences place people on opposite poles. Competition for perceived limited resources separates people along racial, social and gender lines. The need to be right and feel supported separates us from those who hold different views and opinions. Our internal obstacles and external oppositions create a debilitating conflict and limit the coming together of the people of the world. If each of us would take the time to examine our feelings, we would see that "they" are right, too. The nature, experiences and perceptions of individuals help mold the ideals they hold. If we could remember and respect this right for everyone, we could avoid open confrontations. There are so many causes and issues in the world and so many ways to approach them, it is unlikely we will all agree on one way. Unity does not mean we will all believe in or do the same thing. It means we will agree to do something without battling over how and why.

All roads lead to the end.

Natural beauty comes in all colors, strength in many forms. When we learn to honor the differences and appreciate the mix, we're in harmony.

—Unknown

Spiritually, we are all family. We are mother, father, brother, sister and children of one another. As spiritual family we are inseparable. We all breathe the same air that is connected to the same Source; we are all connected to the same Source by the rhythm of breath. Just like a family, we will have our differences, yet we can be different and still be a family. Just like a family, we will have our rebels and outcasts, but we must still include them in the family circle. Just as a family sits and eats together, we must make certain that there is enough for everyone. Just as a family comes together and shares, we must stop holding back and taking away from the family. Blood may be thicker than water, but it is the water of life that will keep us connected. As we learn to see each other through our spiritual eyes, the physical differences will cease to matter.

Today I will honor all of my relations.

I am the one whose mouth is pure and whose hands are clean.
— *The Book of Coming Forth by Day*,
translated by Dr. Maulana Karenga

As we pass through the sea of life, we meet many types of fish. Mud fish sling dirt in order to keep themselves clean. Guppies have big mouths that are always moving, but guppies are always being eaten up by bigger fish. Barracudas knock you out of the way, get in the way and never go away. Eels slither around on their bellies, eating what others leave behind. They do nothing for themselves, so they want what you have. Crabs move from side to side. Today they are on your side, the next day they are not. Flounder have both eyes on one side of their heads. They can only see things one way. Crayfish move backward. Sea horses eat their own. Whales blow air out of the tops of their heads. Sharks attack all other fish. Angel fish float around with no idea of what is going on. Then there are the salmon. They always swim upstream; and no matter how far they swim, they never forget how to come home.

I know who I am in the sea of life.

The bumblebee's wings are so thin and its body so big, it should not be able to fly. The only problem is, the bee doesn't know that.

—David Lindsey

Most of us do not know what we cannot do until someone tells us. We are willing to try almost anything, go anywhere, stretch ourselves to the limits in pursuit of our dreams. And then we talk to other people. We are reminded of how dangerous it may be, how ridiculous it sounds, what a chance we are taking. People have no problem informing us of all the downsides and pitfalls; they cannot see how we will ever reach the goal. They put us in touch with our faults, limitations and habits. They remind us of all the others who didn't make it, and in vivid detail they tell us why. They give us warnings, cautions and helpful hints about alternative things we can do. When they are finished, we have been effectively talked right out of our dreams. Bumblebees do not talk and neither should we. If we have a dream we want to come true, the only way to it is through it. We must take a chance, a risk and a leap. If we believe in ourselves and our ability, we will be taught how to fly.

I can do it because I believe I can do it.

If you can learn to be a hole in the wall, things will happen through you, not to you.

—John Randolph Price

Nothing ever happens to a hole in the wall. Everything passes through it. Things happen around it. Things happen above it and below it, but the hole remains the same. Even if the hole is covered, it remains; never losing its identity, doing what it was created to do. Nothing gets stuck in a hole in the wall. Everything comes into the hole; nothing stays in the hole; the hole defines itself by being a hole. Things come to the hole in the wall. Light. Air. Darkness. Sound. It takes from everything that comes and willingly allows everything to go. How would you define a hole in the wall? Is it nothing? Is it everything? Is it something? Is it all things? A hole in the wall cannot be defined; therefore, it cannot be limited. You cannot identify a hole in the wall; it has an identity all its own. Is it a big hole? A small hole? A black hole? A white hole? The only way to define the hole is based on how you see it.

Today I Am a hole in life's wall.

You must structure your world so that you are
constantly reminded of who you are.

—Na'im Akbar

Your subconscious mind is a twenty-four-hour photographer, recording every item you see. It is important to your mental, emotional and spiritual health that the things you see create images in your mind of who you are or what you want to be. Your environment should reconfirm your identity and the things you want. Is your home peaceful? Orderly? Safe? Are there pictures and artifacts that reflect the images you aspire to live up to? Does your work environment promote your creativity? Does it foster healthy communication? Does it look like a place you want to be? Like to be? Need to be? Is your social environment relaxing? Are you with the type of people you want around you? Do your family and friends support you and make you feel welcomed? Important? Free? Or are you restricted? Oppressed? Unproductive? You can only live up to the images in your mind. Make sure that what you see does not keep you in a place you do not want to be.

My world promotes my growth and true identity.

Life has two rules: number 1, never quit!; number 2, always remember rule number 1.
—Duke Ellington

*L*ife is going to be a challenge. There will be rough times, difficult situations, things to fall into, major obstacles, hurdles, stumbling blocks, forks in the road, knives in the back, mountains to climb, things to get over, oppositions to resolve, unpleasantness to face, feelings to understand, disappointments to accept, mysteries to solve, wonders to unfold and promises to keep to yourself. Now that you know what to expect, prepare yourself. Get ready. The only way to get to where you want to be is to do what needs to be done to get there. Do it fast. Do it slow. Do it right. Do it up. Do it in the daylight. Do it by the moonlight. Do it alone. Do it with others. Do it for free. Get paid to do it. Do it for yourself. Do it for the world. The moment you give up on doing it, it will never get done.

I Am doing it and doing it and doing it.

Everything that has happened had to happen.
Everything that must happen cannot be stopped.

—Dwayne Dyer

*E*verything that we experience, everything we think, feel and do is in divine order. It is part of the universal flow that helps us discover who we are. If our thoughts and emotions did not manifest as actions, how else would we see who we are? The world is not happening to us. We are happening to it. We are molding it, shaping it, creating the good and the bad. Sooner or later we will get tired of what we are doing and will do something else. When we get tired of hate, we will stop living in fear. When we get tired of injustice we will stop judging one another. When we get tired of violence we will stop aggression in all forms. When we get rid of criticism, cynicism and victimization we will live in truth, take responsibility for what we do and stop blaming each other. When we get sick and tired of the chaos in the world perhaps we will begin to love our brother as we love ourselves.

I happen to be creating a better world.

No one can give you wisdom. You must discover it
for yourself, on the journey through life, which no
one can take for you.

—Sun Bear

*T*here are so many wonderful secrets and sciences in the
world we can use as tools to better our lives. Some of them
have been hidden from us, others we have flatly rejected.
We have rejected our own culture and traditions, yet without investigation we accept the world of others as truth.
When we close any portion of our minds we close off a
part of the world. Is it fear that keeps us locked in? Is it
hopelessness? Or is it stubbornness. How can the descendants of genius be so closed to new information? How can
the children of the first civilization be lost and hopeless?
What will it take before we open our hearts and minds to
the world that awaits us? What would our ancestors think
if they saw us lost and struggling, unable to do with so
much more than they had?

*Today I will open myself to another
part of the world.*

May 28

You must be willing to die in order to live.

— Yoruba proverb

$\mathcal{M}$ost of us have been taught that death is the ultimate end. Death is frightening; it is dark, the unknown, beyond our control. We resist death; we brace ourselves against it; we run away because we do not understand death merely means change. When single people marry, their single life dies. As people age, their days of youth are gone. Death is the prerequisite of change. When we become willing to change, we learn to accept death as a meaningful new beginning. We may never like the idea of death; it may never make us comfortable; however, when we want to change anything in life, we must be willing to face death.

*I move peacefully through the darkness
into the light of change.*

> You must do your own independent
> investigation of truth.
>
> —Baha'i teachings

*M*ost of us believe only what we can see. Our eyes limit us in our perception and experience of reality. Yet, do we realize, whoever controls what we see or experience can, in fact, control our perceptions of reality? How then can we determine what is truth and what is not? We must investigate, we must probe. We must ask questions. We must seek. We must know truth intuitively, with our hearts and minds in harmony. The moment we accept what is given to us as truth, we lose our conscious reality. We are living through the eyes of someone else. How can we expect to find peace, harmony or self if we live through the perceptions of another? We can't. Whether religion, career, personal liberty or life itself, we must investigate; we must seek. We must probe. We must ask questions. We must be in charge of our own reality and know our own truth.

I have a right to know.

May 30

I am the thinker that creates the thoughts
that create the things.
—Dr. Johnnie Coleman

There are no circumstances around you more powerful than the power within you. You are responsible for your life through your consciousness. Racism, sexism, homophobia, ageism have no power over you unless you believe they do. A belief is the most contagious influence you possess. If you believe in circumstances, they can and will defeat you. If you believe in yourself, you are assured victory. There is a wonderful inner world at work within each of us. It knows no color, gender or age. We fuel this inner world with initiative, ingenuity and a picture in our minds. The world responds and produces according to how we fuel it. If we picture poverty, oppression, failure, disease and doubt, we cannot expect to enjoy wealth, success and health. When we put the forces of our inner self to work with good thoughts, it will produce according to our system of ideas. If we can keep our inner world clean, fertilize our minds with productive positivity, the powers within will create, with dynamic force, all that we believe is possible.

*Today I fuel my inner world with positive
possibilities.*

May 31

True power comes through cooperation and silence.
—Ashanti proverb

*H*ave you ever heard the sun come out in the morning? Did you hear the moon come out last night? Can you demonstrate the sound made by the fusing of the sperm and egg to create the miracle of life? We have been taught in this society that power is loud, forceful, aggressive and somewhat intimidating. It is not. In silence the Creator works. His creations all appear in silence. In silence one becomes attuned to the energies and forces that are unseen and unheard. In silence one learns to cooperate. We must cooperate with the flow of activity. In silence one learns to bring the head and the heart into cooperation in order to move with the strength and power of the forces in the flow. Keep silent about your hopes and dreams. Cooperate with yourself by doing only those things that will bring them about. Be silent about what you are doing and when you are doing it. Cooperate with those who will silently support you. In the silence of the night, your dream will come true and when the chatterboxes come to look for you, you will be gone.

Silence is my best friend.
I cooperate fully in its presence.

Force against force equals more force.

—Ashanti proverb

*T*here is nothing more infuriating than being in the presence of someone who makes a racial slur. Whether it is in the form of a joke, mindless comment or blatant disrespect, ignorance should carry no weight with you. The comment is a reflection of fear and shame. To respond means giving into fear and surrendering your power. Remember, what you focus your mind on will grow. When you allow yourself to be drawn into the ignorance of another, you will undoubtedly say or do something of the same nature. As hard as it may be, the best response is no response. In the silence of your comment, the sting of the words is sure to hit home.

I Am in charge of my words and deeds.

Nothing ever strikes without a warning.
— Danny Glover

Whenever we have a negative encounter, we wonder, "How could they do this to me?" The reason is because you let them. Basic human nature makes us see people and situations the way we want them to be, not the way they are. We allow others to take advantage, manipulate, and in some cases, abuse us, because we don't want to "believe" what our senses are telling us is true. We listen to the same old line, accept the same dead promises, follow them down the same road, in the hopes they have "changed." We listen to what they say and hear something else. We see what they do and turn our face. When the bottom falls out, we quickly place the blame for the pain on the other person. We shift our anger to them rather than accept our responsibility for the role we played. There are three keys to successful relationships: Never make anyone else responsible for your happiness; trust what your inner self feels, sees and says; and pay close attention to the warning signs.

I listen to what is said, not to what I hear.

June 3

Bad luck picks its company by invitation only.
— African-American folklore

For anyone who has ever said, "My luck is so bad." To those who have ever asked, "Why do these things always happen to me?" For anyone who has dared to say, "I give up!" Get a pencil, a piece of paper and write this down: What you ask for, you get. What you see, you are. What you give, you get back, someday, somehow, sooner or later. There is no such thing as bad luck. The ancient Africans said, "With your own hands you make your success. With your own hands you destroy it." We say things return to us. We do things we know are not good for us. We think things that create situations we don't want. The only way to create success or luck is to think, speak and act in ways that support ourselves.

I make my own luck.

Things don't just happen, they happen just.
— Dr. Johnnie Coleman

When we face disappointments, challenges and obstacles, the first thing we ask is, "Why me?" We don't always realize that things happen to us according to our dominant thoughts, words and deeds. Even when we work really hard to keep ourselves in a positive frame of mind, things happen. When events occur that we don't expect, they increase our faith, strengthen our ability to endure and bring forth our hidden talents, abilities and strengths. Why me? As Les Brown would say, "Why not you? Would you like to recommend someone else?" Why you? Because you can handle it. Because you really do know what to do. Because you need a little nudge every now and then to keep you on or put you back on track. So the next time something happens to you, remember, things don't just happen. They happen the way they should, at just the right time, to the right people. Our job is to know we are equipped to handle it.

Divine order prevails in my mind and my life,
right here, right now.

A new life will come forth from the womb of darkness.

—Na'im Akbar

*E*very new situation we face in life sends us back into the womb of darkness. Like an embryo, we must go through changes in order to become whole, healthy and complete. We may feel alone, confused or frightened. In reality, we are growing, developing, evolving. In the womb of newness, we learn what we can and cannot do, given the space we are in. Yet we must continue to stretch and flex as we grow. We come to acknowledge our limitations knowing they are temporary. There is eventually a way out. In the womb, we are nurtured, fed and protected by an unseen, unknown force. We are watched over and prayed for by the ancestors. They know what it is we must do. The womb is the place where we are strengthened and primed by the people we do not yet know. They are waiting for us to be born and share with them all the things we learned in the womb.

Out of this new darkness, there will come a light.

Give not that which is holy to dogs. Neither cast ye
your pearls before swine.

— Matthew 7:6

Should we wear our most expensive outfit to a mud fight? Why then do we continue to place ourselves in jobs, situations and relationships that ruin our peace, health and self-value? Should we leave our most valuable possession unguarded in a public location? Why then do we place our minds and bodies in the reach of those persons and situations with a demonstrated history of abuse or neglect? We are, to ourselves, the most valuable possession we have. Yet we waste our time, energy and sometimes our lives in worthless situations among people who are unworthy. We must value our ideas, our energy, our time and our life to such an infinite degree that we become unwilling to waste who we are. If we put on our best and go to a mud fight, we can expect to get dirty. If we place our head in the lion's mouth, we should expect to get eaten.

I Am very valuable to me.

If you are on a road to nowhere, find another road.

—Ashanti proverb

*W*hen we are following the wrong teachings or philosophy, we get stuck. We do not evolve. Life just doesn't seem to come together. We see the same people saying and doing the same thing. We may all be in agreement, but we still are not growing. We may know there is something better, somewhere. We may want or need more. But because we don't know exactly what "it" is, we stay stuck in what is familiar. Could it possibly be that it is time to move on? Shift gears? Get back to basics? Open our minds? Try something new? Well, we will never know until we try. The only way to really be sure we are on the right track is to derail ourselves for just a moment and see what new direction beckons.

I Am willing to make a change.

I am thankful for the adversities which have
crossed my path and taught me tolerance,
perseverance, self-control and some other
virtues I might never have known.

—Anonymous

When we are faced with a problem, we seem ready,
able and willing to do battle. Yet sometimes we enter the
battle not being clear of the goal. The best way to ensure
that we make it through the battle is to focus on the outcome, not on the war. Focus crystallizes and directs the
powerful energy of the mind. Focus galvanizes the mental,
emotional and physical energy to such an exact degree
that our efforts cannot miss the mark. When we focus on
the goal and not the obstacles that can and do come about,
we ensure victory. We should not spend our energy worrying about what the "enemy" might be doing. Like the
mighty Ashanti, if we focus our thoughts, take our steps
with confidence and move forward, we may stumble but
we cannot fall. Focus gives the elk its grace. Focus gives
the gazelle its speed. Focus gave the Ashanti strength and
a tradition as undefeated warriors.

I remain focused on the goal,
even in the midst of battle.

If rain doesn't fall, corn does not grow.

—Yoruba proverb

*E*very farmer knows a good hard rain is needed to make a healthy crop. It will strengthen the roots, fatten the stalks and produce a healthy yield. A responsible farmer prepares for rain. He prepares the field by clearing away all remnants of past crops. He irrigates the field so the rain water can run off. He carefully guards his crop to keep away the birds and insects. Through it all, he has faith in his ability as a farmer knowing he is doing all that he can. Our lives are much like a field of corn, our challenges are the rain. We don't mind planting the seeds, working the field or planning for the harvest, but we have a tendency to complain about the rain. If we focus our mind on the goals, we are putting on our raincoat and boots. If we cleanse ourselves of negative emotions, we are covered by an umbrella of strength. If we keep faith in ourselves regardless of what others say, we have all we need to weather the storm.

The harvest I reap is measured by the attitudes I cultivate.

If you fall, fall on your back.
If you can look up, you can get up.
— Les Brown

When was the last time you watched a toddler learning to walk? They take a few steps and fall. Then get up and try again. Sometimes they bump their heads, bust their lips or pull things down onto their heads. No matter. They keep falling and getting up, until one day they make it clear across the room. How did we lose that fierce tenacity to make it no matter what? Most of us consider ourselves much more capable than a toothless toddler, yet they seem to have something we don't. The toddler seems to know that it's okay to fall. They are always willing to roll over, get up and try it again. A toddler who stumbles doesn't always fall. Stumbling actually moves them ahead faster. A toddler will grab on to anyone or anything until they get their balance. When they do, they let go and move on. They don't seem to care how awkward they look, whether or not people laugh at them or how many times they fall. They do it over and over until they get it right. Isn't it funny that those of us who know how to walk are always afraid to fall?

I Am willing to do whatever it takes.

June 11

To be who you are and become what you are capable of is the only goal worth living.

—Alvin Ailey

*L*ife is not hopping from one mountaintop to another because there is a valley between. At times, the valley is a job you hate but need to feed the family. The valley might be a failing or toxic relationship. The valley could be a child who goes astray or a friend who betrays you. The valley could be an illness or the death of a loved one. The valley is dark, bleak, ugly and frightening. But there is value in the valley. When you are in the valley, you begin to muster the strength and power buried deep within you. In the valley you begin to think, pray and tap into your incredibly divine self. The valley gives you a time to rest, to heal, to rejuvenate your being. It is an opportunity to look up, to see and remember those powerful mountain climbers who made it before you: your grandmother, your hero, even yourself. You have been in the valley before. Remember what you did, how you got up and out. Let the thoughts and memories of that success be the rope you use to pull yourself up.

I Am taking time to learn the value of the valley.

Most people think they know the answer. I am willing to admit I don't even know the question.

—Arsenio Hall

*L*ife is a series of mysteries we must each unravel at our own pace. Our task is not to solve the mysteries but to use them along our way. No one can tell us what is good for us just because it worked for them. If we allow someone to give us our answers we create conflict deep within. Sometimes it gets confusing trying to figure out what to do. If the confusion is on the inside, the answer is there, too! No human being has all the answers, if they did they would not be here. One of the greatest mysteries we must unravel is our purpose, because that makes us clear. Let us take more time to listen to our hearts, filtering through the offerings that come in. Let us not be so willing to say "I know" when we have no idea where to begin. Let us know deep down that God loves us and use that knowledge along the way. Let us approach the great mystery of the meaning of life with a little bit less to say.

I Am on the path to knowledge.

Power concedes nothing without a demand.
—Frederick Douglass

*H*ave you noticed how long hard times seem to last? And don't rainy days seem to go on forever? Do life's difficulties appear to multiply rapidly? When hard times, difficulties or rainy days appear, do you give them all your attention? If you are like most of us, you probably do. And like most of us, you give difficulty power. Nothing is ever as it seems. What looks bad today, can be a blessing tomorrow. Challenges come so we can grow and be prepared for things we are not equipped to handle now. When we face our challenges with faith, prepared to learn, willing to make changes and, if necessary, to let go, we are demanding our power be returned.

My willingness to grow is my demand for power.

Predict Life's Alternatives Now.

*P*lan. Do you have a plan? What is your plan? Have you failed to plan? Can you carry out the plan? If you do not have a plan, what do you plan to do? Life is much too precious to waste time on wonder and worry. You can predict your life's alternatives now, if you take the time to plan. Plan your moments to be joyous. Plan your hours to be productive. Plan your days to be filled with peace. Plan your weeks to be educational. Plan your months to be filled with love. Plan your years to be purposeful. Plan your life to be an experience of growth. Plan to change. Plan to grow. Plan to spend quiet moments doing absolutely nothing. Planning is the only way to keep yourself on track. And when you know where you are going, the universe will clear a path for you.

I plan to be all that I Am.

As soon as healing takes place,
go out and heal somebody else.

— Maya Angelou

*N*o man is free until all men are free. No woman is healed until all women are healed. These are more than profound statements worthy of thought. They are the clues to the moral responsibility we all have for one another. Many of us hold on to our pain, afraid to reveal it. Ashamed to admit it. Others hold on to healing information because we believe it is ours to own. We may fight for the freedom of people of color, but we say nothing when gays or women are oppressed. We owe it to ourselves and everyone else to see that all people live painlessly and free. It is our duty to share what we know if it has helped us to move beyond some darkness in life. We can talk it out or write it out, but we must get it out to those in need. We can support someone and encourage someone else to take healing steps or paths or ways. We should think about where we would be if there were no books or people to guide us when we need it. Then, with an open heart and extended hand, we can pull someone else along.

I Am a valuable tool in someone's
healing process.

And He sent them out . . . to heal.

—Luke 9:2

We must realize that the healing power of spirit is within each and every one of us. We each have the power to heal not only ourselves, but our world and all those around us. Spirit expressing through us as a kind word, a caring touch or a simple smile may be all it takes. When we realize who we are, the blessings we have been given, the power we embody, we have tapped into the source of our healing ability. Every day we have at least one opportunity to help a friend, a loved one or even a stranger. Regardless of the color of our skin, our economic status, our social or political philosophy, it is our responsibility to do what we can, when we can, to assure that someone else does better. Today, let us become aware of the healing power within and dedicate ourselves to uplifting those we touch.

Through the healing power of the spirit within,
I bless others today.

Do not follow the path. Go where there is no path to begin the trail.

—Ashanti proverb

*I*t takes courage, strength and conviction to go against the grain. But if someone hadn't done it, we wouldn't have wheat bread, chocolate chip ice cream or radios in our cars. It is often difficult to get other people to follow your train of thought. Stop trying. It's your train. You are the engineer and the conductor. We usually want and need help, support and comfort when we are doing something new. If we do not get it, so what! Does it mean we should stop what we are doing? Absolutely not! The path to success is paved with road signs, warning symbols and obstructions. But when you start a new trail equipped with courage, strength and conviction, the only thing that can stop you is you.

I Am a trailblazer.

No one can uproot the tree which God has planted.
—Yoruba proverb

When we think our enemy is gaining on us, we want to run and run. When we believe someone wants what we have, we squeeze the life right out of it. When we believe "they" are out to get us, we find "their trap" at every turn. Yet if we would just stop running, squeezing and suspecting, we would understand who "they" really are. They are the thoughts that beat us down, causing us to behave in unproductive ways. They are the doubts and suspicions we carry within us that take the life out of the very thing we want. They are the fears that we fall into, showing us the very thing we don't want to see. They are us when we don't have faith because faithlessness is the greatest enemy. No one can get what is meant for you. The universe will not have it the way it should not be. We have been put on this earth to be a certain way, have a certain thing, accomplish a certain task. Until we have been, done and had what we came here to be, do and have, we are the only ones who can get in the way.

What is mine is mine alone.

The main point in the game of life is to have fun.
We are afraid to have fun because somehow that
makes life too easy.

—Sammy Davis, Jr.

We live in a world that thrives on fear. Fear of living, fear of dying; fear of having too much, fear of not having enough. When people find our weaknesses we become fearful of them. If we demonstrate our strength, people become fearful of us. Fear is an accepted way of life. We are fearful our past will be repeated. We are fearful that we have no chance in the future. We are fearful of one another. We are fearful of those who are fearful of us. When we allow fear to control our daily lives we run the risk of remaining where we don't want to be—in fear. We must confront the things we fear, people and situations, believing the spirit of God is with us. By doing the very thing we fear, we tap into a force that directs and protects us, unleashing the power that has brought us this far. When we give in to our fears and avoid taking chances, it is unlikely we will ever overcome the very things we fear.

As my sense of power increases,
my fear about life decreases.

And the earth was without form, and void; and
darkness was upon the face of the deep.

—Genesis 1:2

*A*re you afraid to face the darkness of something new?
Do you want to know everything right now and be able to
see what is before you? Well, just imagine if the Creator
had waited for a model to shape the world. Who? What?
Where would you be today? When facing the darkness,
have faith. Active faith works through you and for you.
When we approach something new, surrender. Surrender
your desire to be in control. It is the eagerness to know,
the desire to control and the inability to surrender that
creates fear. Remember, the same force that created the
world without a model is the substance upon which you
stand. Stand firm in the darkness knowing there is something solid there.

I surrender to the power of the divine within me.

Love is the light. Forward is the motion.

— BarbaraO

God is love, a presence who enters our lives the very instant we pass from the darkness of the womb to the light of the world. Birth is a forward movement from the known to the unknown. It is a forward thrust from the warmth to the cold. It is a journey from unknowing to knowing and to recognition of the light. God never asks us to move backward. We are simply asked to grow. The love light of birth remains with us until the earthly task is complete. Then we move forward into the realm of the known. The source of the light. The cause of the love. No matter what situations we are given in life, the light of love is there. As long as we are in the light the movement must be forward. The more we love, the greater the light. The greater the light, the easier the birth.

In all situations, under all circumstances,
I will stay in the light.

Exploring the question brings more wisdom than
having the answer.

—*A Course in Miracles*

*I*f you attack a problem, you are going to get your butt
whipped. Anything you attack will fight back. Chances
are, if you have a problem, it is bigger than you; it crept up
on you or you didn't know what you were doing in the
first place. Don't attack your problems. Face them, confess them, understand what they are—that is the process.
The process teaches and brings a richness that will help
you avoid future problems. When you attack a problem it
means you want a solution. The solution is not always the
answer, but the process is. The process keeps you in the
moment and you must be in the moment to fully experience the solution. When you wrestle, attack or fight a
problem you are focused on a place you are not—the future. You are here, in the moment, exactly where the
problem is. So calm down, understand what is really going
on and then surrender to the process.

Today I will not attack a problem,
I will go through the solution process.

Self-hate is a form of mental slavery that results in
poverty, ignorance and crime.

—Susan Taylor

*W*hen you don't feel good about yourself, it is hard to
feel good about anything or anyone else. You see everything with a jaundiced eye. You miss the value and worth
of every experience. You limit yourself because you don't
feel good about who you are or what you do. You hold
yourself back because you don't believe what you want is
worthwhile. You put yourself in situations that are abusive
or unproductive. You feel bad about yourself because of
what you've done. Self-hate is a vicious cycle that leads to
self-destruction. It fills the world with hate and people
with despair. The only way to get out of the cycle of self-
hate is to allow yourself to believe the world is waiting for
who you are becoming. What the world must do is let
every being know they are appreciated and welcomed
simply for being who they are.

I Am loving myself for being a lovable being.

Males understand power by doing powerful things.
Females just understand power.

—Stuart Wilde

It was an ancient tradition in an African village that the women choose the leaders. As time passed on, modern ideas prevailed and the men refused to adhere to tradition. The men picked the new leaders and within nine months the village riches had been sold, the temples were invaded and 85 percent of the elders, women and children were killed. The symbol for male ♂ indicates an outward action. It is aggressive. It must have something to do. The symbol for female ♀ is downward and inward. It is a container that receives what is done. If we are to achieve the world balance and harmony we seek, men must step back and honor and learn from women. If we want to stop the aggression and destruction of the world, women must individually and collectively honor themselves.

*Today I will support,
honor and respect the feminine power.*

Six million women were abused in 1991.
One in every six was pregnant.
—Sally Jessy Raphaël

*A*buse against women is more than a crime of violence. It is a statement about society's view of women and itself. Women have been viewed as property, tools of pleasure and underlings. The people who support these views forget that women are the mothers, daughters, aunts, sisters and nieces who raise the fathers, sons, uncles, brothers and nephews. Women are the creative force of the world. The world's treatment of women will be reflected in the things men create. Every man of color has an ancestral obligation to get clear regarding his views about women. Childhood pains, adolescent disappointments, adult misconceptions must be mended and forgiven. Every woman of color has a responsibility to all women of color to reveal the violence against her, to heal her wounds and do everything in her power to make sure another woman is healed.

I Am every woman.

Advice is what we ask for when we already know
what the answer is, but wish we didn't.
—Erica Jong

*E*ach of us is born knowing everything we need to know. It is programmed in our genes. It is connected to our mission and purpose in life. People of color in particular are genetically coded for genius. We are, however, programmed to self-destruct. We are taught we must be authorized, qualified and sanctioned by someone else. Unfortunately, we believe it. We don't trust ourselves. We search for the support and acceptance of others. We question what we know unless we can identify someone else who taught us. We forget we have a built-in mechanism of information, protection and guidance. We move outside of ourselves, then lament when we get lost. If we are to survive we must accept and understand what we already know. The key issue becomes "Do I have the strength and courage to do what I know is right for me?"

I know that I know that I know I Am knowing.

> The passion for setting people right is,
> itself, a dis-ease with the self.
>
> —Marianne Moore

Many of us have a need to be right. Usually this stems from the inner cry, "There is something wrong with me." We then set out to make ourselves right by making someone else wrong. We may plan what to say. We may canvass others to elicit their support. In some cases, we simply attack, letting others know how wrong they are and why we think so. Self-righteousness is an affliction. It is an inner desire to be accepted and valued. It is a camouflage for feelings of worthlessness. No matter how wrong another may be, it will never make you right. Self-value, self-worth and self-esteem cannot come as a result of being the only right one. It must come from knowing who you are from within and feeling good about it. Europeans being wrong will not make African people right. Women being wrong will not make men right. White people being wrong will not make Native Americans right. We must get right with ourselves. Once we do, we will have so much to do, we will not have time to keep track of who is wrong.

I'm okay, you're okay, now let's get to work.

[V]ictory has a hundred fathers and
defeat is an orphan.
— John F. Kennedy

*P*eople sure do remember when you do something that's out of line, out of character or just plain dumb. They have a way of letting you know how shocked, surprised or disappointed they are. There are even those times when someone will believe that you committed the error or mindless act just to strike out at them. They may want to berate, scold or chastise you, probably giving very little consideration to how you feel. You are probably beating up on yourself and do not need the help of others. But you get it and that's how the shame, guilt and anger set in. No matter what you do, you must never lose sight of the fact that it is your lesson. It does not matter what anyone else thinks or believes; you are the one growing and learning. You have nothing to feel guilty, ashamed or angry about, you must be ready for the lesson, otherwise you would not have had the experience. Rather than focusing on what "they" are saying, identify what you have learned and remember how awful it felt to be criticized the next time you start to criticize someone else.

*No one has to tell me what an important
lesson I am learning.*

If you are not totally free, ask yourself, why?
—Stuart Wilde

Mhite people like violins, Black people like drums. White people play bridge, Black people play blackjack. White people eat caviar, Black people eat pigs feet. White people play squash, Black people play football. People do not do what they do because of the color of their skin. They do what is familiar to them, accessible to them and what vibrates in their soul. It's about ancestry. It's about tradition! It's about what feels good and what doesn't. And it's all okay. Once we begin to understand that we are so much more than color, we can begin to accept our individual differences. We can eat what we want, play what we want, go where we want, do what we want—because we choose to. No one thing is better than the other because of who does it. What makes an activity attractive and available is how it is supported by the people who do it. Do what you do because you like to do it, not because your color keeps you from doing something else.

It's a soul thing. You have to do it to understand.

One love. One heart.
Let's get together and feel alright.
—Bob Marley

True power, our power, is in our diversity and difference. It is not in the illusive power we chase in money and things. It is not in what we call unity. We are already unified through breath. We want to deny our unity because we look different, act different and we believe we want different things. The elk, oak and pine live together to create the mighty forests. The shark, dolphin and whales live together to create the wealth of the oceans. The blue jay, hawk and robin sing together to create the melody of the sky. The lion, elephant and jaguar live together in the wonderment of the wild. They all want the same things: food, protection for their young and the opportunity to move freely. The animals do not blame or judge. They live without anger or fear. Are the animals just stupid? Or have we become too smart?

Today I will honor and
respect the power in difference.

Others

Everyone in our lives is a mirror of who we are, what we think and what we do. They reflect back to us our secret thoughts and feelings. More important, they come to show us what we need to learn. People do not come into our lives to hurt us, they come because they love us. The people in our lives love us so much, they come to show us what we must do to grow beyond the thoughts and emotions that cause us pain. The best thing we can do for ourselves and the people in our lives is to love them unconditionally, forgive them without reservation and to accept them exactly as they are. What we must always remember about others is that whatever we give to them or do to them will come back to us tenfold.

The love we desire is already within us.
—*A Course in Miracles*

God is love. That is where we must begin. We cannot expect to have a loving relationship with our family, mate or children until we heal our individual relationship with God. In the ancient traditions of people of color all life was centered around the Creative Force and its elements. Our ancestors had a wholesome respect for the Creator and all creations. They honored the earth for support, the sun for the life force and themselves as expressions of creation. Today we relate to one another's ego. We want to please one another because of who we are or what we have. We hold people in awe; we want people to fulfill our needs; we demoralize ourselves and one another for what we believe is love. God is love. That's it! God does not give presents. God does not have needs. God does not argue. God does not make threats. God does not feel abandoned. God does not deal with rejection. The only thing God does is love you and that is the only reason you are here.

The only relationship I will seek today is a relationship with love.

Having begun in the spirit, are you now to be made perfect by the flesh?

—Galatians 3:3

*T*he most accurate measure of our worth is how much we value ourselves. When we value who we are, we are sure to draw to us others who value us as much. When we are needy, deficient, lacking confidence and self-esteem, we will find ourselves in situations and among people that reinforce those views. The first step in building relationships is learning to value who we are. We cannot convince others how wonderful and marvelous we are if we do not believe it. We must first convince ourselves. If we repeatedly find ourselves in situations where we are treated badly, we are responsible, not the other person. When we find ourselves in situations where we do not feel wanted, we must have the courage and confidence to leave. Our sense of worth must first come from within. When we have that, we can expect those in our relationships will value us as well.

The wealth of my spirit is the light of my world.

You must have love in your heart
before you can have hope.
— Yoruba proverb

*A*t a very early age, we are taught to depend on someone else for our basic needs. When we are bald, toothless
and helpless, it should be that way. As we mature, we
must learn to become self-supportive and self-loving. A
balanced, productive being is one who learns love of self.
Loving yourself has nothing to do with being selfish, self-
centered or self-engrossed. It means that you accept yourself for what you are and that you are willing to put your
best foot forward, even if the foot is big. Loving yourself
means that you accept responsibility for your own development, growth and happiness. It means you set the standard for how you want to be treated. Loving yourself
means accepting your strengths and weaknesses, making a
commitment to work on building and correcting what
needs to be done. When you love yourself, you pave the
way for all you want and need to come to you at the right
time in the perfect way.

I love me.

Forgive and you will be forgiven.

—Luke 6:37

*E*verybody has had someone who has "done them wrong." When someone hurts us, we want to hurt them back. We live with anger and thoughts of revenge. We want to see them suffer. We want them to feel what we have felt. We want them to know they can't get away with what they did. But they did get away if your anger keeps you stuck in the situation. When the table turns, we make mistakes, we create pain for others and we cannot understand why they do not or cannot forgive us. Perhaps it is because there is someone we need to forgive. Forgiveness frees us from the pain of the past and moves us beyond our mistakes in the future. What you give you get. When you forgive, forgiveness is there for you if you need it.

I forgive everyone for everything,
totally and unconditionally.

If you are willing to deal with the past,
you can make the moment you are in rich.

—Oprah Winfrey

We are products of our past, the environment of our childhood. For those of us who had painful childhoods, we are determined to get away from our memories. We cannot. Our past is a part of our today. We carry it in our hearts. We model what we saw, heard and experienced as children. It is called a pattern. We do what was done to us. We behave the way we saw others behave. Unwittingly, with a great deal of denial, we repeat the physical, emotional and mental patterns set by our families. The only way to stop the cycle, to break the pattern, is to go back and deal with the pain. We must relive the memories before we can erase them. We must confront the people in our minds and say now what we could not say then. We must explore the feelings, unpack the guilt and free ourselves from the baggage we picked up at home.

The buck stops with me.

July 6

You cannot belong to anyone else,
until you belong to yourself.

— Pearl Bailey

*F*inding and beginning a new relationship can be difficult. It is particularly difficult when we are carrying baggage from past relationships. We are told that it is not
good to carry past relationships into the current ones. You
know that. But how do you free yourself from that which
is a part of you? You don't! Yet you can unpack the baggage. You can take a look at the pain, guilt, fear. You can
look it dead in the face and see what it is, for what it is—
the past. It's over. Without shame, without blame, you
must look at what happened and know it does not have to
happen again. It is only when you refuse to look, refuse to
release, that you will have experiences added to your baggage collection. There is another point you often forget
when moving into a new relationship: No matter how
painful the past has been, you made it through.

Today, I Am unpacking.

Don't look back and don't cry.
— El-Hajj Malik El-Shabazz (Malcolm X)

Are you stuck in your first relationship? Your fifth? Your last? Most of us are stuck in the memory, ideals, pain or trauma of a past relationship. We hold everyone responsible for the things someone did to us in the yester-year. We can't seem to put the baggage down, overcome the disappointment or forgive the past. And we can't figure out why we end up in a similar relationship, the identical situation or with a broken heart. What we draw to ourselves is what we are! If we are hurt, angry, in pain, confused, disappointed or lonely, we will attract mates who will bring more of what we already are. We can only draw to ourselves the beings on our ray. If our ray is dark and dismal we will attract our reflection. If we want to move beyond the pain of past relationships, we must stop crying about them. Stop thinking about them. Stop drawing them to us. Forgive, let go and move on. When we move beyond where we are, the past cannot follow.

I'm moving up, out and beyond.

To understand how any society functions you must understand the relationship between the men and the women.

—Angela Davis

*W*hat type of relationship did you have with your parents? How do you really feel about them? Whatever your relationship is or was with your parents will be reflected in the types of relationships you have in your life. It will be difficult for you to have a good relationship with women if you did not have a good relationship with your mother. Whatever the image, thoughts and feelings you have about your father will be reflected in your relationships with men. Your relationship with them is your model of what to expect, what is and is not acceptable. When the memories of our parents are disappointing, frightening and/or painful, we may repeat these patterns in our lives. We can break the pattern when we forgive our parents. They did the best they could based on the pattern and model they lived with. They have hurts and pains and bad memories, just like we do. Our parents are just people who did the best they could with what they knew.

I forgive my parents and release their patterns.

July 9

A man is an idea in Divine Mind;
the epitome of being; the apex of creation.
—Charles Filmore

*T*he following is a list of adjectives used by a group of a hundred women to describe men. A man is: a dog; a liar; irresponsible; unfaithful; hard to communicate with; a good worker; strong; a pain in the neck; lazy; sloppy; inconsiderate; unemotional; unreliable; not to be trusted; cheap; a user; manipulative; hard to please; messed up in the head; too aggressive; too possessive; confused about what he wants; out to take advantage of women; the only thing that can really hurt a woman; hard to love; a good lover; a sex fiend; stupid; hard to catch; difficult to keep; not worth the effort; a disappointment; a waste of time; cute when he's sleeping; better off without a woman; a joke; okay to his mother; too smart for his own good; the last thing on my Christmas list.

Twelve of the women were in long-term, loving relationships. Sixty-three of the women did not know their fathers.

A man is a mind thing.
Whatever is in my mind I will find in a man.

A woman is the intuitive perception of truth
reflected as love in the soul.

—Charles Filmore

*T*he following is a list of adjectives used by a group of a hundred men to describe women. A woman is: a bitch; a liar; fickle; hard to please; a sneak; a credit wrecker; a pain in the ass; a mother; a helpmate; God's gift to man; weak; stupid; here to serve man; nothing without a man; a sexual object; a tease; something I don't want to have anything else to do with; spiritual; nice to have around; a tax deduction; greedy; a heartache; a heartbreaker; capable of anything low down and dirty; frightened; jealous; too mouthy; angry most of the time; confused; sweet; nice to look at; hard to handle; my mother; a fool; thinks she's smarter than men; my best friend; a gossipmonger; able to make it in the white man's world; a welfare recipient; too emotional; unsure of herself; the reason I work two jobs.

Forty-seven of the men were in long-term loving relationships. Eleven men loved and admired their fathers. Forty-three admired their mothers.

A woman is a mind thing. Whatever is in my mind
I will find in a woman.

July 11

Your divine mate is seeking you and
you can only meet divinely.
—Jewel Diamond-Taylor

*Y*our divine mate already exists. You are being prepared to meet one another. Through your many growth experiences, and the purpose that is etched in your soul, the day will come when you will meet face-to-face. It will be crystal clear that this person is the right one. She will not need fixing. He will not require work. You will be touched in a place in your heart and soul that, until that divine day, has been untouched. As you allow yourself to accept the reality that your divine mate exists, it will unfold as a reality to you. You can stop looking, forcing and trying to make it happen. You need not fret or worry or allow yourself to be lonely, because your divine mate already exists. You can stop looking out for him or her. Instead, spend your time looking within. When you get to the place in yourself that is peaceful divine love, your true mate will be revealed.

My divine mate will be revealed to me in the divine
way at the divine time.

July 12

If you are having a bad day, get another one
and get it quick!

— Rissie Harris

*I*f you are having a bad day, it is a personal problem the world does not have to deal with. If you get up on the wrong side of the bed, it is no one's fault but your own. If it is that time of the week, month or year for you, what would you have the world do? It is never an excuse for being rude, cruel or abusive to anyone, to simply say, "I am having a bad day." It is not appropriate to scream, swear, lash out or do things that have no place among civilized people because "you have something else on your mind." We cannot abuse or traumatize others because we are facing a challenge. *LIFE IS A CHALLENGE!* African tradition tells us that it does not matter what difficulties we face. Our worth is measured by how we face those difficulties. If we are to grow and reach our fullest potential, we have no time to waste on bad days.

Today is a new day.
I refuse to get off to a bad start.

The ruin of a nation begins in the home of its people.
—Ashanti proverb

If you have an argument at home, chances are you will have one at work. If you feel unsupported at home, your friends are likely to abandon you. If you are uncooperative, unreliable and disrespectful at home, you carry that same energy everywhere you go. Home is the foundation of everything we see and do in the world and relationships. For people of color, culture mandates that one make home the primary concern of the heart. The heart creates love, support, cooperation, nurturing and peace. Home is our first school. Let us put our hearts, minds, bodies and souls back into the home as the first step toward eliminating the violence in the streets.

My home is my salvation.

The needle pulls the thread.
— Yoruba proverb

When we make strides in life we face obstacles and challenges. There are times when that which is most familiar to us will present the most challenging opposition — our family. If our life moves away from what is familiar to our family, they become frightened we will leave them. They may use their fears and concerns as a reason not to support us. They may not understand why we cannot do things the way they've always been done. The way they are comfortable with doing things. We want our family to support and encourage our dreams, but if they don't, it is okay. Sometimes we must step out alone, make a new way, start the path others will follow. Our job is to let our families know that we love them, keep them as informed as they care to be; when possible, we should invite them to join us in the process. However, if they choose to stay on the same old beaten path, there is no obligation to march with them.

I am weaving the fibers of a new world.

People come into your life for a reason, a season or a lifetime. When you figure out which it is, you know exactly what to do.

—Michelle Ventor

*W*ouldn't it be wonderful if our first love could be our one and only love, forever and ever, amen? Well, surely you know by now that life is not like that. People come and go in our lives, taking a little piece of our heart with them. As difficult or painful as it may be, that is exactly what they should do. We have more than enough love to share and spare, and we should give it freely. When we love for a reason it feels good to give love, because we get what we give. When we have a seasonal love, it is a whirl-wind love, preparing us for something better. When those very special people come into our lives, we can and do love them forever. Loving is not what causes our emotional damage; it is the attempt to throw people out of our hearts and minds. When we love reasonably for the season we are in, we will undoubtedly enjoy a lifetime of loving.

*I know why you are in my life and
I love you for that reason.*

A reason . . .

When someone is in your life for a reason, it is usually to meet a need you have expressed outwardly or inwardly. They have come to assist you through a difficulty, to provide you with guidance and support, to aid you physically, emotionally or spiritually. They may seem like a godsend, and they are. They are there for the reason you need them to be. Then, without any wrongdoing on your part or at an inconvenient time, this person will say or do something to bring the relationship to an end. Sometimes they die. Sometimes they walk away. Sometimes they act up or out and force you to take a stand. What we must realize is that our need has been met, our desire fulfilled; their work is done. The prayer you sent up has been answered, and it is now time to move on. Next!

When a prayer is answered,
there is no need to cry.

July 17

A season . . .

When people come into your life for a season, it is because your turn has come to share, grow or learn. They may bring you an experience of peace or make you laugh. They may teach you something you have never done. They usually give you an unbelievable amount of joy. Believe it! It is real! But only for a season. In the same way that leaves must fall from the trees, or the moon becomes full and then disappears, your seasonal relationships will end at the divinely appointed time. When that time comes, there is nothing you can say or do to make it work. There is no one you can blame. You cannot fix it. You cannot explain it. The harder you clutch, the worse it will feel. When the end of a season comes in a loving relationship, the only thing for you to do is let go.

For everything there is a season.

July 18

A lifetime . . .

*L*ifetime relationships are a bit more difficult to let go of. When a parent, child or spouse is involved, the wounds are very deep. When the end of a lifetime relationship comes, you may feel that you would be better off dead. The pain seems to grow, the memories linger, a part of your life is dying. You relive every painful moment in an attempt to understand. Your job is not to understand. Your job is to accept. Lifetime relationships teach you lifetime lessons; those things you must build upon in order to have a solid emotional foundation. They are the most difficult lessons to learn, the most painful to accept; yet these are the things you need in order to grow. When you are facing a separation of the end of a lifetime relationship, the key is to find the lesson; love the person anyway; move on and put what you have learned to use in all other relationships.

A new life begins when a part of life ends.

The most frightening part of helping
is getting involved.
—Dianne Ridley Roberts

With all that goes on in our daily lives, we may believe we don't have time to get involved with other people and their issues, yet we must. Perhaps we think if we do not see or hear about the problems, they will go away, but they will not. People of color are a communal people. That means the community is our lifeline. African, Latin, Native American and Asian cultures are cultures of "we" not "I." We cannot consider ourselves free, prosperous, successful or at peace as long as anyone who looks like us suffers. We cannot help everybody, but you can help somebody. We cannot do everything, but you can do something. If we each participate in a cause, if we each battle an ill, if we each contribute time or money to someone for something, a great deal could be done. If we each shoulder a bit of the responsibility for us, we can progress faster.

I will do my part for us.

Someone was hurt before you; wronged before you;
hungry before you; frightened before you; beaten
before you; humiliated before you; raped before you;
yet, someone survived.

—Maya Angelou

*W*hat do you do when it seems as if people want to stay
in their pain? They have a story to tell, and they tell you
every chance they get. It may get to the point that they become so entrenched in their pain that they stop looking for
a way out. Well, believe it or not, they may like where they
are. Our job is to leave them there. You can point the way
out of pain, but you cannot force them to get out. You can
support the move beyond their limitations, but you cannot
make the move. Movement requires learning from painful
experiences by recognizing the role we have played. If we
continually tell the story without drawing a conclusion,
we become the victims of the drama of the pain.

You can do anything you choose to do.

July 21

No person is your friend who demands your silence
or denies your right to grow.

—Alice Walker

*H*ave you ever wondered why people hide their dirty
laundry in the closet of your mind? Somewhere deep inside, you may feel honored when you are entrusted with
another's downside. What you fail to realize is that knowledge creates responsibility. When you are asked to remain
silent about the secret or hidden acts of another, you are
lured into collusion. If people demand your loyalty, presence or participation in that which is detrimental to them,
you create a detriment for yourself. When you abandon
your dreams, swallow your truth, give the will of others
precedence over your own, you sell yourself out. Be aware
of the person who asks you "not to tell anyone" the thing
they cannot keep to themselves. Be responsible to yourself
and let them know.

You are talking to the wrong person.

It goes without saying that your friends are
usually the first to discuss your personal
business behind your back.
—Terry McMillan, from *Mama*

*I*f there is anything you don't want people to know
about you, don't tell anyone. We give people too much responsibility when we entrust them with our business.
Sometimes they repeat the information mindlessly; other
times they use our story to make a point. We should only
tell our problems to people who can help. Eighty percent
of the people we talk to can't help us; the other 20 percent
really don't care. We are quick to accuse our friends of be-
traying us, but do we consider how we betray ourselves?
We lie to ourselves and on ourselves and then allow ourselves to believe it will not come back. It does, through the
mouth and actions of someone else. In those special times
when you must talk about your private affairs, ask the
other person if he is willing to keep your confidence. If he
repeats it, then the responsibility is his—not for telling
your business, but for not keeping his word.

I will only tell you what I want everybody to know.

Two men in a burning house must not stop to argue.
—Ashanti proverb

It is not your duty or responsibility to change the minds of other people. The nature of their thinking is advanced or limited by their experience. In your presence, they have an opportunity to learn about you and, perhaps, to grow. Allow them to experience you as a well-grounded, compassionate being who is capable of listening, learning, sharing and growing. That is your responsibility to yourself, your life and the other person. You can be an example of the peaceful, vibrant, valuable contributor your ancestors were. Like them, you can contribute to the enlightenment of the world when you spend less time worrying about what others think and more time creating positive change.

Every experience is an opportunity to grow.

Offensive words that come from your mouth, if
repeated, can make bitter enemies.
— *The Husia*, translated by Dr. Maulana Karenga

*E*very mouth has two lips. The high lip gives to praise, the low lip gives to gossip. When we do not guard what we say or to whom we say it, we can never be sure which lip will repeat the words. The ancient Egyptians gave warnings about the unguarded movement of the mouth. They understood the destructive potential of words on the wrong lips. We may not be familiar with those ancient teachings, but we do know the impact of low-lipped speaking. Speak highly of everyone or say nothing at all. Repeat only that which you have a duty to repeat and repeat it with a noble intent. If something you say comes back the wrong way, correct it immediately. If you quarrel with family or friends, speak to them directly. Temper your words with a consciousness of empathy. Speak the way you would want to be spoken to. Remember that your parents gave you the blessing of lips; speak to them with an attitude of gratefulness.

I have spoken truly and done it righteously.

July 25

No investigation. No right to speak.
—Confucius

*V*ery often we find ourselves involved in conversations of the "he said, she said" variety. We may not know the parties involved or we may have heard some other version of the same story from another source. The sad thing is we use this information as the basis for our opinions and interactions with the people involved. There's an old African saying, "Ears don't pass head," which means we should never let what goes into our ears override good common sense. Common sense tells us we should accept people for who they are based on our individual experience with them. All too often the side of the story that is not told is the other person's side. It is in our best interests to give everyone a fair start, regardless of what we have heard about them. We should make our own mental inventory, identify any negative experiences we have had. If there are none, we should commit ourselves to be open and deal with people as they deal with us.

I am willing to give everyone a fresh start.

No one can judge you unless you let them.
—Swami Nada Yolanda

Don't "should" on other people and don't let them
"should" on you. Should is a judgment we make based on
our experiences and perceptions. When we pass that on to
other people, we are judging them. Should is an expression of fear. It says that our way is the right way; if you
move beyond that, you might prove I am wrong. Should is
the way we control others, to make them think or behave
the way we want them to. Should takes us on a guilt trip
and limits our capacity to grow. If we only do the things
we should do we will never learn another way we could do
it. Should limits us to what is comfortable. Should keeps
us in a place that is familiar. Should makes us responsible
to someone other than ourselves when we know that is not
the way we "should" live.

*I "should" do only those things
that feel right for me.*

What is the quality of your intent?
—Thurgood Marshall

*C*ertain people have a way of saying things that shake us at the core. Even when the words do not seem harsh or offensive, the impact is shattering. What we could be experiencing is the intent behind the words. When we intend to do good, we do. When we intend to do harm, it happens. What each of us must come to realize is that our intent always comes through. We cannot sugarcoat the feelings in our heart of hearts. The emotion is the energy that motivates. We cannot ignore what we really want to create. We should be honest and do it the way we feel it. What we owe to ourselves and everyone around is to examine the reasons of our true intent.

My intent will be evident in the results.

July 28

Each time we have sex we must be
innocent and open.

—Ebun Adelona

Sexual intercourse is an act of profound creation. It is
the meshing and weaving together of the Mother/Father
force of the Creator. Whatever we hold in our heart the
Mother and our mind the Father, during the sexual act,
will be created in our lives. Sex in anger will create angry
words and angry situations that must be resolved. If we
are in denial about ourselves, who we are or who our mate
truly is in our life, then sex will create denial in the relationship. Sex in self-sacrifice will create a doormat. Whoever makes the sacrifice will be walked on. Sex in
confusion creates chaos and more confusion about how
and why we want sex. Unconscious sex, doing it just to be
doing it, creates a violation in the subconscious mind.
When we create children during misguided intercourse,
the child brings to life the state of our being at the time of
the act. We can heal and strengthen ourselves during our
conscious sexual activity, but we must know what we are
doing and why.

Sexual intercourse is a creative expression
in which I fully participate.

Instant intimacy is very often followed
by desperate disillusion.

—May Sarton

We can become so emotionally charged by a person that we allow ourselves to be intimate before we know who the person really is. When we give our bodies to another being, we are giving them a piece of our souls. We might want to take the time to find out if they deserve it. Sexual activity is not the only way to let someone know we like them. Sharing information, supporting each other's goals, giving of our time and energy without expectations sends a much stronger message than sex. We must take time to know the other person; understand what they want, where they are going and figure out if we want to be in the same place. When we let down our hair too early in the game we are apt to end up with a messed up head.

I will choose time over intimacy.

Everything, even darkness and
silence has its wonders.

—Helen Keller

A history of abuse and labeling has created a tremendous strain on the sexual consciousness of people of color. The ancestral memory of being labeled as animals to be studded and bred has made us fearful of our sexuality. What we must accept and learn to understand is that we can be sexual and still be spiritual. Even in the abuses of the past, people of color were capable of loving and sharing that love as a sexual expression. We prayed for our freedom and the safety of our lives, and we still made love. Although the abuses have changed, many of our fears have not. Right now, there are many people of color who become anxious, nervous and uncomfortable in conversations about sex. We do it, but we hide it. We make jokes about it in private; we tell stories about it in secret; when it comes to talking and sharing openly about sex, we shy away. Try this. Sex is wonderful. Sex is good. I like sex. Sex likes me. But don't take my word for it; try it for yourself—with the lights on.

I Am free to be a sexual being.

Let them wait. And wait they do.

—Jackeé

All relationships are like contractual agreements. Each party expects to receive certain things. In our intimate relationships, sex is like a signature on the contract. Unfortunately, many of us sign the contract without reading the fine print. By the time we discover what kind of deal we are being offered, we are bound by our signature. Some contracts have a ninety-day grace period. This gives the parties the opportunity to examine the merchandise, test the service, make any necessary adjustments or bow out of the agreement. It makes sense to apply a grace period to our intimate relationships. We may need time to assess behavior, true intentions and the performance history of the prospects. The fine-print issues such as habits, motive and background cannot be seen with closed eyes.

I Am willing to read the fine print.

If you eat well, you must speak well.

— Yoruba proverb

When we become angry, upset or disappointed with someone, we forget the good they have done. We seem to think people must prove themselves to us again and again. If ever they fail to live up to our expectations, we are quick to voice our dismay. The ancient Africans taught that if a person is good to you, you must forever speak good of them. They believed the good always outlives the not so good. In order to keep the good flowing, you must speak of it. The ancestors taught that we must honor those who helped us when we were in need, regardless of what they do now. We must honor those who taught us, even if we no longer use the lessons. We must remember with a kind word the road someone else has paved for us, no matter where or how they travel now. Everything we receive in life is food for our growth. If we eat from the plate, we must give thanks. Remembering, without that food, at that time, we may have starved.

I remember only the good that has been done.

Go behind the apparent circumstances of the situation and locate the love in yourself and in all others involved in the situation.

—Mother Teresa

*T*he moment we have a negative experience we get stuck in what was done and how it was done to us. We must learn not to take life so personally. People are not really out to get us. Events are not waiting to befall us. We are all moving to get where we want to be. As a result, we will sometimes step on each others' toes. When we find ourselves in a conflict or confrontation we must know how to love ourselves out of it. Love means recognizing fear as an operand condition that sometimes makes us do and say things we really don't mean. Love means opening our hearts and minds to our best, regardless of what is going on. Love means not attacking but supporting, not defending but seeking clarity. Love means knowing that, in the end, we will all be okay even if it means we have to give up a little of something. Let us learn to give up anger and fear by replacing those things with love.

I Am loving you and me out of this situation.

Each of us is stamped with vibratory signature of
our own state of consciousness.

— Paramhansa Yogananda

We become very offended if someone says we don't
measure up or if they criticize our actions. We think they
are picking on us because of our race, gender or because
"they" have a problem. We must consider what they are
actually saying before we dismiss what could be valuable
criticism. Consider the things we think about ourselves:
"I'm not good enough," "I'm not smart enough," "I didn't
do it right," "So and so did it better than me," "I need
someone to tell me how good I am," "I hope I don't mess
up, like I did before," "If I do it like this, they will like me,"
"I don't know what I'm doing," "I'm not good at this," "I
can do better than this." Life is an accurate reflection of
our consciousness. People will usually say to us the very
things we think to ourselves. If we want others to speak
well of us, we must first think well of ourselves. The next
time someone criticizes you, think, "Where have I heard
that before?"

*I think positively about me and
speak positively to me.*

If you love 'em in the morning with their eyes full of crust; if you love 'em at night with their hair full of rollers, chances are, you're in love.

—Miles Davis

*W*hen was the last time you were in love? Really in love? Do you remember feeling silly? Giggling and grinning whenever you saw the object of your affection? Did you feel like skipping, running, jumping in the street? Maybe spinning around and rustling your hair? Did everybody look better, act nicer, seem beautiful because you were in love? What about playing? Didn't you want to stay home and play with your love mate rather than go to work or school? And didn't you want to go to bed early? Do you remember getting dressed up and wanting to look nice because you felt so good? Did you feel as if you could do anything because you had somebody at your side? What about feeling nurtured, supported, protected? How about being needed, wanted, valued? And didn't it bring a smile to your face just to think that somebody loved you? Did it make you feel young again? Well then, why do you think children don't know when they're in love?

Loves come to all ages.

August 5

I wish I woulda knowed more people. If I woulda
knowed more, I woulda loved more.
— Toni Morrison, from *Beloved*

We have an unlimited capacity to love. Actually, loving
is not something we do to or for other people. It is a blessing, a gift we give to ourselves. Love opens us to endless
possibilities. It increases our resources and our capacity to
give. Love fine-tunes our vibrational frequency, which enables us to create. Love keeps us alive long after we have
departed and gives meaning to who we are, what we do
and how we do it. The only thing that limits our capacity
to love are the conditions we place on loving. When love is
based on what we get or how we get it, our love ability is
stunted. When we love under circumstances rather than in
spite of them, our love is limited. When we love what was
rather than what is, we have no real idea what love is
about. When we love just for the sake of it, giving who we
are without excuses or apologies, taking what comes and
making the best of it, we open our souls to the abundant
blessings of the strongest forces of life.

*Today I will pour love into everyone
and into everything.*

August 6

We are each born with a limitless capacity for
pleasure and enjoyment.

—Sondra Ray

*R*elationships do not just happen. No matter how we
meet our mate or who makes the introduction, we create
all the relationships we experience. We each have the capacity to bring to ourselves the exact relationship we
want. Unfortunately, most of us are not willing to do the
work. We must begin the work by looking at the "self" and
getting clear about how it feels. We cannot expect to attract a loving, generous mate if we are angry and withholding. We must stop blaming the past for our condition
now. Wherever we are, what we have or don't have is no
one's fault but our own. If by chance someone else made a
contribution to the mess we were creating, forgive them
the mess and move on. Finally, we must give thanks for all
we have been; all we have had; all we are becoming. When
we take the limits, restrictions and fears off our hearts, our
cup of love will run over.

I will look at me before I look for love.

August 7

Your mate is your mirror.

$\mathcal{M}$any of us think we are lucky or blessed when we find just the right person to love. By now we know that nothing in life is an accident, including our selection of a mate. The people who come into our lives are a reflection of who we are. They reveal to us those things we cannot or refuse to see about ourselves. The very thing we don't like about our mate is the thing we need to change. The thing we love about the other person is a hidden, undeveloped or unrecognized asset that we have. We can only draw to us those people who are on our ray, our level of energy and development. They reflect back to us the very things we do. Most of us reject this idea. But then most of us reject criticism, too. We find it difficult to accept those things about us that others see. We do, however, feel completely justified when we criticize our mates. Here's a question for you: How would you know what to call what you see in your mate unless you had seen it somewhere else?

I am looking in the mirror of self and making adjustments in me.

The person who seeks to change another person
in a relationship basically sets the stage
for a great deal of conflict.

—Wesley Snipes

*V*ery often we go into relationships with the idea that we can make somebody better. We see their flaws or short-comings and take it upon ourselves to help them fix what is wrong. Our task in our relationships is not to fix one an-other. Our job is to love what we see and support one an-other in doing better. Fixing is telling what is wrong, why and how to fix it. Supporting is allowing us to make our own choices, being there if things go wrong and support-ing us in doing better next time. Fixing is forcing us to do it their way when our way doesn't work. Supporting is sharing with us their needs and trusting we will take them into account. Fixing is nagging. Supporting is nurturing. Fixing is anger when things get rough. Supporting is knowing things will get better. Supporting is seeing us ex-actly as we are. Fixing is seeing in them what we refuse to see in ourselves.

I love and support you exactly as you are.

Only choose to marry a woman whom you would
choose as a friend if she were a man.

—Joseph Joubert

We often have such unrealistic expectations of our mates that it is as if we do not want them to measure up. We want them to be like, act like, behave like some idealistic model we have cooked up in our minds. The problem is that we never reveal to them what the model is. We hold them accountable and responsible to satisfy our desires, but we forget to tell them what our desires are. We must remember that our mates are people. They are not mind readers. We are asking for disappointment when we do not share with them our expectations. We complain to friends, compare them to family members; why not talk to the one person who could probably help set things right? We should talk to our mates as if they are our friends. Reveal to them those parts of us that we have hidden from the world. And if in our heart of hearts we cannot do this, we need to ask ourselves, "Why am I with this person?"

I want more than a mate, I want a friend.

If you know what you want, you will recognize it
when you see it.

— Bill Cosby

When we convince ourselves that we can't find the right mate, we try to make the one we have into the one we want. There are two ways to do this. First, we need to see who we have and tell ourselves they are someone different. The other way is to try and fix what we have. Neither idea works. When we are not honest with ourselves about who our mate really is, we end up disillusioned and disappointed. It is not their fault, it is our own. We must be clear about what we want from a relationship whether it is social, business or intimate. Then we must make a decision to wait for exactly what we want. If who we have is not who we want, say so! It is not our job to change the other person. If we buy a pair of shoes and they do not fit, should we wear them and suffer or take them back to the store?

Who I want is important enough for me to wait for.

Would you marry you?

We are always looking for the perfect relationship. The goal is to find that perfect someone who will make our lives a better place to be. It is unfortunate that we don't realize perfection runs two ways. In order to find that perfect somebody, we must believe that, whatever perfect is, we have already achieved it. No one can give us what we don't already have. Mr. or Ms. Right cannot be to us what we are not. If we are unhappy, unfulfilled, not pleased about who we are, we owe it to ourselves to stop looking. We have to ask ourselves: Would I marry me? Am I doing my best, giving my all, being the best I can be to myself? If not, why are we pawning ourselves off on someone else. We need to take time to do some homework on self-love, self-esteem and self-confidence. When we can pass the test of self-acceptance, the perfect someone who will complement all that we already are will walk right through the door.

The love and harmony within me reaches
out and draws my mate.

Do not envy the oppressor,
and choose none of his ways.

— Proverbs 4:31

*W*hen someone does you harm, it seems only natural
that you should do the same to him, right? Wrong! You
can never get even with someone who has harmed you.
Any attempt to do so puts you behind the eight ball, again.
Two wrongs never make a right. Nor can you right a
wrong by committing another wrong. You may be able to
justify your actions politically or socially, but spiritually
you will be held accountable for what you do—why you
do it doesn't count. The pendulum of life swings both
ways and brings rewards at both ends of the spectrum. If
you use your mind, time and energy to cause harm to anyone, the pendulum will sooner or later move in your direction. If your slate is clean, when it swings toward you, you
will not have to worry about being knocked down.

I settle all of my scores in the court of
universal justice.

Let go!

When we believe we are losing control, we grab on tight. If we want to avoid pain, we hold on for dear life. When we are in fear of losing, looking bad or being abandoned, we tighten our grip. When our greatest fear comes upon us, we clench our fist and teeth, close our eyes and hold on. We must learn how to let go. We have the capacity to live through any adversity if we simply let it go. We cannot stop time or destiny. Whatever is going to happen has already happened; we must learn how to see it through to the end. When we hold on, we prolong the pain. When we dig our feet in, we must be uprooted. When the time comes for growth and change, we must have the courage and faith to let go.

*Whatever leaves my life makes room for
something better.*

If you cannot find peace within yourself, you will
never find it anywhere else.
— Marvin Gaye

Where do we get the idea that if a relationship or a
marriage ends, we have somehow failed? The ending of a
relationship is not a sign of personal failure. Actually, it is
a courageous step. It is a loving gesture. It is a responsible
move. It takes courage to admit when a relationship is not
working. When we are locked in a relationship that is not
working, it can be very painful. We must love ourselves
and our mates enough not to want them to stay in a situation that is causing pain. When we are willing to take personal responsibility and the necessary steps to free
ourselves from the pain of a relationship, we are showing a
willingness to grow. Looking at things from this perspective, how can we consider ourselves failures? There comes
a time in every situation when difficult decisions must be
made. Making the decisions may make us feel miserable;
not to make them is what makes us miserable failures.

I am not a failure. I am ending a relationship.

Rejection can be killing. It kills faster and more effectively when the victim is already lacking in some vital way.

— Patti Austin

Nobody likes being rejected, but rejection does not mean there is something wrong with you. An early rejection can save you a great deal of grief later on. Then there are those times when what you have is not really what you want, but you convince yourself to settle for it anyway. Well, if the other person rejects you, you are saved from having to run away. Rejection is only damaging when you start out believing you are not complete. When you enter a relationship needy and unfulfilled, rejection can be a damaging blow. In those situations you must not shrink away feeling defeated and afraid; you must ask what is it that this person has, and why you don't think you can get it anywhere else. If you understand that you can only draw to yourself what you already are, you can see rejection in another light. When you enter any relationship, you want to be and feel the best you can. If you get rejected, it might simply mean you have a little more work to do.

When I accept me no one can reject me.

No one can see their reflection in running water. It is only in still water we can see.

— *The Wisdom of the Taoists*

*D*ivorce or separation following a long-term relationship creates many feelings. One of the strongest is "something is wrong with me." If your mate becomes involved with another person or gives what you consider an unacceptable reason for moving beyond the relationship, the feelings of inadequacy deepen. Why? What did I do? How could you do this to me? Somewhere in the process you lost sight of the fact that people have a right to change their minds. You may not want them to do it. You probably won't like it when it happens. But people have a right to change their minds, and it has absolutely nothing to do with you. Time marches on. People change. As people change, their needs change. When people have a need, it is their responsibility to themselves to see their needs are met. And it has absolutely nothing to do with you.

There is nothing wrong with me.

Spend time alone in objective thought as you
consider the direction of your life.
—*I Ching (The Receptive)*

*T*he entire purpose of life here on earth is for people to
be free. Why then do we spend so much time acquiring
things to make us comfortable and tie us down? Our possessions keep us in bondage to jobs, debts, situations and
conditions. We spend precious time fighting with one another as to the right way to fight for the freedom we want.
Women want to be free. We sit idly as men control the
markets, industries and services that are essential to our
survival. Women complain that men oppress them, yet at
the same time they believe the things men say women cannot do. Men say they want to be free. The average man
spends his average day watching someone else, wondering
what someone else is doing, believing someone else is
waiting for an opportunity to take what he has. What's the
matter with these pictures? We will never be free as long
as we need something or someone else to give it to us.
Freedom is a state of mind, not a tangible condition.

I surrender everything to my freedom.

You have to love enough to let go.

*T*here are times when loving someone means we must let them go. It is not healthy or productive to remain in a relationship that makes us happy sometimes, sad most of the time. Yet we hang on. We hang on believing that something bad will happen to the person if we let him or her go. That is our ego telling us what we want to hear. We hang on in fear that no one else will love them or us the way we want to be loved. This time the ego is telling us that we are not good enough. We hang on because we don't know who or what may come along. We believe there is a lack of available mates. We hang on wishing, hoping, trying to make it work—afraid it will not. When a relationship is over, it is over; but the love can live on. Loving someone means you want him or her to be happy. If that person can be happy without you, love enough to let go.

I know when to let go.

Friends borrow your books and
sit wet glasses on them.
— Edwin Robinson

Sometimes the people we care about the most are the people we treat badly. We don't always mean to or want to. At times we just don't think. Other times we do it because we know we can get away with it. We must learn to value and honor those blessings we call friends; they are few and far between. They come to share a part of life with us. How we treat them is a reflection of our thoughts about life. When we tax our friendships with abuse, neglect or mindless actions, we shut ourselves off from the support that makes life easier to bear. When we fail to nurture our friendships, it is a sign that we do not nurture ourselves. When we treat our friends with kindness and respect, they are obliged to do the same. When we hold our friendships in high regard, we learn to feel good about ourselves. When we value our friends and the relationship, they know it, and they will do their best to keep things in balance.

I will treat my friends as well as I treat myself.

It is said that love is blind. Friendship,
however, is clairvoyant.
—Phillipe Soupault

A friend, a real friend, someone you love and trust, is going to tell you all the things you do not want to know about yourself. A friend tells you when you are right and helps you understand how you could be wrong. A friend will yell and scream, but when you need him, he is there. A friend is someone you cannot and do not lie to. She knows your secrets and holds them in confidence. A friend never judges, yet will let you know when you are doing it "again." A friend sees your mistakes and, without covering them up, steers you in another direction. A friend pushes you, shoves you and drives you real hard. Just when you think you are about to break, he whips out the Band-Aids, patches you up and starts pushing again. A friend always says things that make no sense until you hear a stranger say the same thing. A friend is someone you can look at and see yourself and know you are really going to be all right.

When I see my friend, I see myself.

I was secure enough in my relationships
with my children that I did not have to fight my
mother for power.

—Gladys Knight

*M*others and daughters have many hurdles to overcome. There's the mother's view, the daughter's view.
There's the mother's opinion, the daughter's opinion.
There's the mother's fear that the daughter will not succeed. There's the daughter's fear that she will not be supported in what she wants. There's the mother's incessant
nagging to do things the "right way"; there's the daughter's
view that the mother's way will not work. There are mothers who have not grown up. There are daughters who
have grown up too fast. Then come the grandchildren, a
chance for the mother to do it again, better this time. Now
there is a way for the daughter to prove that the mother's
way does not work. The mother sees herself in the daughter—there is pride and celebration. The daughter does not
want to be anything like the mother—there is disappointment and embarrassment. Mothers and daughters reflect
each other, they repel each other, yet in spite of it all they
love each other. Sometimes they should tell each other.

I Am my mother's daughter.

We survived slavery because we held onto one another. The moment we found independence, we began to commit suicide.

—Dr. Tesehloane Keto

*T*here is a metaphysical principle that says whatever we do to someone else, we actually do to ourselves. This principle supports the golden rule "do unto others." We forget this and when we do, we create an imbalance in our own being. When we malign another person, we are talking about the self. When we deal dishonestly with someone, we are cheating the self. When we abuse, neglect or abandon another, we are doing it to the self. Why? Because we are connected by the one Creative source. This source creates a responsibility for, accountability to and dependence on one another. The moment we allow the self to believe it can do without other people we create the kind of loneliness, depression and disconnection that makes life not worth living.

I Am one with the Source.
I Am one with mankind.

Potential means —you ain't doing nothing now.
—Michelle Ventour

*O*ne of the greatest downfalls in our relationships is banking on the potential of someone else. We go to great lengths to understand what someone should do, could do, has the ability to do but is not doing. Very often what we see of the person prevents us from seeing that the person is doing nothing. Parents, friends and spouses have lost millions of dollars and valuable time saying, "I see the good in you." We usually want so much for our loved ones that we forget to ask what they want for themselves. You cannot want more for someone than they want for themselves. If they want it, it is up to them to go out and get it; you should not have to drive or take them to find it. Do not be concerned with what a person could do; pay close attention, listen intently to what they are doing and saying right now.

I see you in this moment.

Emotional independence begins with the
development of inner resources.

—Anonymous

We have been taught that a relationship is a fifty-fifty proposition. A more accurate view is that two incomplete people can come together and find completion. This is a false premise that has had a disastrous impact on our relationships. Each person must come into a relationship a whole, complete person who is able to handle the responsibility; willing to share in the responsibility for mutual growth. Fifty-fifty relationships usually do not work. The premise is simple: What if both parties are missing the same thing? A relationship must not be a crutch. We want to develop complimentary unions where strengths and weaknesses have support. We want to be able to stand on our own, but stand a little taller in a relationship. We want to bring an identity to the table and have it reflected to us a little brighter. In a relationship, two halves do not make a whole, and we cannot allow anyone else to take responsibility for our completion.

*I am bringing 100 percent of who
I Am to the love table.*

> There is really a very little difference between
> people; it is called attitude; and it makes a
> really big difference. The big difference is
> whether it's positive or negative.
>
> —W. Clement Stone

*P*eople are not always out to get you, but there are times when they do. Chances are the person was close to you — best friend, relative, parent, lover, child or spouse. There's an even better chance that you deeply loved and trusted the person. Perhaps they betrayed you. Abandoned you. Stole from you. Or failed to return the emotional commitment you made. No matter how traumatic the wrongdoing or end of a relationship may be, the good always outweighs the bad. If you have one bad memory, you have two positive ones. If you learned one new thing about yourself or another person, you know more than you did when you started. If you learned in this relationship what not to do in the next, you are better for it. If you learned patience, faith, trust, humility or what a truly strong and powerful person you are, you have treasures you will never lose.

The difference between me and
them is I am positive.

It is your moral duty to be happy; however, you cannot exercise this duty by clutching unrealistic beliefs, struggling with unworkable assumptions, juggling painful images, jumping to false conclusions, running with impulsive decisions or massaging hasty judgments.

—Sufi Hazarat Inayat Khan

*T*oo often we expect happiness to come as a result of our relationships rather than as a premise upon which to build one. If we truly wanted to be happy, we would not be so eager to sacrifice happiness for nonsense—jealously, possessiveness, anger, fear or any other function of the ego. Nonsense renders us downright miserable. Happiness requires that we be honest, trusting, trustworthy, respectful and mutually considerate. We cannot realize true happiness when we entertain nonsense in our hearts and minds. Individually and collectively, we must work to clear ourselves before entering a relationship. If we wait until we are in the process and wading through the nonsense, the ego will be well on the way to eroding the happiness we seek.

I will exercise my duty to be happy.

If you want to know the end, look at the beginning.
—African proverb

*W*herever you are in your heart and mind at the outset of a relationship is where you will be at the end. Whatever you bring to the start of the relationship is what you will have to clean up in the end. You cannot begin a relationship in dishonesty and deceit and hope to experience an honest end. If you run into a relationship to get away from another, you will run into another one to get away from this one. If you enter a relationship in fear, anger or grief, you stand a pretty good chance of finding more of the same. If you enter a relationship in sadness, desperation and pain, guess what? You will find it again. If we want to put an end to angry, bitter and ugly separations, we must begin our relationships with the open, loving honesty we say we want. If we do not know who we are and how we feel at any time, it is best that we stay alone.

I will be better at the beginning to avoid anything worse at the end.

Anything dead coming back hurts.
—Toni Morrison, from *Beloved*

If you keep going in and out of the same relationship, chances are you are going to get hurt. People come together in a relationship to learn. Once you learn your lesson it is time to move on. Take your lesson from the last time and move on to something new. If you insist on drinking from the same used cup, you will eventually get sick. You can do the same old things in just so many ways until you lose track of what you are doing. How many ways can you cry? How many ways can you hurt? How many ways can you convince yourself that you can make this work? When a relationship is over, you must learn to let go. No matter how much you love the other person, or how afraid you are that you will never love again, you cannot squeeze juice from a piece of dry fruit, so don't bother to try.

When it is over, I am on to the next thing.

Is this love? Is this love? Is this love?
Is this love that I'm feeling?

—Bob Marley

*H*ow do you know when you are really in love? First of all, you would not have to ask the question. Love is knowing, it is not a condition or state of mind. When you are loving, you are not doubting, judging or fearing; you are in a state of acceptance. You accept yourself first, for who and what you are, and then the person you love, without question. You do not want to fix him, change him, control him or help him. You want for the person you love exactly what she wants for herself. When you are in love, you feel vulnerable and know that it is okay. You do not hide your feelings, change them to fix what you think the other person wants, and you do not question what you feel. When you are in love, you give, expecting nothing in return, not even love. Love is an inner process between you and yourself that you want to share with someone, everyone. Love is free. If your quest is to own, control, hold on to, protect, or take care of someone, they cannot be free and you are not in love. Love is never wrong, seldom right. It just is.

Love is in the midst of me.

When self-respect takes its rightful place in the
psyche, you will not allow yourself to be
manipulated by anyone.

—Indira Mahindra

*L*oving, wanting or being with someone else is absolutely no reason to abuse, neglect or disrespect yourself. In all of our relationships, we can only give what we have. When we have a sense of self, an honest consciousness of our needs, a clear concept of what we want, we can respect ourselves. We set the standard of how we want to be treated; it remains our responsibility to make sure that anyone and everyone who comes into our lives treats us as well or better than we treat ourselves. If we are not honest with ourselves, how can we expect others to be honest with us? If we are not nurturing and supportive of ourselves, why would we expect it from anyone else? If we do not expect and give the best to ourselves, from where do we think it will come? Our relationships can only be reflections of the relationships that we have with ourselves.

*If I love, honor and respect me—you must
do the same.*

You cannot throw a loved one out of your heart
and mind.

—Betsey Salunek

No matter what they have done to you and said to you, you cannot stop loving them. No matter how much they disappoint you, neglect or abuse you, if you think you love them, you probably do. It does not matter what others say about them, how others feel about them or how bad you feel about them; if you love them, admit it. Do not tell yourself you don't love somebody if you do. What you might want to do is make a choice about whether you want this person to be a part of your life. It is not necessary to stop loving people if you don't like them. You can choose the type of relationship you want to have with the people you love. You can love them from a distance. You can love them and not live with them. You can love them in the deepest part of your being and choose to move on. You can figure out why you love them, if you love them and still choose to move on. You can love them for who they are and what they are and stop complaining.

I can choose how I want to love you.

Everything was fine but the beans were salty.
—Mother Jefferson

There are people in your life you can never please no matter what you do. There is always something wrong with you, with the world and with them. Criticism is the way adults cry. When we are in pain, nothing looks or feels good, particularly those close to us. We strike out because we cannot tune into what we are feeling. Criticism is our way of saying something is wrong with us and we see it in you. Do not take it personally when a loved one continuously criticizes. They are never upset for the reason they say they are, and whatever it is, it is not your issue. Do not strike back when you are criticized. Remember, you are with someone who is in pain. Be gentle with them, love them, gently ask them to talk to you about what they are really feeling.

I Am all right with me.

When one door closes, another one opens.
— African-American folklore

Many people ask, "Why can't I find a good relationship?" Perhaps it is because they haven't truly ended the last one. We hold on to people in our hearts and minds long after they have gone. We may hold on to anger, hurt and pain. We may be holding ideas of revenge and destruction. We hold on to romantic memories and special times using them as measuring sticks for anyone who comes along. We hold on to our hearts, protecting them from pain, our minds filled with memories and doubts. We believe our dreams are shattered and will never come true. With all of the stuff we hold on to, how can others get into our hearts? We must learn how to close the door on old relationships. We must sort through the rubbish, clear out the garbage and freshen up our hearts and minds to receive a new guest.

I Am closing the door on the past.

If you believe you are to blame for everything that goes wrong, you will have to stay until you fix it.
—Zora Neale Hurston

Some of us, particularly women of color, set ourselves up to be martyrs. We are to blame. It is our fault. We just can't seem to do anything right, so we don't. We create mess after mess, crisis after crisis. This allows others to use us as doormats. Smart move! As long as we are to blame, we cannot be held responsible or accountable for what we do not accomplish. We are too busy fixing the mess, figuring out what to do, or if we should do anything at all. As long as we have something or someone to fix, we cannot fix ourselves. We will never fix the fear of our power. We will never fix the fear of our beauty. We cannot fix our pain or confusion or desperate feelings of isolation. We don't have to face our fears or try to fix them; after all, it's our fault we are like this. And as long as we are to blame, we will never have to face the thought that others must share in the responsibility of getting things done.

The only thing I will fix today is me.

It doesn't matter what road you take, hill you climb, or path you're on, you will always end up in the same place, learning.

—Ralph Stevenson

*T*here is nothing more devastating to the human psyche than what we call a broken heart. He done me wrong! She put me out! He cheated! She lied! I can't eat! I can't sleep! I see her face! I hear his voice! Please let him call! I've got to see her! Wait! Hold it! Hearts don't break! We love with our heads, not with our hearts. We develop an idea of what a relationship should be, how our mate should behave and what we want to feel in the process. If things do not go the way we planned, our hearts are broken. There is a secret to this love thing—we must learn how to love honestly with no preconceived notions. Loving honestly means being who we are, accepting our mates for who they are; demanding nothing in return for our love. Under these conditions, if things do not go well, it has nothing to do with our hearts; it's our poor choices that have caught up with us. The only thing we can do about a broken heart is fix our head.

My heart is unbreakable.

The only way to have peace in a relationship is to
know how to butter your own bread.

— Ra-Ha

*I*f you are in a relationship that causes you imbalance
and anguish, get out. If you are in a relationship that does
not support you or lowers your energy, leave it alone. If
you are in a relationship where you give more than you
get, where what you give is not respected, where the security you seek is costing you peace of mind, you've got
nothing else to lose — so leave. We come together in relationships to grow, not to live in misery. Our relationships
should be sustaining, energizing and growth-supporting.
When they are not, our growth is stunted, our energy is
depleted and our personality is distorted. A solid, loving,
supportive relationship is like a shot of life. It is a source
of inspiration, it provides a spark of motivation to encourage you onto the highest evolution of your selfhood. If you
are in a relationship in which you are happy sometimes,
sad most of the time, struggling to figure out what to do
and how to make it last, you are out of place.

I know when to quit.

Make all your relationships an "eight" or better.
—John Salunek

On a scale where one is low and ten is high, we want to live as close to ten as possible. We want to give and get the best in our relationships. Whether it is a friendship, love affair or business relationship, we must not allow mediocrity to be the standard. When we have no standards our lives become so crowded with people, demands and unrealized expectations that we run the risk of losing ourselves. An "eight" relationship is one where there is mutual support and respect. We can be who we are and know we are accepted on that basis. There are common goals; even when we disagree on method, we can support the intent. In an "eight" relationship we give for the joy of giving. We share for mutual growth. We give and get complete honesty. We take what we need and do not fail to give back. An "eight" relationship is one that we do not work on. It is one we work with and for, striving for better as a mutual benefit. "One" means you don't have it. "Six" is just making it. An "eight" means you are definitely on the way to the top.

There is no reason I must settle for less.

Vulnerability is the gift I give to those
I trust when I trust myself.
— Terry Kellogg and Marvel Harrison

*J*ust because people are nice to us and don't ask anything in return, does not mean there is something wrong
with them. It is often hard for us to believe people can like
us simply for who we are. Benny, a White man, was willing to give Frank, a Black man, a kidney. Frank wouldn't
accept it. He had known Benny for three short weeks.
Frank knew very little about Benny. But he knew Benny
must have a hidden agenda. Nobody gives a kidney away
for nothing. Frank confronted Benny with his anger, sus-
picion and fear. Quietly Benny replied, "I know you like
to go fishing. I know you are a good father and a loving
husband. I know because that's what you've shown me.
Based on what I've seen, I know you don't deserve to die."
Frank accepted the kidney. Benny moved to Arizona and
never saw Frank again.

Blessings come in all colors.
I get the ones I deserve.

Love creates an "us" without destroying the "me."
—Leo Buscaglia

*L*ove really is about people coming together to support each other. All the little tricks and games they play to get their needs met are just that, tricks and games. It would be so much simpler if we honored ourselves and trusted our partners enough to ask for what we need. Instead, we wait for them to figure it out; if they don't, we hold them responsible. What a cruel trick! When we let our partners know up front what we need, we have a greater chance of having the need met. We must know that our needs are important. Whether it's hugs and kisses, foot rubs, reassurance or Hershey syrup and whipped cream, our needs do matter. Once we let our partners know what we need, we must accept their honest answer as to whether or not they can meet those needs. If they cannot, we must then decide if these are the people we want in our lives.

*I honor my needs by letting my mate
know what they are.*

Loving someone and pleasing someone are two different things.

—Jerry Jampolski

The mother knew that her teenage son was involved with some unsavory people and affairs. She remained silent when he started wearing expensive clothes. She turned her head when he flashed the money. She drew the line when she found the bloody clothes and the gun in the basement. The next morning she called the police and had her only son arrested. When the social worker asked her how she felt about what she had done, she replied, "It is a lot easier for me to visit him every week in prison than it would be for me to take one trip to the cemetery." In all of our relationships there comes a time when we must do what we know is right. If we love someone, we want the best for them. It may not make them happy; it probably won't be easy; but loving someone does not mean allowing them to hurt themselves. It certainly doesn't mean you must allow them to hurt you.

In loving you I will not lose myself.

Consider those whom you call your enemies and
figure out what they should call you.
— Dwayne Dyer

*Y*ou cannot choose sides in a round world. You are either in it, a part of it, or you are off. When you have enemies you are a part of the very things you accuse them of.
An enemy opposes your interests or position. An enemy is
hostile, unkind or unfriendly. And what are you doing
while all of this is going on? If you consider them your
enemy how can they approach you to get things clear?
You are in the middle of what stands between you and
your enemy. It is not what they have done or said, can do
or might do; it is you. It is your thoughts, your judgments,
your fear, your condemnation, and if you did not feel
guilty you could not attack those you call your enemy. You
believe the enemy is wrong, not to be trusted, unworthy of
love; you prepare yourself for the defense, projecting onto
the enemy the very things you do yourself. When you
have an enemy, look at your own hatred; understand how
the hostility disturbs you and ask yourself, do I really
want to attack the very thing I fear?

The only enemies I have are the ones I attack.

For a love to grow through the tests of everyday
living, one must respect that zone of privacy where
one retires to relate to the inside instead
of the outside.

—Kahlil Gibran

*E*verybody needs a little time and space where they can
go to be alone. What this is called in a relationship is "the
danger zone." We all need those few little things that we
have for ourselves. It could be a thing, place, an activity or
something we cannot share. What this can look like in a
relationship is "what is mine is theirs." Everyone has that
special thing that they just love to do. What this feels like
in a relationship is "I'm going out without you." If you
want your relationship to grow and flourish and your
loved one to remain loving and kind, give them the time,
space and opportunity to go and make contact with their
own minds.

Today I will let you be with yourself.

When the law of an eye for an eye operates, all the people will end up blind.
—Bishop Desmond Tutu

*Y*ou simply cannot pay anyone back for something they did to you. Look for the lesson and move on. If one man treats you badly, rejects you, abandons you, abuses or disrespects you, you cannot hold all men accountable. Look for the lesson and move on. If your ex-wife took your money, lied to you, neglected your children and your home, it does not mean no woman can be trusted. Look for the lesson and move on. If some White people are racists; some Black people thieves; some intellectual people condescending; some uneducated people lazy; some light people uppity; some dark people ignorant; it does not give you the right or the authority to treat all people who look the same or act the same any way you choose, based on your past experiences. Ask yourself, What can I learn from this situation? What can I do this time that I did not do before? If there is nothing, simply move on.

I am doing the best I can right now.

Every woman is every other woman trying to
figure out who she is.
—Nana Korantemaa

Women of color have been led to believe that they must
be everything to everyone. As a result, we do not know
how to ask for support when we need or want it. We become angry with others when they are not there for us,
but we must realize people cannot, will not and do not
know how to help if we do not know how to ask. Take
sixty seconds for yourself and ask yourself what you need.
If it is assistance with a project, a shoulder to cry on, a
special something you need or want for yourself, let other
people support you. We make judgments about what people can or will do and we move on our assumptions. We
never really know what a person is willing to do or capable of doing until we ask. Nothing is too big or too small to
ask for if we need it. When we don't ask for what we need,
the need keeps getting bigger.

If I need support today I will ask for it.

If you can find someone you can really talk to, it can help you grow in so many ways.

—Stephanie Mills

*W*e all need the time, space and opportunity to vent our anger, frustration or dissatisfaction with the world. Unfortunately, those closest to us bear the brunt of our emotions when we do not release them. If loved ones take their frustration out on us, we must try not to take it personally; and never, never tell them they don't really feel that way. We must learn to honor others' feelings and support them in expressing how they feel. If they say things to us that are painful or angry, we must separate what is truth and what is unreal. Parents must find a way to express their feelings without taking it out on the children. If we are tired, we should say so. If we are angry, we should take a walk before we go home. If we allow ourselves to say what we really feel, when we feel it, and try listening and not responding, we would probably have a lot less to fight about. When we express what we feel the moment we feel it, it won't get mixed in with everything else.

Today I will talk about what I feel.

God is my source and my supply, not my husband.
—Bridgette Rouson

*T*here is only one power and one presence operating in our lives. That is the power of the Creative Source. It operates through our consciousness. It draws to us and provides for us in response to how we think. If we are not aware of the power operating in us, through us and for us, we hold our mate responsible to provide the things we want and need. The Source gives us all that we deserve based on our conscious awareness of its presence. If we pressure our mates to give us things, it means we are out of touch. The Source provides our food, clothing and shelter. It provides us with work; it fulfills our needs. The Source may work through things and people, but the Source is the substance of all things. If we have a mate who is not giving, sharing or providing us with the things we think we need, we must ask ourselves, What am I thinking about in terms of where and from whom I get my sustenance?

God, the omnipresent, provides my every need.

Coming together is a beginning; keeping together is a process; working together is success.

—Henry Ford

*W*hether in business or personal relationships, what makes working together so difficult is the individual need to be right and to have things our way. As long as we have a position to hold on to we cannot come together or work together. If we are not willing to bend, we will somehow get in the way. We must get clear about what we are doing, why we are doing it and who we are working with. Only with an honest examination of our motives and intent can we surrender to any working or loving process. If we enter any collective agreement for only personal goals and with mental garbage, the stability of the group is jeopardized by our dishonest foundation. If we come together in honesty, work together in clarity, we can stay together with respect and meet any goal successfully.

*I respect myself enough to respect
the working process.*

Most people enjoy the inferiority of their friends,
real friends don't notice it.
—Norman Douglas

*M*any people of color believe it is their responsibility to stay in relationships, communities and situations to prove they are true blue. Nothing could be further from the truth! We owe it to our dreams to place ourselves in an environment that provides and supports the things we want. We have a right to peace, prosperity and success, even when it means we leave the "'hood." Does this mean you think the 'hood is bad? No, it simply means the 'hood is not where you choose to be. Growth requires that we move on. Movement does not mean rejection. It means we want to broaden our scope. To move beyond those things and people who are familiar to us does not mean we are leaving them behind. It means we are clearing a path for them to follow, if they choose to.

New friends are silver, old friends are gold.

A friend is a person who dislikes
the same people you do.

—Anonymous

*D*on't hang out with people who are where you don't want to be. Your friends and the environment reflect what you really feel about yourself. Winners hang out with winners. Losers hang out with losers. When you are on the move, you need people and an environment that supports and encourages your dream. You won't find that among people who are helpless and hopeless. You won't find support for your goals among people who whine and complain. You must know and believe that there are people waiting for you in the places you want to be. They will nurture, support and encourage you to keep moving. People you know may not always support your growth. For you to move on means you leave them behind. It also means that you prove what they claim to be impossible is definitely possible.

*I surround myself with people and
things that are good for me.*

When you are kind to someone in trouble, you hope they'll remember and be kind to someone else. And, it'll become like a wildfire.

— Whoopi Goldberg

For some reason which was never fully explained, Robert despised Rhonda. He told anyone who would listen how rotten, no good and downright dislikable she was. He made a campaign of it. He wrote letters. He made telephone calls. When he saw Rhonda, he smiled and said, "Hello." Robert died, suddenly, unexpectedly and penniless. There were many things that needed to be done. No one stepped forward to help, except Rhonda. She made the arrangements, spent the money and took care of Robert's affairs as best she could. Robert will never be able to say, "Thank you." He's not in a position to say, "I'm sorry. I was wrong about you." He will never be able to pay her the money or compensate her for her time. But when Rhonda had a family emergency and needed a car to travel across two states, someone she hardly knew said, "Here, take my car."

When I help you, I help me.

When you are not happy with yourself,
you cannot be happy with others.
—Daryl Mitchell

*E*veryone comes into our life to mirror back to us some part of ourselves we cannot or will not see. They show us the parts we need to work on or let go of. They reveal to us the things we do and the effects they have on ourselves and others. They say to us openly the things we say to ourselves silently. They reveal to us the fears, doubts, weaknesses and character flaws we know we have but refuse to address or acknowledge. We can usually see the faults of others very clearly. We all have people in our lives who anger or annoy us, who rub us the wrong way. They may create confusion or chaos. They may bring pain and disruption. They may reject us, abandon us and create some sort of harm. Before we get busy trying to fix the person or remedy the situation, we should ask ourselves, Why is this person in my life? What am I doing to draw this to myself? How do I do what they do, and how can I release this need? When we cleanse, heal and bring ourselves into balance, everyone in our lives will do the same or disappear.

My relationships are a true reflection of me.

Your children are not your children.

—Kahlil Gibran

*T*ake time today to remember that your children also have a heavenly Mother and Father who are as concerned about them as you. You are the channel used to bring the child into life, but you are not the only force guiding that life. We can become so preoccupied with what we "should have" done that we forget how much we are doing. We can be so absorbed with what is "wrong" with our children that we miss what is right. The fear over their or our failure prohibits our giving them what they need to succeed. Today, focus on the goodness that exists in children! There are things they do well and things they will learn to do better. Know that you cannot fix your children and you cannot plan their lives. What you can do is guide, support, nurture and love them, with all you have, in the best way you can. Once you've done that, know that the heavenly Mother and heavenly Father want as much if not more for them than you do.

I surrender my children to the divine force that moves in, through and for them.

Some kids do what you say. Some kids do what you
say do not do. But all kids do what you do.
— Unknown

A thirteen-year-old was sent to the cleaners. She was
told to go straight there; she did. But she did not come
straight home. On the trip home from the cleaners, she became involved in an egg fight. More than a half dozen
eggs ended up on a $300 suit. She took the suit home,
rolled it up, put it in a plastic bag and hid it in the closet.
Three days later when she was asked about the suit, she
started to cry and produced the bag with the festering suit
from the closet. The child is still alive with all of her limbs
intact. The parent took a deep breath and reminded herself: There are times when I do not follow instructions; I
do not always admit my mistakes and I try to cover them
up. When I am put on the spot, I cry. Whenever I am confronted with something I've done wrong, I usually don't
lie. If we really want to understand why our children behave the way they do, we must take a long, hard, honest
look at ourselves.

When I see my children I see myself.

It doesn't have to glitter to be gold.
—Arthur Ashe

They always want. They always need. They gave you that first gray hair. They eat too much. They sleep too much. They have a loving relationship with dirt. They break the good dishes. They never wash the glasses clean. They really know how to embarrass you in public. They talk too loud. They walk too slow. They rarely do what you ask, the way you want it done. They go away. They come back with friends and dirty laundry. They worry you. They frighten you. They always want to question you. They love you. They hate you. They always have a great use for your money. They grow up. They get better. They get older. They get worse. Now just think how empty the world would be if we didn't have our children to love.

I really do love my children.

Children are God in work clothing.

*I*t is hard for our children to tell us what they really feel. They don't want to hurt us. They don't want to be disrespectful. They may not believe what they think and feel is valuable. As parents, it is sometimes hard for us to let them be who they really are—people, with thoughts, feelings and dreams. We want to protect them. We want to give them the best. We must consider whether the things we want for them are the things they want for themselves. What we fear for them they may not fear for themselves. Our children have the right to choose to search, explore and decide, and they have the stamina it takes to fall on their faces and get up again.

Today I will do more than listen,
I will hear my children.

Think wrongly if you please, but in all cases think for yourself.

—Louisa May Alcott

*O*ne of the many things that drive parents crazy about their children is that children like to think for themselves. Parents do not like that. Most of the time, parents do not understand why children believe as they do; they may also feel threatened when the children do not see things the right way—that is, the parents' way. Parents have experience; they believe children do not. Parents know the dangers and traps in life; children seem not to care. Parents believe that if children are left to their own devices, they will destroy themselves. Parents need to realize the difference between discipline and thinking, disobedience and thinking, disrespect and thinking. Children are just people living through a smaller body. They must learn to express themselves, to understand who they are and grow into who they are through their own thoughts. Just because your children do not think as you do doesn't mean they are wrong.

Ideas are children of the mind.
My children have children.

When you say "I love you," you are actually saying you have awakened a place in me where I am love.
—John Rogers

*D*eep within our being is a place of peace, joy and knowing. It is a place called love. We are not taught to live from that place for ourselves. We are taught to shower it on others. We do for others what we will not do for ourselves. We give to others what we think we do not deserve. We turn to others for the very feeling that comes from the self. We are love from the core of our being. It is the energy by which we were born. We breathe love. We see love. We have our being in love. Why can't we learn to love ourselves the same way we love others? If we can live from our being of love, we can't help but attract more of what we are. Love is what we are. When we know that and live through it, we can live "in love" with ourselves.

I Am love.

A relationship is placing one's heart and soul in the hands of another while taking charge of another in one's soul and heart.

—Kahlil Gibran

*W*hen we enter a relationship, we don't often think or see beyond the physical being. We are attracted to the body, face or personality. We may like what the person does or how they do it and want to be a part of that. We may even experience a pull from within that we can't actually explain. But how often do we stop to consider the true depth of the person we are attracted to? There is a being before us who has a past, present and future. There are flesh and bones, hurts and scars, feelings, thoughts and ideals. When we enter the world of another being we must be willing to be a part of it all. When someone entrusts their heart to you they are giving you a piece of their soul. You cannot treat a soul casually. You must protect, nurture and handle it with care. Our interactions with one another go far beyond the face, body and hair. One other thing we must consider when we enter someone's heart, there is a heart and soul inside of us of which they will play a part.

I respect the heart, mind and soul of my friends and lovers.

Experience is a good teacher
but she runs up big bills.

—Minna Antrim

*I*f life is about learning and growing, why do we think our relationships are beyond life's classroom? Every relationship—family, friendship, love and marriage—is about growth and development. There are certain skills we need. Certain strengths we must develop. Certain lessons we must learn. Our relationships provide the perfect framework for us. We come together to share, learn and grow. Once we have acquired the skill, imparted the information or learned the lesson, it is time for something else. It is time to move on. That may feel like, "You don't love me anymore." What it actually says is, "You don't have anything else to give me." If we could move beyond the emotion of it and look for the growth, ending a relationship, moving out of a family or friendship would be a great deal less painful. We want to learn how to be grateful for everything we get in our relations. Somewhere beyond the grief, fear, pain and disappointment is a mighty lesson just waiting to be learned.

Every encounter is an experience of growth.

I will fear no evil: for thou art with me . . .
—Psalm 23:4

No matter what is happening in your relationships, fear nothing and no one. When you walk with the consciousness of the Creator, there is nothing to fear. Do not fear that people will harm you or leave you. Do not fear people who threaten you. Do not fear obstacles that confront you. Have no fear of harm to your body or possessions, you are walking with the strong arm of the law. Do not fear disapproval. Do not fear criticism. Do not fear judgment. Know that the only energy that has any power in your life is the gift of breath from God. Do not fear places. Do not fear darkness. Do not fear separation or divorce. Do not fear being alone. Do not fear being cast aside. When you walk with the Master, you are in the best company available.

I shall not fear.

Those who don't know how to weep with their whole heart, don't know how to laugh either.

—Golda Meir

When we lose a loved one to death or end a long-term relationship, it is perfectly normal to grieve. We must honor and recognize each stage of the grief and every emotion we have. There will be shock, denial, anger, confusion, fear, helplessness, numbness and, eventually, acceptance. There will be a point when we do not know what to do, but we want to do something. At that point we must understand and accept, there is no death; there is no end; there is only transformation. Our loved one now exists in a new time, new place, new reality—and so do we. The relationship as we knew it has been transformed from the physical to the spiritual, from marriage to separation, from loveship to friendship; it has not ended; it has changed. When we allow ourselves to grieve, we release the negative thoughts and emotions that make it easier to accept the change. When we do not grieve, we get stuck. Grief is natural, normal and to be expected. We owe it to ourselves and the memory of the relationship to grieve and cleanse our soul.

I will take the time to grieve and prepare myself for the change.

Money and Abundance

There is no lack in our lives unless we believe there is. Belief is the key to what we see, what we have and what we accomplish. Everything the Creator has made or given us exists in abundance. Unfortunately, many of us are unaware of this fact. When we are not aware of God's goodness, grace, beauty and unlimited wealth, we accept lack, restriction and limitation as a part of life. The problem we experience has nothing to do with life, it is a function of our vision. If we want abundance, we must think abundantly. If we want wealth, we must believe we are wealthy. If we want to move beyond the struggle, hardships and restrictions we find in life, we must open our eyes and remember, "All that the Father has is mine!"

Success Law #107: Put your butt on the line.

*I*f there is something you want to be, have or do in this life, there is only one sure way to find out if you can have it. Put your butt on the line! All the things you want to have; places you want to go; things you want to experience are eagerly awaiting you. It's up to you to go for it. Put your butt on the line! Say what you need to say. Do what you need to do. Ask for what you want, exactly the way you want it. Don't take no for an answer. Put your butt on the line. All you get is what you give, so give it all you've got. Put your butt on the line. If you're satisfied, but still hungry for something out there, somewhere, go for it! Put your butt on the line for what you believe in. Put your butt on the line for what you stand for. Put your butt on the line just to prove to yourself you can do it. Think of it this way, the worse that can happen is that you will end up right where you started, with your butt on the line.

Faith will save my butt when it's on the line.

October 2

Give thanks!

We have so much in life to be thankful for. We walk, talk, see, hear, think and breathe—usually without effort. Why do we spend so much time dwelling on what we can't do, don't have and what is going wrong? We can instantly recall the negative experiences, people and circumstances without recognizing we have the ability to walk away, get away or make a change. Perhaps we have too many options from which to choose. Or it could be we simply like to complain. Maybe if we spent just a little time saying "thank you" for what we do have, we won't have so much time to dwell on what we lack. Gratitude, praise and thanksgiving activate the divine laws of abundance. When the universe can see we are conscious of and grateful for what we have, it is activated to shower us with more. Even when it seems that the well is drying up, we can affirm, "I can hardly wait to see the good that will come out of this."

My cup runneth over always.

> It is the Father's good pleasure
> to give you the kingdom.
>
> —Luke 12:32

*I*t is time you realized you were born to be successful and to have wealth. You are not only ensured material wealth, but abundant wealth of the mind, body and spirit as well. You have been created in an image of perfection, with an inborn knowledge of all you need to know. In the image of the Creator, it is only right for you to have the abundance of the kingdom. You are a king's kid! Born into royalty! You should not live in lack or a state of desperation and need. It is the Creator's will for you to live richly. It is your duty to claim what is yours. The riches of the kingdom, the wealth of the world, the infinite supply of the universe is your inheritance. Graciously accept it right now!

I have inherited an abundance of every good thing. Thank you.

October 4

In order to cooperate with life you must learn
how to forgive, how to pray, how to give, how to
receive, how to adjust; seeking nothing, giving
everything, loving all people, trusting God,
living each moment fully.

—Donald Curtis

You may not have all the money you want. You may
not live in a fancy house or drive expensive cars. Maybe
you haven't found the right man or woman. You may have
a few extra pounds on your thighs. This does not mean life
is over. Actually, it may not have begun. What we must do
is live from the inside so the outside will become more fun.
Give what you have in order to get what you need. Take
what you get with an open heart. Trust God to bring forth
the desires of your heart, forgive all people for what you
believe they have done. Begin each day with a prayer of
gratitude, love all people for who they are. Possess no
things or persons, speak only of the things that you want.
Life is willing to cooperate with you, but you must know
where to start.

*When I cooperate with life,
the forces of life cooperate with me.*

If you go to God with a thimble,
you can only bring back a thimbleful.
—Randolph Wilkerson

*A*nn spent six and a half months living in a basement with rats and mice. Every day she prayed for a safe place to sleep. Her prayers were finally answered. A friend offered her the living room sofa. After two weeks of living out of shopping bags, she started praying again. "Please! All I want is a room with a bed." Three months later her daily prayer was heard. She found a six-by-nine-foot room with enough space for her body, a bed, and four milk carts to hold her clothes. Why didn't Ann ask for a three-bedroom house with a basement, backyard and garage? Because like most of us, Ann's tendency was to limit God. For some reason we get stuck in our immediate need and we think God is stuck there too. We believe that the one who created the earth, sun, stars, mountains, rivers, oceans and trees has nothing left to give. How long will it take us to realize we have an unlimited account with the universal bank? Our prayers make the withdrawals. Our faith is the deposit.

I will receive exactly what I ask for.

There are four rungs on the ladder of success: Plan Purposefully, Prepare Prayerfully, Proceed Positively, Pursue Persistently.

—African-American folklore

*I*n everything you do, have a purpose. Make sure the quality of your intent is one of truth, honor and love. Prepare to pursue your purpose with prayer. Ask for guidance, protection and direction. Ask that closed doors be opened and that the purpose of those that remain closed be revealed. Give thanks for your answered prayers by proceeding without any doubt. Keep your purpose in mind, trust the guidance you receive, have faith in your ability to succeed and accept all that comes your way. If your purpose is clear, your prayers backed by faith, your outlook sure and positive, never, never look back. You may meet forks and turns in the road, but your obstacles shall all be removed.

I am planning with purpose, preparing with prayer, proceeding positively in persistent pursuit of my goal.

Could it be, He saved the best for last?
— African-American spiritual

*V*ery often we become angry, anxious or fearful when the things we want do not seem to be coming our way. We watch others. We judge whether they have worked hard enough. We criticize them in support of our determination, that they don't deserve to get or have what they want. We doubt ourselves, our ability and worthiness. We blame people and conditions, believing they can stand in our way. The only thing that stands in our way is doubt, fear, criticism and judgment of ourselves and others. As long as we believe someone or something other than ourselves can deny or delay our good, we are not ready to have it. The all-giving, all-knowing Creator is the source of all supply, and He wants you to be ready. When you are strong in heart and mind, when you honestly want for others the good you seek for yourself, you will be well-equipped to have the very best you desire.

*I Am preparing myself
for the highest and the best.*

What you see, is what you get.

—Flip Wilson

When we are in a dark room, we quickly realize it is easier to see with the lights on. If we've ever been imprisoned, oppressed, in bondage to anyone or anything, we develop a yearning desire for freedom. We learn to appreciate good health when we are sick. We respect wealth when we are in poverty. It seems quite natural to define one condition by what appears to be its opposite. Freedom and oppression, illness and good health, poverty and wealth, happiness and sorrow, peace and confusion, faith and fear, strength and weakness, male and female—these are not opposing powers. They are the results of how the one power of life is used. The ancestors knew that everything comes from one source. They knew this source had the only power and everything else was a minor challenge. When we stay centered on the source, the power, we see that there are no opposites. Only light coming out of darkness to help us see where we want to go.

There is only one Power,
one Source operating in my life.

Possession of material riches without inner peace is
like dying of thirst while bathing in the river.
—Paramhansa Yogananda

*H*oward Hughes is a classic example of what it is like
to gain wealth and lose your soul. He and many others like
him should reinforce the idea that money cannot buy happiness, peace or health. This seems to be a contradiction.
On the one hand you need money to get the things that
will make you peaceful, happy and healthy. On the other
hand the pursuit of money can bankrupt your mind, body
and spirit. What is a person to do? Do Not Chase Money!
Do what you do, using your talents and abilities because it
makes you happy. Do Not Do Things for Money Only! In
everything you do, have a purpose, principle or ideal that
you hold dear and will not compromise if the price is right.
Use Things to Help People; Do Not Use People to Get
Things! If what you want or what you are doing is not the
highest and the best for everyone involved, leave it alone.

Prosperous, prospering peace is my money.

Your failures in life come from not realizing your
nearness to success when you give up.

— Yoruba proverb

*I*n setting goals, we sometimes box ourselves into time
limits. Limits are fine when we have everything we need
within our control. No matter who we are and what we
want, we must always surrender the element of time to the
divine timekeeper. When we are not conscious of this element, we may throw our hands up in despair and walk
away a moment before the breakthrough. Our ideas and
goals are the children of our minds. We nurture them with
our thoughts and actions. Like a fetus in the womb, they
develop in just the right way, at the right time. Eventually,
labor will start. It is painful and sometimes long, but eventually the child comes into life.

Time is on my side.

You don't own the future you don't own the past.
Today is all you have.

—Les Brown

*I*t is never a good idea to bank on what we may have to-morrow. It makes even less sense to dwell on what we had yesterday. The only thing that really matters is what we can do right now. One of the greatest stress inducers in our lives is tomorrow, for it is the unknown. We worry if "it" will happen, if "it" would happen, what if "it" does happen. Then we spend time planning for what may never come. We do that because we think we know the past. We remember it so well, particularly the pain, the dark days, the unpleasantness we've seen. We spend our present time and energy protecting the future from the past. We fail to realize one is over and the other has yet to come. What we know is now and we have complete control over it—now. Nothing can be promised, nor can we own what is no longer. If we do our best in this moment, we have no time to worry about what may come or has gone.

I Am living in this moment.

What you give you get, ten times over.

— Yoruba proverb

We have been trained and conditioned to give gifts on specific occasions. Occasionally we give gifts to those who have a special meaning to us. Unfortunately, this kind of giving is more for ourselves than for the person receiving the gift. Usually, we tell ourselves, "I don't have anything to give." We have been miseducated about gift-giving. We believe gifts must always bear a price tag or be given for a particular reason. It is this kind of thinking that causes a drought in our giving supply. The real joy in giving comes when we give what we have spontaneously, with no reason other than for the joy of giving. It is this kind of giving that opens the door for us to receive. When we give for the sake of giving, rather than out of duty, we will begin to understand. We can give our time, our energy, our thoughts. We can give a book when we've finished it, something we can no longer wear or use, pay the toll for the car behind us, or give someone we don't know a compliment. We actually have a great deal to give in many ways.

*I give joyously from my heart just
for the sake of giving.*

Ask for what you want.
—African-American folklore

*T*here is absolutely no reason to ever settle for less than the best. The only reason you get less is because you don't ask for exactly what you want. Sometimes you may think you don't deserve more than you have. At other times we think we want too much. You may believe that if you get what you want, you will lose something else or something bad will happen to take what you already have. It's as if a waiter spirit is waiting and asking, "How would you like it?" Let your mind scan life's menu, make a decision knowing whatever you want is available. Ask for what you want, the way you want it. From that moment on, believe it is yours.

I make my requests from life clear,
specific and plentiful.

Stop doing. Start being.

*H*ave you ever noticed that the more you try to do, the less you get done? The reason is that doing requires evaluation and activity on the physical level. The physical part of us is limited by perception and personality. Our perceptions tell us what we can do, can't do, will do, won't do and what others will think, do and say about our "doing." Doing is an intellectual exercise. The more we value our intellect, the more we think we must do. The key is to stop doing and start being. We must accept our goodness right where we are and stop thinking of it as something we must wait to get. Whatever it is you want to be is waiting for you. You can be healthy, organized, loved, prosperous, fulfilled and free without "doing" anything. It begins with a single thought and a simple statement—

I AM.

No matter what you can see, there is always more.
— Dennis Kimbro

*T*ake a ring of keys, place them in front of you. What do you see? Keys, right? Wrong. What is a key? What does it represent? A way in, a way out. A home. A car. Employment. Businesses making keys, providing shelter and protection for families. A steel mill, workers burning ore, machines creating heat, extracting metal used for keys. Migrant workers in mines, minimal wages providing food, small villages with dusty roads, ragged huts that don't need keys. Steel-industry inheritance, caviar, a Jaguar; mansions with many doors, many locks that need many keys. Hot steel being shaped, not enough air, black lung disease. Fire extracting metal, interstate travel, truckers moving metal, making machines, to make keys. The key is never what you see. There is always more.

I Am not fooled by appearances,
the best is yet to come.

It is the fool whose own tomatoes are sold to him.
—Akan proverb

*P*eople of color are great and creative producers. Yet they are even more consistent consumers. We have given so much to the world and for some strange reason, we keep buying it back. We cannot complain about what we lose if we allow it to be taken. We cannot complain about what others do to us if we are not doing for ourselves. If we as a people are ever to stand, we must give credit to one another for the things we create. We must take every necessary precaution to safeguard what is ours. Buy in our own communities first. Educate our children well. Protect the women and elders at all costs. Give to our own expecting nothing in return. Above all, do not allow the love of money to supersede our pride for our people.

I recognize the value and value all that I have.

Sooner or later it catches up with you.
— African-American folklore

The universe is so intelligent, it never asks us how or why. Our thoughts, words and deeds are quietly recorded and we are always paid our due. There are times when we can't figure out how we got to where we are, or why we go through what we do. We just can't seem to figure it out, but the universe knows. There is an invisible bank of law and order into which we all deposit. At just the right time, in just the right way, we are given an account. We must be careful of what we ask for because we will always get it. What we do unto others, shall be done unto us. What we hold in our hearts stays with us. That on which we focus our thoughts will grow. Get the idea?

I thank the universe for revealing what
I am thinking about and feeling.

October 18

What makes you think the world
owes you something?

—Gwendolyn Brooks

So many people go through life believing they are being cheated or that the world owes them something. This world owes us nothing except the opportunity to express our highest self. The world does not owe us a house. We are not owed a car. We are not owed money, furs or diamonds because the opportunity to have is ours at birth. The Creator has wisely provided us with the most important things in life—the air to breathe, the sun to warm and nurture, the abundant beauty of nature and the opportunity to choose. Divine guidance and inspiration are available to all whenever they are needed. By believing that certain things are only given to certain people, we get stuck without realizing all is available to all. We must ask those who believe they are owed something from whom do they think it will come?

All that I am owed comes to me by choice.

You get what you expect.

—Alvin Ailey

We often say we want many things while deep inside we doubt it will come to us. The universe does not give us what we say we want; it gives us what we expect to get. You cannot fool Mother Nature. She gives birth to your deepest thoughts and the principle is this: Everything happens twice—first on the inside, then on the outside. We must literally create the energy of what we want within ourselves before we can have it in the physical world. How does it feel to be wealthy? In love? In perfect health? Totally free to do anything we choose? We must let the feeling well up inside and live as though the very thing we want is the thing we have. We must feel ourselves being and enjoying the very best life has to offer. We must think about it, talk about it and expect it every moment. We must impregnate our total being with the expectation of what we want. As the feeling grows, the day will come when we give birth to exactly what we want.

I expect all the best right here and now.

He'll give you as far as you can see.
— First Church of Deliverance

We have the ability, right and power to create whatever we want in our lives. All we have to do is see it. We can choose to see the unlimited possibilities, rich opportunities and uncharted waters. We can choose to see that doing what we want with ease, having what we want with joy and being where we want can be used for projection and perception. When we use our eyes to project what we want into the world, we send forth the creative power of the soul's force. When we use positive perception to interpret what we see, we avoid falling prey to doom and gloom. If we can look beyond today, its challenges and obstacles, we can create a better tomorrow. If we can see, it must come to be. That is the law.

I Am willing to see my good.

When you focus on the problem,
the problem gets bigger.

*T*he mind is such an incredible power that it literally expands whatever it touches. When we are faced with a challenge, obstacle or problem, our tendency is to nurture it. We talk about it. We describe it vividly. We monitor its progress day by day, imagining how much it is growing and how its effects are devastating every aspect of our lives. What we are actually doing is giving the problem more value than it's worth. When confronted with a difficulty, we must immediately shift our attention from the problem to the solution. We can think, speak and bring the best possible outcome into existence by focusing on where we are going, not on where we think we are.

*My positive, faithful attitude
quickly brings my good.*

Stretch your hands as far as they reach,
grab all you can grab.

— Yoruba proverb

*Y*ou look inside a packed moving van, but you cannot find a place for the last box. You take a chance, climb over all the other boxes and find there is just enough room at the top. If there were only room for one at the top, we would have only one brand of chocolate chip cookies, one brand of tea and only one kind of potato chips. We must never allow ourselves to be guided or stopped by what anyone else is doing. We must never allow ourselves to think we can only go so far because others are already there. When we reach up, stand on our toes, stretch our hands out and grab as much as we can hold. If we want to keep our hands full and the goodness flowing to us, we must never, ever forget to say "thank you" for every little thing.

I Am grateful there is always room for me.

Money is in abundance, where are you?
— Reverend Ike

*D*o you know that you are as rich as any individual walking the earth? Do you know that you have the keys to unlock unlimited inexhaustible wealth? Do you know gold, silver and piles of warm, loving money are yours, right now? If you answered no to any of these questions, you have not developed a prosperity consciousness. Prosperity is a state of mind. It goes beyond money or the things money can buy. It requires you to release the anger, hurt and disappointment of yesterday in order to embrace the goodness in your life today, without fear of the uncertainties of tomorrow. Prosperity is freedom, peace, good health, simplicity and love. Prosperity is knowing who you are, loving it and doing what you love. When you think prosperity and act prosperously you will contract bountiful wealth.

My prosperity begins as a state of mind.

If you want to be a millionaire,
you have to think like one.
—Dr. Johnnie Coleman

ost people want to be rich. They spend so much time wishing the money would come that they cannot figure out how to bring it to themselves. The rich-wishing people don't seem to realize that if you want to be rich you have to think richly. People who think richly do not believe in lack. People who think richly know nothing costs too much. People who think richly believe they are worthy of the best—that is why they always get it. People who think richly don't always have money. What they have is a rich consciousness. Unless we have a consciousness that mirrors what we want, we cannot draw it to us. Unless we believe we deserve the things we want, our thoughts will push them away. We must not limit ourselves to what we think we can have. We must allow ourselves to think we can have it all. Millionaires are born in the consciousness. If you are living in lack, what are you thinking?

I Am making millions in my mind.

Decide that you want it more
than you are afraid of it.

—Bill Cosby

So many times in life we allow fear to stop us in our tracks; the sad thing is we don't always recognize we are afraid. We find excuses and rationalizations. We create responsibilities, true and false, we must tend to before we can move forward. We create challenges and obstacles so real in our minds that they manifest in our lives. Behind it all is fear. Fear we are not good enough. Fear we won't be liked. Fear that if we do it once, someone will ask us to do it again and we won't be able to. What are our excuses? Who or what is stopping us? How many times do we talk ourselves out of what we say we really want? What are we afraid of?

I put desire above fear every day.

Pray for a continuous flow in the now,
rather than a contingent flow in the need.

— BarbaraO

Need represents lack. It says we are in some way deprived, unable to provide for the self. Need feels desperate and often we get stuck in that desperation. We don't always realize that God provides for our needs without any effort on our part. We need food, clothing and shelter, of which there is an abundance. The issue is, do we want what is available? Usually not; so we think we need more. We think we need a new coat, a VCR, a late-model car. We want these things, and that is fine. Want places us in the driver's seat. It says we are open, ready and willing to receive. Want says we have a dream, a goal or an idea we desire to manifest in our lives. Need makes us fearful. Want helps us to become creative and responsible. When we strive only to meet our needs, we are never satisfied. When we strive to satisfy our wants, we become alive.

All that I need comes to me easily.
I want the best.

Life doesn't have to be a strain or a struggle.
—Marian Anderson

Sometimes we make life very difficult for ourselves. We have a great ability to create our own stress. We may refuse to see the good in anything or anyone. We sometimes refuse to count our blessings and complain about lack. We will criticize, judge or blame others because we forget when our choices were not wise. What we don't seem to realize is that when we voice words of struggle and strife we draw more of it into our experience. We create our own well-being according to the way we conduct our mind, mouth and heart. When we expect the best, we get it. When we speak of good, we see it. When we cleanse our hearts of fear, anger and strife, we place ourselves on a higher vibration. If we choose to struggle with the issues of life, they will be very willing to fight us.

I Am going to create a great day.

Don't show an indifference to money.

—Reverend Ike

*H*ow many times have you passed a penny on the street without bending down to pick it up? Don't you think a penny is money? Penny has a mother; her name is dime. Dime has a father; his name is dollar. Dollar has many relatives in all different sizes. Dimes and dollars are very peculiar about how you treat penny. A person with a million dollars who loses a penny is no longer a millionaire. A person who needs a penny to buy a loaf of bread may not eat. We pick and choose the kind of money we want. We may not realize money has a vibration, and if we treat money right it will draw like unto it. The next time you find a penny, do not be indifferent; pick it up, value it, take it home and realize you now have in your possession a close relative of the dollar.

My money vibrates, drawing like unto like.

You can't have what you want
until you have what you want.
— Horace Harris

*T*he universe is extremely responsive to our strongest thoughts and emotions. The forces of life are eager to bring us the very things we give force to. When we are unhappy, dissatisfied or unfulfilled, we give a great deal of energy to the condition we are in. We must realize that complaining about where we are or what we have is the best way to ensure things stay exactly as they are. We will not attract better or do more until we respect and appreciate what we have now. When our needs and wants seemingly go unmet, we should remember what we do not need. If we consider that we have ended up with the shortest end of the stick, we should consider those who have no stick at all. The only way to prove ourselves to the universal forces is to be grateful and appreciative of what we have now. When we are grateful for the minor, the powers that be carry us over to the grand.

I Am grateful for now.

If you do not re-verse your ways of thinking,
speaking and doing, you will remain on
the wheel of no motion.

— Ralpha

*T*here are universal laws that govern our ability to multiply and have supply. The law of forgiveness, when put into action, infuses the mind with natural, healthy ideas that take away the darkness and bring in the light. The law of obedience governs our movements, requiring that we act in order and harmony. The law of sacrifice says we must give in order to receive. For everything we give must be returned, as a sacrifice never goes unnoticed. The law of increase requires that we give praise and thanks for all that we have. The law of receiving gives us exactly what we expect. The law of attraction brings to us without delay the desires and thoughts we hold in our minds. The law of supply provides all of our needs and desires, based on our belief of its existence. When our efforts do not multiply, when our supply is not sufficient, it is quite possible that we are breaking the law.

I live within the boundaries of the law.

When "I" am here, God is not.
When God is here, "I" am not.
—Bawa Muhaiyaddeen

If God is the source of life, shouldn't we be able to find the essence of the source in our lives? Yet when we examine our lives, in what part do we find God? What part is the "I"? God is love, peace, abundance, power, strength, mercy, truth, balance and joy. For many of us, life is lack, limitation, strife, stress, chaos, confusion, oppression and hate. Your race, my race; their goals, our goals; your religion, my religion have replaced the sense of oneness known as God. Did God create this mess? No, "I" did. The small part of "I" that wants control and power. The "I" that is fear, arrogance, anger and pride. The "I" that holds on to pain because "I don't know what to do." The "I" that wants it my way because "I can take care of myself." The "I" that can't figure out which part God is and which part "I" am because "I" have forgotten that all that God is I Am. If only "I" would let God do His part, we would be fine.

God, how can I serve you today?

Inhale the future, exhale the past; inhale the good,
exhale the goop!

—BarbaraO

*I*nhale. Exhale. Inhale. Exhale. What a wonderful gift of life. Inhale. Exhale. Inhale. Exhale. The beginning and the end. Inhale peace, exhale confusion—it is just that simple. Inhale faith, exhale worry—that is all you have to do. Inhale order, exhale confusion—get into the flow of life. Inhale love, exhale anger—feel the warmth flow through your being. Inhale strength, exhale fear—now put your mind to rest. Inhale silence, exhale chatter—feel your body settle. Inhale freedom, exhale restriction—let your mind follow the dream. Inhale victory, exhale defeat—prepare yourself for the best. Inhale acceptance, exhale judgment—feel your self opening. Inhale confidence, exhale doubt—enjoy the rhythm of who you are. Inhale. Exhale. Inhale. Exhale. Breath is the gift of grace. As long as we have it, we have the divine opportunity to go it again.

I accept the gift of breath as a gift of life.

*If we never faced adversity, our well-being
would not be as sweet.*

—Terry Kellog

*I*s there a persistent problem plaguing you? Does it seem to just loom over your head waiting to swoop down and devour you? Is it a money problem? A relationship? A choice or decision you can't seem to make? Do you feel as if you have been backed into a corner with no way out? Good! That is exactly where you need to be! Now take your mind off the problem and laugh. That's right, laugh. Stare adversity in the face. Stop trying to figure out what to do. You are probably thinking this is your punishment for something you did in the past. Or maybe you think it's some more of your "bad luck." Well, just throw those thoughts out of your brain and replace them with "I know there is a power for good in the universe and I call that power forth right now to perfect every condition in my life." But of course this sounds too easy, too good to be true. You want it to be hard, right? Well, here's something hard for you to work on: "Be ye transformed by the renewal of your mind!"

Just for today I will laugh in the face of adversity.

The finger of God never points where the hand of
God isn't somehow making a way.

—Rev. Alvin Kibble

*W*hen you have a deep burning desire to do a thing, do
it! "De" meaning "of," "sire" meaning Father, is the very
thing God wants for you. The urging is from the soul and
is the only fuel you need. It is a blessing. It lets you know
that you have been chosen for a special task. The Creator
knows you can and wants you to do or have whatever it is.
It cannot be too difficult! It is not beyond your reach! It is
connected to your soul! That's where all the power is!
Trust those urgings. They are the best friends you could
have. Learn to move beyond what appears to be the
essence of what you are. Is it a good thing? Will you and
others benefit? If so, go for it! Don't let others talk you
out of your desire. It is not for them to see or know. They
cannot feel it the way you do; don't expect them to. Nurture your desire in thought, word and deed; never doubt it
will become your reality. If you do your part, the Father
will do His part and guide you to the wellspring of your
desire come true.

*I can't do it. I Am the conduit through
which it will be done.*

God would not give us the ability and opportunity to
be successful and then condemn us to mediocrity.
— Debra Anderson

*E*verything in the world was, at one time, just an idea
in someone's mind. The chair you are sitting on. The
clothes you are wearing. The car you drive. The multime-
dia instruments that bring information to us. They were all
ideas that someone took the time, had the faith and made
the commitment to bring forth. How many good, no, great
ideas have you had lately? Do you have ideas about things
you would like to do? Ideas about the quality of your life?
How to make life better for someone else? Why then are
you not acting on those ideas? Ideas are all we have.
That's what we get from the One on high. We already
have the ability, skill and access to information. What the
Creator does is generate ideas. Many people get the same
idea at the same time. Some of us act, others don't. The
next time you are wondering what you are supposed to do
in life, remember all the idea blessings you let go.

Go ahead, God, talk. I'm listening.

If your brain can move your body with a split second
command thought, imagine what it can do with
concentrated and directed thought.

— Dr. Therman Evans

*E*veryone wants to know the secret of a long, happy, prosperous and successful life. It's no secret. It's an attitude. An energy. A formula. Want to know it? Here it is: (1) Do all things in peace; (2) Achieve personal unity of heart and mind; (3) Learn truth; (4) Maintain your body; (5) Correct character imperfections; (6) Be free from fear; (7) Live in harmony with all people; (8) Eliminate worry; (9) Be poised; (10) Give love; (11) Admire, respect and trust yourself; (12) Know God; (13) Express God; (14) Know what works for you; (15) Help others; (16) Make, have and keep good friends; (17) Solve your own problems; (18) Find your proper place; (19) Have a true marriage; (20) Discover and use your personal talents; (21) Acquire knowledge; (22) Share what you learn with others; (23) Relax; (24) Sleep well; (25) Awake with enthusiasm; (26) Stop unwanted habits; (27) Think positively; (28) Always give thanks for everything you have!

I will prosper because I give thanks.

The moment you move out of the way, you make
room for the miracle to take place.
—Dr. Barbara King

You will never accrue the wealth, experience the success, do the things you really want to do as long as you worry about it. Chances are you are thinking in terms of what you do not have and cannot do. Your good cannot get to you if your mind is filled with lack. You have no room for blessings if your words are laced with limitations. You will not notice or be open to new experiences if you are stuck in the old ones. What you want may be totally new to you. It may be way beyond your highest expectations. How can it get to you if you keep getting in the way? It's time for you to move, realizing that the thing you are seeking is also seeking you. If not, you wouldn't want it. That is the law of compensation, what you give out will be returned to you. Get rid of your bad thoughts, inferior attitudes and limited behaviors and good will be attracted to you. It's not easy. It's not magic. But it works, miraculously.

I will not stand in the way of my own good.

Work is love made visible. Keep working with love.
—Anonymous

*H*ave you ever watched people who love what they do? They work with a smile on their faces or a song in their hearts. They move with grace and ease. They attend carefully and lovingly to every little detail. They never tire of what they do. They do it willingly, joyously for themselves, for you and for anyone else who shows the slightest bit of interest. They talk about what they do, they read about it, staying up on the latest trends, teaching it or some part of it to newcomers and converts. When you love your work, it's like a love affair. You do it with a passion. The lust for it rises up from within your soul and makes you giddy. You want to do it all the time, in as many ways as possible. Wherever you go, whomever you're with, you want to do what you love because it feels so good.

I love what I do and I do it with a passion.

Your wealth can be stolen, but the precious riches
buried deep in your soul cannot.

— Minnie Riperton

*D*o you like money? Wouldn't you like to have some? Or even better, wouldn't you like to have a lot of money? Do you find yourself chasing it? Doing things to get money or wondering how much money you will get for doing things? Do you see things you want and remember you don't have money? Do you think about the places you would go if you had money? The longer you think about money, the more you chase money, the longer you will do without it. Money is very much like a hard-to-get lover. It eludes you. It teases and tempts you. It gets your blood flowing and then it runs away. Money will drive you crazy. The more you want it, the less you will have of it. It will fight your advances. It will turn on you. It will leave you high and dry. The best thing you can do to money is ignore it. Don't chase it. Don't lust after it. Don't let it invade your mind. Do what you do without giving any thoughts to money and when you least expect it, money will fall right into your lap.

Unexpected doors are open.
Unexpected channels are free.

If you keep your pockets full of coins,
you will always have small change.
— Yoruba proverb

*I*f you expect to get something for nothing, or if you feel good when you get something without paying for it, you are violating the law of abundance. The law of abundance says you must pay for what you get. You cannot benefit from the mistake or loss of another. If you do, you will someday be forced to pay. Are you a bargain hunter? If so, you are violating the law of vibration. Cheap thoughts bring cheap returns. When you place yourself in low vibration, you draw things that vibrate on the low level. Do you begrudgingly spend money? Do you hate to pay your bills? If so, you are violating the law of correspondence. What you withhold from the universe will be withheld from you. If you give begrudgingly, people will begrudgingly give to you. It is not what you do not have that makes or keeps you poor. It is what you do with what you have that opens the door to more. Pay your way or at least offer to pay. Expect the best and give it to yourself. Release your money happily, being grateful that you have it to give.

The laws are on my side. I am blessed.

Imagine what a harmonious world it could be if
every single person, both young and old, shared a
little of what he is good at doing.

—Quincy Jones

We all come into this life with talents, gifts or abilities
which, if we put them to use, they would be profitable to
us and useful to the world. Yet, we allow ourselves to be
told and we tell ourselves that we're not good enough or
that no one is interested in what we can do. Many of us
spend the greater portion of our lives seeking authoriza-
tion or recognition, never developing or using the goodness of the things we do naturally. If we would trust life
and ourselves a little more, we would do what comes naturally, what we are good at, giving it all that we've got. If
we would stop looking for fame and fortune we might find
we are sitting on a goldmine of ideas and abilities. If we
would stop blaming others and being ashamed of ourselves, there would be no way we could expect or accept
anything less than the best from ourselves and for ourselves. If we would stop chasing castles in the sky and do
what we can do, where we are, the world would probably
appreciate it and reward us greatly.

I am willing to give the world
who I Am naturally.

I could do better if I wanted to!

— Dr. Oscar Lane

There is a natural, universal force called the law of correspondence. According to this law, you will attract to you that which you are. The law is activated by your dominant thought patterns. The purpose of this law is to show where you are in your consciousness and to give you the opportunity to lift yourself to where you want to be. You can do any good thing you want to do with the right adjustment of your thoughts and actions. If you want prosperity and success, you must change your thoughts to reflect the things you want. Many people live and die never experiencing anything greater than what is handed down to them. If you are born amidst lack, failure, struggle and limitation, you do not have to stay there. Do not claim inherited limitations. The law of correspondence can and will move you to the heights of your consciousness. You cannot attract better, however, until you can better lift your thoughts. Lift your expectations. Lift yourself. Train yourself to mentally look for the good things you want and the good will respond.

I see myself with all the best.
I see myself with it now.

When people say it's not the money it's the principle,
it's the money.

—Stuart Wilde

*P*eople of color don't like to talk about money; we do not want others to know how much we have. We are ashamed to admit when we don't have any. We can talk all day about politics, sex or religion, but when it comes to money, the room gets very still. We don't like to charge money for the things we do. We don't like to collect money for the things we've done. We don't like to give money. We get very nervous when the money we expect does not come when we expect it. Where did we get the notion that there is something wrong with money? Is it our childhood trauma? Is it what we think money can do? Is it our experience of not having much? Is it a fear that having money will somehow cause us harm? Perhaps somewhere deep in our consciousness we realize that money demands respect. And that is something we are not quite ready to do.

I can freely and openly talk about money without shame or fear or guilt.

The abundance you desire to experience must first
be an experience in your mind.

—Ernest Holmes

*O*pen your mind, heart and soul to accept that it is the
Creator's will for you to have plenty. How else can the creative force glorify itself? If you are expressing lack, how
can you express faith and love? Today, continuously affirm, "My income exceeds my outgo." As you affirm,
know that you are receiving a substantial increase in your
income. It will exceed your greatest expectations. It will
exceed all of your financial commitments. You have plenty
to spare. New doors of opportunity are opening to you.
New ideas are pouring forth. As you open your mind to
accept your glorious new good, you find new ways to express faith and love. Abundance may be a new experience
for you, but if you open your mind, you will come to understand that the creative source finds great pleasure in
giving you plenty.

*I Am an abundant being experiencing
the gift of plenty.*

If you think poor, you are poor.

—Wally Amos

It is said that the mind is a terrible thing to waste. Thoughts of poverty and lack are a waste of the valuable power of the mind. In order to experience wealth, success and well-being, it is necessary to train the mind to think positively. Positive thinking is more than a cliché. It is an attitude that embraces the wealth of the human experience. The mind is a tool that can turn a negative into a positive with a stream of progressive thoughts. Many of us have no idea about the true wealth of the universe. We are so accustomed to lack that we see everything as not enough. It is only through the mind, the power of thought, the transformation of perceptions that we will move from being poor to a state of conscious wealth. Take a penny and commit to collecting 999,999 more. In the end you'll have more than a bunch of pennies. You'll have the beginning of a fortune.

Today I will think abundance, prosperity and wealth into my experience.

Guilt, shame and money go hand in hand.

*P*arents of all races have berated and belittled themselves over what they could not do for their children because they didn't have the money. Children have the warm, loving, nurturing relations with their parents in exchange for shame over what their parents couldn't afford. There is something wrong with a nation that places monetary value above the greatest gift of life—love. There is something wrong with the people of a nation who continue to measure self-worth in terms of net worth. It is true that money can make life a little easier, more comfortable and perhaps exciting. Money, however, does not make life. Love, supportive parents, good health and a well-ordered mind are absolutely free. And they are nothing to be guilty about or ashamed of.

Money cannot make me and will not break me.

Have you had it? Owing? Borrowing?
Can't have it? Can't buy it?

—Les Brown

Something is wrong when, as children, we are kept in the dark about money. So often, because our parents view money as an issue to struggle with, they do not talk to us about it. As children, many of us were not allowed to question anything, so we never asked about financial issues. To some, money was used as a punishment or reward. This molded and shaped our views about it. In other cases, our parents used money as a weapon against each other or against us. How can we expect to be financially responsible if we never received positive instructions about money? Well, now it's up to us. We owe it to ourselves, our self-esteem and our future to get the right idea about money. Many of us feel ashamed, guilty or uncomfortable when we ask questions about money. What we need to accept and realize is that those who ask questions do not lose their way.

Money is nothing to be afraid of.

When you get the bills in the mail, it's like
you just can't breathe.
—Michael Phillips, from *The Seven Laws of Money*

*W*hen you are experiencing financial chaos, your primary goal is to be free of debt. This requires discipline and structure. You may rebel against the notion of discipline because it feels as if you are being punished. But you must realize that you are punishing yourself. When you love beyond your means, if you spend without a budget, if you live without a plan you are punishing yourself and your creditors. When you are in debt, spending money without discipline means you are spending other people's money. You are withholding from the flow. You are blocking your abundance. If lack of discipline put you in debt, only discipline will get you out. As hard as it may be, as unfair as it may seem, your money is not your money when you are in debt. Give what you have to those whom you owe if you want your money to be rightfully yours.

*When I am patiently disciplined
my progress is assured.*

Never settle for the crumbs of life.
—Og Mandino

*I*f you are not happy with where you are in life, you don't have to stay there. Don't you deserve better? Don't you want better for yourself and your future? Well, you are the only one who can make it happen. Sure, you've had some pretty rough times, even some pretty devastating ones. There is nothing that says that must be the norm. There are some very difficult challenges and negative attitudes you will confront, but you are equipped to handle it all. There may be some pretty stupid ideas about who you are, what you can do and how far you can go. So what! People also said the world was flat and the moon was made of cheese! The only thing that really matters is what you think, what you believe and what you want. If you have the desire and the will, you will be shown the way.

Greater is that within me than the problem in the world.

Lack of money is the root of all evil.

—Reverend Ike

*E*ach day, around the country, thousands of people become ill from the stress of not having money. Once they become ill, they are subject to inadequate health care because they don't have money. Each day, hundreds of creative, talented people sit wasting away because they don't have money. Don't have money to do what? To think? To take care of themselves? To create? We are conditioned to believe that if we don't have money, we have nothing. That is an evil thought. It's evil that robs us of our faith in ourselves and in the process of life. The darkness of it dims the light of human potential. We abandon our dreams, live below our own standards and allow a variety of opportunities to slip right out of our hands, because we think if we don't have money we are worthless. If you believe that, if you think like that, you have been possessed by an evil spirit. You need faith, love and a passionate desire to excise that beast from your being.

I am not lacking the things that really matter.

Let not what you cannot do tear from
your hands what you can.
—Ashanti proverb

Staying focused on a project or plan is one of the most difficult challenges we face. There is always the house to clean, calls to make, laundry to fold, movies to watch, news to catch up on, deadlines to meet and expectations to live up to. There is so much pulling on us, distracting us, keeping us from doing what we say—no wonder it never gets done. Actually, there is only one thing that keeps us from our goals, that is lack of focus. Very often, lack of focus is caused by fear. Lack of focus/fear means you can find a million reasons not to do what you say you want to do. Lack of focus/fear means if you do what you say you just might succeed. Success means you would move out and beyond your comfort zone. Somehow, somewhere deep inside, that is frightening. The key is if you would just stay focused, all of those frightening little details would miraculously be taken care of. Before you know it, you would be exactly where you say you want to be.

*When I stay focused on the end,
the details are handled.*

Know your friends and then you prosper.
— *The Maxims of Ptahhotpe*

*A*bundance has absolutely nothing to do with how much money you have. Abundance is about feeling rich and having rich feelings. Abundance is rich relationships, rich experiences, a rich mind and rich ideas that provide you with a sense of meaning. To understand abundance is to create what you want without fear. Abundance is knowing the glass is always half full no matter what is going on. Abundance is feeling good about who you are, where you are and what you have because you realize you don't have to stay there. When your mind is an abundance of ideas, when your hearing is an abundance of love, when your life is an abundance of good people doing good things with you and for you, you are rich beyond words. Abundance begins in mind, extends to the deeds and brings rewards you can bank on even if you cannot put them in the bank.

My abundant source is unlimited.

I am receptive to the inflow and
outpouring of the universe.
—Eric Butterworth

The world is truly abundant. There are enough trees to give shade and create oxygen. There is enough grass to picnic on and feed the worms. There is enough water to swim in, fish in and feed the animals all over the world. There is enough sun to shine on everyone. There are enough animals, plants and minerals to feed everyone and everything. There truly is enough for us all. We can have as much as we want if we have faith, courage, determination and perseverance. We are the dealers of our own hands in life. Our thoughts are the cards we play with. If we approach life as if we have a full house, we will reap an abundant jackpot. We must remember that our experiences can be like baggage. It is a reality, but if we want to move through life abundantly, we must unpack, sort out and distribute the baggage to its proper places. We must talk about what we want, knowing it is in abundance. We must give thanks for universal abundance, letting the world know we are open and ready to receive as much goodness as is available.

There is so much abundance for me.
I can have it all.

We must learn to love everyone,
everything, everywhere.
—John Randolph Price

*I*magine if your job, business or school schedule were a hot new lover you had a lustful interest in. How would you handle it? At the very thought of it you would dress yourself up, sweeten up those secret places and go for it. You wouldn't take "no" for an answer. You would chase it, pursue it, follow it and find creative ways to get yourself noticed. You would probably fantasize about it, utilizing all your thought sensations. You would imagine how it would feel and smell and even taste if you could just get it to the place you want it. What would you say to it? And how would you want it to see you? Attractive, powerful, successful, in control? And what would you do to your hot new lover once you got your hands on it? Would you stroke it? Fondle it? Caress it? Or would you give it a big crushing embrace while you whispered sweet nothings in his or her ear? Just for today, treat whatever you are doing as if it's a hot new lover. You may find, just for a day, your wildest dream comes true!

I Am in pursuit of a new love.

Your attitude about who you are and what you have
is a very little thing that makes a very big difference.
— Theodore Roosevelt

*C*an you see, hear and speak? Can you walk, move
around and do things for yourself? Did you eat today?
Yesterday? Someday last week? Can you pick up a telephone? Turn on a light? Stick a key in a door and have a
place to sleep? Are your feet adequately covered? Do you
have something to wear? Are your lungs and kidneys
functioning? Can you breathe without assistance? Can
you move your hands, arms, legs and do the things you
want to do? Is there someone who will help you if you
need help? Is there someone from whom you receive love?
Is there someone you know who will be there no matter
what you've done? Can you laugh when you want to? Cry
if you need to? Does your mind let you know the difference between the two? Is there a tree you can touch? A
flower you can smell? Can you stand in the rays of the
sun? Give thanks for every "yes" you can give and remind
yourself that you are truly blessed.

Thank you! Thank you! Thank you!
Thank you! Thank you!

With money a dragon. Without money a worm.

— Chinese proverb

Many people of color believe that if you have money, you can do any and everything. You cannot. Other people believe that if you don't have money you cannot do anything. They are also wrong. Money is only the visible effect that shows what is going on in your mind. The richer, stronger and clearer your thoughts, the greater your supply of currency. Money doesn't always show up as dollar bills and coins. People you can call on, resources you can draw from, thoughts and attitude — these are also wealth. What you yield in your physical life is the result of how you think. You are your own money. Money is: my own natural energy field. Your thoughts, words, feelings and actions determine your own worth. The quickest way to make money appear is to love yourself, respect yourself and put yourself to work.

I Am money. Money is me.

When you are employed by God, Inc., you never worry about unemployment.

When you work to obtain greater awareness, knowledge and understanding of yourself, you are working for God. God's goal is for you to be the best you can be with what you have been given and to share what you do with the world. When you do the thing that makes you happy to the best of your ability you are working for God, Inc. The only reason we have come to life in a physical body is to work for and serve the true self within. That is the part of us that is all-wise, all-knowing, all-loving and infinitely creative. When we do what we love, we are happy. When we do what we are good at, we are at peace. When we use what God has given us to create our own work, our rewards do not come from man. Every living person has a desire to do or be something. When you follow that desire, using your gifts, talents and abilities, you can never be out of work.

I Am employed by my God self,
which is unlimited.

A man's true wealth is the good he does in the world.
— Mohammed

*I*n many ancient African, Asian and Native American traditions, a person's wealth is measured by the well-being of his or her children. Tradition mandates that you bring children into the world to continue your work and to make additional contributions to the good of the world. If you have no children, your wealth is measured by what you do. Do you sell good products? Do you create good crafts? Do you provide a good service? Do people speak well about you? Do people seek you out to obtain what you have? Do you deal with people honestly? Are you a person of your word? Are you dependable? Reliable? Can you be trusted? Your reputation is your wealth. Your work is a part of your reputation. If you want to pile up riches, give your best to what you do.

I Am my greatest product.
I Am my greatest service.

If a job isn't worth dreaming about,
it isn't worth having.
— Deborah Gregory

*Y*ou cannot and will not acquire wealth working at a job you do not like. Whatever you spend your life's energy doing, you must be willing to give it your all. The more of yourself you put into your work, the greater it will reward you. We are trained to think in reverse: If you pay me better, I'll work harder. According to the laws of abundance, it doesn't work that way. Your job, work, life assignment must be the spark that fuels your fire. It must be a passion that you pursue. You must want it enough to do it for free. You must be willing to stick with it, taking the ups and downs, giving it all that you are for as long as you can! You've got to taste it, smell it, know it whether you are awake or asleep. If you do not have a lustful passion for your work, you really need to find something else to do.

I Am willing to work at what I love.

Wealth consists not in having great possessions
but in having few wants.

—Epicurus

*Y*ou must make yourself content with who you are and what you have if you want to be truly wealthy. Contentment does not mean you must stay where you are; it simply means you have no desperate needs. Contentment does not mean you cannot want and do more for yourself; it means you are at peace. The peace that contentment brings is a quiet peace of mind. With a peaceful mind you can think and dream; you also get information about what to do. When your mind is not filled with desperation and doubt it is primed for inspirational ideas. Our wants rob us of the peace of the moment; they keep us locked in deprivation and lack. When we are wanting we are not grateful because we cannot see what we have. We must learn to be content in the abundance of where we are if we ever want to move beyond that spot.

I Am wealthy right here and right now.

You must begin wherever you are.
—Jack Boland

*I*f you are waiting for something to happen before you begin what you want to do, it will never happen. If you are waiting to get something before you do what you say you want to do, you will never get started. If you are waiting for the right time, the right person, the right circumstances, you could be waiting forever. How about this, what can you do right now? Can you write a letter? Make a call? Finish a plan? Structure a goal? Can you pick a name? Paint a wall? Ask a question? Sweep a floor? Can you structure a schedule? Can you project a date? Can you fulfill a promise? Can you read a book? Can you stop doing all the things you do that keep you from doing the one thing you want to do? Can you pray? Can you sing? Can you dance right where you are? Whatever you can do, you better do it now. Now is all you have to work with.

I Am going to live in the moment.

December 1

It is only through order that greater things are born.
— The Wisdom of the Taoists

*T*here is no way goodness, abundance and success can come to you if your affairs are not in order. The universe is an orderly system of activities and events. Things flow in and out and through. When our home, environment, accounts or activities are not in order, the universal flow will move right past us without stopping. We must recognize and practice divine order if we want ultimate success. We must pay our bills in a timely manner, keeping an organized, structured record of what we pay and when we pay it. Give everyone their due. If we are in debt to someone, pay them. If we cannot pay the agreed upon amount, pay something—and pay it consistently on time. Think of it as giving to God. If we don't give to God, how do we expect God to give back to us? One of the greatest enemies of success is living hand to mouth. Believing we don't have enough, we fail to pay, save and give. In the universal flow, hand to mouth does not work. If we are not living in order we will continue to meet our open mouth with empty hands.

I do have enough to pay, save and give.

There is a soul force in the universe, which, if we
permit it, will flow through us and produce
miraculous results.

—Mahatma Gandhi

*E*ach of us on some level tries to elevate ourselves to a
new height, a higher standing, a better way of living. Unfortunately, that is why we don't get where we want to be,
because we are trying to do it. The power is right where
we are. The power is the essence of all that is good. The
power is divine. When we believe in the power and seek to
make conscious contact with it, the power, not the self,
will bring into our lives the very things we are struggling
to do. The power will operate in all of our affairs, going
before us to prepare our path. The power wants joy,
peace, perfect health, abundant wealth and loving relationships for us. The power is the living spirit within
buried beneath the personality, ego, perceptions, fears and
doubts. The power is the truth of who we are. The power
is available; all we have to do is invite it forward and move
out of the way.

*Today, I Am one with the living spirit who will do
the work through me and for me.*

People with ten million dollars are no happier than
people with nine million dollars.

—Hobart Brown

*Y*ou do not want to be rich and have a diseased body. You do not want to be healthy and broke. You do not want to have good health, abundant wealth and poor relationships. You want to have all of the good. You want to enjoy every aspect of life abundantly. You want it from expected and unexpected sources. You want to have more, give more and get more. In order to do it, you must think abundantly. Speak abundantly. Do everything in an abundant way. Rest well. Dress well. Eat well and act right. You cannot achieve abundance with ugly thoughts, words and deeds. Abundance is a direct reflection of your preparation to live abundantly. People who are abundant do not worry about what others are doing. People who expect abundance do not make themselves content to live in lack. People who are ready for abundance keep their heads up, their eyes open and give thanks for everything they get.

I want it all abundantly prospering me now.

Life is not a problem. If we live, we live; if we die, we die; if we suffer, we suffer; it appears that we are the problem.

—Alan Watts

What is prosperity? A mental state. A functional attitude that draws to you an abundance of every great thing. How do you get prosperity? Expect it. Always ask for the highest and the best; never doubt that it will come. What does prosperity look like? Look in the mirror. You are prosperity. Prosperity is your birthright. It is up to you to recognize your free access to an inexhaustible supply of all things good and desirable. You were born into prosperity. It is your inheritance as a child of the kingdom, a child of the universe. You have been given a body capable of doing almost anything. It is up to you to convince your mind that you can. You have been given power, dominion and authority over everything in the world. It is up to you how you use it.

When I look at me, I am looking at prosperity.

Are you one of the human beings who knows there is more to being human than paying bills and not paying bills?

—Rev. Frederick Price

Go ahead, take a moment to pinch yourself. Go ahead, pinch yourself. Feel that? You are alive. You have another opportunity to get this thing together. If you have it together, you have more opportunities for keeping and demonstrating how good you are. Go ahead, pinch yourself again. You have not been carted off to the cemetery. They have not thrown dirt in your face. You can still feel the snow on your face, the rain on your head and the fire under your bottom. You are alive. That is really all it takes. A little time, the opportunity and the desire. If you want abundance, pinch yourself. If you want success, pinch yourself. If you want good loving relationships, pinch yourself. If you really want something good in your life, stop pinching yourself and go out and get it.

All it takes is a little life.

We don't have to be at the bottom.
We were born to be at the top.
— The Thunder Brothers

Do you know people who say, "I don't want a lot of money." They seem to think if they have a lot of money, people will want things from them. If they have a lot of money, they should be willing to share. What about those people who claim "Money isn't everything." They are right; money isn't everything, but if you don't have it, you won't have anything. Have you heard, "Money causes trouble." Don't believe it. It is what people do with money, do for money, do because they don't have money that causes the problem — not the money. What about, "I can't seem to hold on to money." You shouldn't hold on to money. You must keep it in the flow, use it wisely, spend it freely, give and share it lovingly. Money has a face. It has eyes and ears. If you are not careful about what you say about money, it has a way of staying away from you.

Money is all right with me.

Act the way you want to be and
soon you will be the way you act.

—Dr. Johnnie Coleman

*T*he next time someone says, "How are you?" try this answer on for size: I am whole. I am complete. I am perfect. I am happy. I am dynamite. I am lovable, loving, getting lots of good love. I am well off and doing well. I have it all together. I am basking in the riches of life. I am prospering right here and right now. I am being richly rewarded, even in my sleep. I am a miracle worker expecting a miracle right now. I am peacefully peaceful. I am walking the walk. I am talking the talk. I am claiming the victory right now. I am successful. I am wealthy. I am living by pure grace. I am a believer. I am standing on faith. I am on my way to the top. I am what I am because I just can't help myself. And how are you doing, my dear?

As I speak it, I Am it.

NOTICE TO GUESTS: If there is anything you need and don't see, please let us know, we will show you how to do without it.

— Mary McWilliams Fadden

*H*ow many times have you let an opportunity go by because you thought you were not prepared? If you sit there waiting for something to happen, when it happens over here, you will be sitting there. If there is something you think will make you better off than you are right now, go find it. See the challenges, face the obstacles, pick up the stumbling blocks, test the waters and imagine the very best that could possibly happen in every situation. It is only when you allow yourself to dream, to see, to feel what you want that it will ever come into existence. Everything happens twice. First on the inside, then on the outside. You must create what you want inside of your heart and mind before you can hope to see it in your world. You cannot build the life you want based on outside stimuli. If it is not in your world, that is because you have not created it. So what in the world are you waiting for?

There is a world inside me waiting to happen.

You don't need anything to experience prosperity.
—Dwayne Dyer

*Y*ou might feel that money will make life more simple. You can begin designing a simpler life right now, without money, by developing such qualities as inner peace and becoming more organized in your life. Whatever you feel money is going to bring, you can begin to feel those qualities within yourself right now and radiate those qualities outward through your thoughts, words and actions. Rich feelings draw rich experiences. As you think, the very substance of the universe creates the set of circumstances to bring forth the experience. Thinking and feeling go hand in hand. Thinking is the masculine faculty within us all, feeling is the feminine faculty. When you integrate your thinking and feeling you have a marriage that will produce children—ideas. With an idea you have an opportunity to create for yourself the exact thing you desire. Begin, today, to think and feel your good into existence.

All that I want I have right now.

You survived 100,000 other sperm to get here. What do you mean you don't know what to do?
— Les Brown

The best-laid plans and strategies are useless unless you expect to win. And you must know you are going to win before you start. When you know you are going to win, you can prepare your victory speech and what you will wear to the awards dinner the day before it is announced. When you are a winner, you learn how to take a win no matter how it comes — whether by default, an interception, a fumble or when it comes right to you through the air. Never let a win catch you unexpectedly. Take your wins in stride. Know they are an everyday occurrence for you because you expect to win from the beginning. Never let words of doubt or fear cross your mind; they are the only things that can steal your win. Win big. Win small. Win it for yourself. Win it for others. Know what a win will look like for you, and when it comes, chalk it up to life.

I Am the winning kind.

A sequential chain of events called growth will bring
forth the fruits of the seeds.

—Rev. Joe Hill

A good farmer does not worry about the weather. He
plants his seeds well, takes great care to till his soil and
knows the seeds will produce. A good farmer does not
plant when the winds are blowing; he waits until there is
peace and calm. He then carefully digs the holes and
places the seeds down with love and prayer. You are a
farmer. Your thoughts are the seeds you plant; they are the
cause of every condition in your life. Your success, health,
wealth and all of your relationships are the fruits of the
seeds you have planted. If you want an abundant harvest
and healthy fruits you must carefully turn the soil of your
consciousness. Get rid of the weeds of doubt, fear, criticism and judgment of yourself and others. Clear your
mindfield of the rocky areas; whining, complaining and
blaming other farmers for spoiling your crop. Plant every
thought with care and prayer if you want a vast harvest of
healthy crops.

Today I am planting a mindfield of goodness.

> We don't know how to celebrate because we don't
> know what to celebrate.
> —Peter Brock

*G*uess what? We are having a party today in celebration of you. You are one of your favorite people in the world. You are what life is all about and you know it. So let's celebrate. Let your hair down! Kick off your shoes! Open the windows, the curtains and the blinds! Pump up the volume and let's do it for you! Let's celebrate your victories big and small. Let's celebrate the things you did that you thought you couldn't do, but you did them anyway— and they worked. Let's celebrate because millions didn't make it, and you were one of the ones who did. We're going to invite everyone in the world to celebrate in the being of you. We're going to have a low-down get-down in honor of you. This is what life is all about. Living, laughing and loving; not worrying, working and whining. So come on, get loose, get free, get up so we can get down in celebration of you—let's boogie!

Today is my day to let the good times roll.

Go and open the mansion of the soul;
when you find the powers of heaven,
you shall sit with them.
— *The Book of Coming Forth by Day*,
translated by Dr. Maulana Karenga

Where your treasure is there your heart shall be. Your heart is a place of silence and communion. Your heart houses the secrets of your soul; the path of your destiny. Your heart covets your desires and places them strongly in your mind. It is the key of all you want to be. You must have faith in your heart and trust all that it says to you. Never betray your own heart or you will find yourself lost. Your heart is the gatekeeper to your soul. It will never judge you, never doubt you, for your heart knows exactly who you are. Keep your heart light from grief. Let it guide you in all your ways. When things are not as you know they should be, retreat quietly to the resources of your heart. You make your heart a mystery. You fail to ask its advice. When your heart is heavy about a matter, you believe others can lift you up. If you really knew your heart you would never doubt its value to you. God speaks to us through our hearts because all that God is, is love.

God is in the midst of me.
Wherever I Am, God is.

Talk plenty. Think plenty. Give plenty thanks.
—Rev. Joe Hill

*O*pen your closet. Do you see shoes, sweaters, pants, dresses? Now, remind yourself you have plenty. Look out of the window. Do you see a tree? Grass? The sky? Now, remind yourself you have plenty. Look at a child. Look at the children, the ideas yet to come, the experiences to be had, the things that must be learned. Now, remind yourself you have plenty. Look at the sun, the moon, the ocean, the stars. Think of the summer, the winter, the spring, the fall. Now, remind yourself you have plenty. Turn on the water in the sink. It comes whether you say thank you or not. Now, remind yourself you have plenty. Take a look at the newspaper and ask how many trees it took to make it. Now, remind yourself you have plenty. Think of your heart, lungs, kidneys and liver. Now, remind yourself you have plenty. Remember that the computer is an attempt to re-create the human mind. You have a mind. Now isn't that plenty?

I Am enough. I have enough.

Success is a journey, not a destination.

— Ben Sweetland

*E*rnest and Julio Gallo have told us for many years, "We will sell no wine before its time." Life treats us much the same way. We are attached to making it quickly. We want everything right now. We make plans and schedule what we want and how it will come. When things do not go our way, we consider it a failure. No matter how hard you push or insist or demand, everything happens when it is supposed to happen; everything comes in time. We really are not in control of the universe, it is so much bigger than we are. Our ego tells us to take control of our time, but what we really do is create confusion and stress. We cannot rush our victory; we cannot cut short our pains. Everything happens when it needs to happen; everyone is always where they need to be. You will never miss out on what is meant for you, even if it has to come to you in a roundabout way. When we relax and follow our inner guidance, everything we should have is all that we get. When we rush around trying to make it, disappointment may be all we get.

I have the time to take my time.

All you have to do to receive your divine inheritance
is change your old way of thinking.
—John Randolph Price

*T*here is this thing going around. If you are not careful
it will attach itself to you. When it does, it will drain you of
everything you have. It will suck you dry and leave you to
die. This thing is called the Spirit of the Do-Do. It attacks
your brain. It can drive you insane. It never lets you rest.
It is constantly telling you what to do. Do this! Do that!
Do it faster! Do it better! Do it quick! Do it now! Do it
today! Do it for me! Do it for money! Do it or else! Do it
again! You better do it! You better not do it! They saw
you do it! You should do it! You should not try to do it!
When will you do it? How will you do it? Why would you
want to do it? You can't do it! You'd better do it! Don't
you ever do it! There is only one way to rid yourself of the
Spirit of the Do-Do. Close your eyes, take a deep breath
and repeat one hundred times:

Father/Mother Source,
what would you have me do?

I can't afford to go around saying it's hard for me
because I'm a woman.
—Brig. Gen. Marcelite J. Harris

*Y*ou know by now that what you focus your mind upon
grows. This is key for women. Women do not have it any
more difficult than anyone else. It is a matter of what they
believe. Women must move into a deeper understanding
of their own creative powers. Women create, men direct.
Women are the co-creators with the God force; they can
manifest life. Women bring to life what is planted through
the nurturing power of love. If women want success, prosperity, health or good relations in their lives, they must
learn how to make them manifest. Not pushing, forcing,
demanding they come. Rather move into your sacred
place and space; use your mind's eye, nurture and love
yourself and everyone else and let the power of love flow
through you.

Today I will love myself healthy and wealthy.

Giving and receiving are one in truth.
—*A Course in Miracles*

*T*here is only one mind. The mind of the Creator. Each living being is an idea in Divine Mind. We are not separate, as it seems. We are linked through the mighty power of breath. Since we are one, you cannot give anything away; you can only give to yourself. Whatever you give, whatever you do, you are giving and doing to an expression of the one Mind. If you give good, you will receive good. If you do harm, you will feel its effects. If we understand the concept of Divine Mind, we know there is no such thing as stealing from anyone. You can only take away from yourself. Whether the guilt, shame or fear cause the pain, you will take away from yourself that which you believe you are taking from another. When you give, you receive. When you receive it is a reflection of what you give. Since we are all one in Divine Mind, we should make a commitment to always give the best.

Today I will give lovingly and freely to myself.

I wish I knew how customs got started, it would
make it easier to stamp them out.

—Martin Lane

*R*ight now, in the midst of a so-called recession, many
people are still able to, and do, demonstrate wealth and
abundance. These individuals have overcome the dominant thoughts and beliefs of the mass consciousness that
money is in short supply. Unfortunately, many people still
believe they can't live day to day; they won't make it
through the week; they can't make ends meet; they don't
know what to do to get some of the shrinking money supply. Many people who believe this way are people of color.
We have been duped into believing we will never be self-
supporting, self-sufficient, capable of standing on our own.
We are dependent on the system to get better, give us a
break, take care of us. Many of us still believe the system
can and will provide the economic healing we need—*Until
today!* Now hear this, *God does not have a money problem!*
Everything God made is self-sufficient, including you. If
you want to know what to do about money, ask God.

*Dear God, thank you for providing
my every need.*

Money was exactly like sex, you thought of nothing
else if you didn't have it and thought of other
things when you did.

—James Baldwin

$\mathcal{E}$very day, our five senses deliver millions of messages
to our brains. We do not remember the messages because
they are filtered through the conscious mind into the unconscious mind. They are filtered, they are not gone and
they, the unconscious thoughts, govern our attitudes and
behaviors. I need some money . . . Everybody is broke
. . . Money is tight . . . Prices are too high . . . Cut spending. . . . The messages we receive stagnate our abundance
consciousness. It is very difficult to think and feel prosperity when the appearance of lack and limitation is swallow-
ing us at every turn. Yet until we change our minds about
what we are hearing and thinking, we will continue to be
money miserable. Create the pictures of what you want in
your mind. See your life the way you want it to be. Write
the checks and envelopes for the bills before payday.
When you are in the company of money-miserable people,
let them know that lack is not your issue.

Prosperity is my state of mind.

I like work, it fascinates me,
I can sit and look at it for hours.
—Jerome K. Jerome

*M*ost of us do not work because we want to; we work because we think we have to work for money. The problem is that is all we do. We forget that life is more than work. Life is also about balance. In order to have balance, we must do more than work. What about fun? We need fun to keep our minds off work. How about rest? Not just sleeping to get ready for the next day's work, but resting the mind and body from all activity. What about solitude? Take an hour or perhaps a day away from the hustle and bustle of life and people. It's called a mental-health break. Let us not forget the mind. Education. It helps to keep the gray matter upstairs from getting dusty. Work is necessary but it is not the only thing required to get ahead. All work and no play may give us a balanced checkbook, but it can also give us an unbalanced mind.

Today I will rest, relax and have some fun.

If you don't do it excellently, don't do it at all.
Because if it's not excellent,
it won't be profitable or fun.
—Robert Townsend

$\mathcal{I}$t takes about as much time to do something really well as it does to do whatever works. What works is not the best you can do. Excellence is. If you want prosperity, wealth, abundance in every area of your life, do what you do with excellence. Excellence requires a commitment, a force from your soul. Excellence is a power source and a sure way to ensure that your product or service will be in demand. Excellence requires order, the first law of prosperity. When you are committed to excellence you must think orderly, behave orderly, conduct yourself in an orderly manner and perform your tasks in order. Excellence is flexible. It does not get stuck in the right way but uses the best of all ways to get the job done. Excellence is cooperation with nature and the forces that be. When you are committed to excellence, the goal helps to keep you focused, not what everyone or anyone else is doing. Excellence is the way to perfect your skill, create a demand and put dollars in the pocket. Do it with excellence.

I Am committed to excellence in all ways.

There is enough in the world for everyone to have plenty to live on happily at peace and still get along with their neighbors.

—Harry S. Truman

*T*he quickest way to block your in-flow of good is to begrudge someone else what they have. We may somehow believe it is our place and duty to judge what other people do. When they receive or achieve beyond our expectations, we become even more judgmental—and sometimes angry. Is the anger really fear that the person will go away and leave us? Or is it fear there is not enough to go around? There are three principles of prosperity we must observe to ensure we receive our good: (1) Ask for what you want; (2) Give what you want away; (3) Be willing to see someone else get what you want before you do. When we follow these principles, we demonstrate our faith that no matter what we have, there is more than enough to go around.

I behold my good in your good.

Prosperity is living easily and happily in the real world, whether you have money or not.
—Jerry Gillies

*I*f you have many things you are not free to come and go in life; you are not prosperous. If you have things to do and protect that you think others can take away from you, you are not prosperous. If you are not comfortable with yourself no matter where you are, you are not prosperous. If you believe others can take your ideas, your mate, your things, you are not comfortable. Prosperity is a state of mind. When worry or fear crowd your mind, you cannot be prosperous. If you know you will eat even when you don't have a dime, you are prosperous. When you can love and give all that you have, you are prosperous. When you do what you love without pay or reward, you are prosperous. When you do what you can because you can, not for money only, you are prosperous. When you love all people for who they are, not for what they can give you, you are a wealthy being. Prosperity is a state of mind.

The richer I think, the richer I Am.

Make a prayer acknowledging yourself as a vehicle
of light, giving thanks for all that has come today.
—Dhyani Ywahoo

*J*ust for today, allow yourself to embrace all that you are
every moment. Know that you are a vessel of light. Allow
yourself to release all doubts about your ability, the mistakes of the past, the fear of the future. Just for today, remember that you have grace. It is called breath. You have
a connection to the Divine Mind, the power source of the
world. Just for today, remind yourself, "I am one with
God." "I am one with all the power there is." Just for
today, be a little child. Know the world is safe. Know that
you are loved. Know that just where you are, God is. Just
for today, be free. Be peace-filled. Be loving to yourself
and all others. Know that you shall not want for any good
thing. Just for today, give praise and thanksgiving for
everything to let the universe know you are ready to receive more.

Let the light shine on me today.
I give praise and thanks.

Let there be everywhere our voices, our eyes,
our thoughts, our love, our actions,
breathing hope and victory.
— Sonia Sanchez

In the twenty-first century the power is with the people. The people are the force that will make or break the world as we know it. The people are the only voice that will matter. The people have the power to create the world they want to see. The power is their thoughts, their words, their actions toward one another. Who are the people? Not the priests, the heads of state, the presidents. The people are those who can surrender their ego, embrace themselves as they are and do what they have been sent to do. The people are those who know they are not in charge; rather, they give praise to the Creative Source of life. The people are those who control their breath, know their bodies and use both to teach others how to do it. The people are the children. The people are the women. The people are the elders. The people are the men who love, nurture and protect the children, women and elders. The people are the light.

Today I Am a person of power.

In this world it is not what we take up but what we
give up that makes us right.

—Henry Beecher

*T*here is a very simple principle that people cannot seem
to get the hang of—as you give, so you receive. People
find it difficult to believe that it is necessary to give first
and give righteously. If you only give to get, you will not
receive. If you give out of fear, you will not receive. Many
people of color do not believe they have enough to give.
That is because they may be thinking in terms of money
only. If you do not have money, give of your time, talent
and energy. Give a smile. Give a prayer. Give anony-
mously without expectation of recognition. The spirit in
which you give determines the manner in which you receive. If you give freely, joyously and willingly, you will
receive abundantly. As you give what you have, what you
are not using, you make room to receive something else in
its place. Give of yourself, your knowledge and the information you have received, then prepare yourself for an
outpouring of blessing. And by the way, do not expect it to
come back to you from the person you gave it to.

Today I lovingly give my all to all who may need.

Unhappiness is not knowing what we want and
killing ourselves to get it.

—Don Harold

*C*an I continue to live in lack and limitation, denying
myself the abundant goodness of the world? Or can I
make a plan, follow a dream, do what I can, where I am,
with what I have? Can I? Can I? Can I continue to buy
into the belief that there is not enough, I am not enough,
settling for whatever I can get? Or can I do my best in
every situation, expecting the best from every situation,
recognizing that what I put out must come back to me tenfold? Can I? Can I? Can I continue to live in fear, complaining about what I do not have, cannot do, criticizing
myself and others? Or can I take a chance, find an opportunity and know in my heart what I want to do is possible? Can I? Can I? Can I blame the world, hate my
enemy, feel sorry for myself as an excuse not to do what I
desire to do? Or can I raise my consciousness, pour love
into every situation and take responsibility for myself?
Can I? Can I? Can you?

I Am responsible for doing all I can do.

Wealth is not in making money but in making the person while they make money.

—John Wicker

Do I see anything that needs to be done for me that I am not doing? Or do I only see what others could be doing and are not? Do I? Do I? Do I support myself by nurturing myself, accepting what I feel and letting my needs be known? Or do I shrink under criticism, blame others for my conditions and look for the easy way out? Do I? Do I? Do I recognize my truth and speak it when I feel the need? Or do I allow fear and people pleasing to silence me? Do I? Do I? Do I continue to do the things I know are not good for me and do not bring me what I want? Or do I examine myself, correct myself, accept myself but commit to get better? Do I? Do I? Do I know what I want, believe I can have it, do everything in my power to bring it about? Or do I accept what others tell me about my limitations and limit myself to what they believe? Do I? Do I? Do I have faith in spirit, faith in myself, faith in things unseen? Do I? Do I? Do you?

I am not what I used to be.
I am doing much better.

If money is your hope for independence,
you will never have it.

—Henry Ford

*W*ill I make it through the difficult times? Or will I give up? Will I? Will I? Will I get up this morning with a positive attitude, greet everyone with a smile and be glad to be alive? Or will I take a bad attitude into the world and have everyone wish I were not? Will I? Will I? Will I accept the people I encounter today for who they are and encourage them to become part of the group? Or will I seek out the people I feel are superior to the rest and alienate myself from those I judge beneath me? Will I? Will I? Will I do my part and give of myself to create my own independence? Or will I accept the crumbs that keep me dependent on people, conditions and situations? Will I? Will I? Will I trust myself and follow my first thought? Or will I look for others to validate me? Will I? Will I? Will you?

Today I will know me, honor me,
support me and trust me.

Your crown has been bought and paid for. All you must do is put it on your head.

—James Baldwin

*T*here is nothing you need that you do not already have. There is nothing you need to know that you do not already know. There is nothing you want that does not already exist. There is nothing that exists that is too good for you. There is nothing anyone has that you cannot have. There is nothing more powerful, more intelligent, more sacred than you. You are the stuff life is made of. You are the essence of life. You have been chosen at this time, in this place to be among the living. You come from a long line of successful living beings. You are one of the king's kids. Born into the world to inherit the kingdom. You are equipped to handle anything. You live by grace, built by love. You are the cause and the reason of everything you see. You are one with the Source. You are creative. You are alive. What else could possibly matter?

Today I claim my Divine inheritance.

Index

Faith in the Valley

Valley

*Lessons for Women
on the Journey
Toward Peace*

Acknowledgments

A ll of my work is a community effort: the community of people who love and support me, give me the inspiration to continue on the path. I salute you! I honor you! I love you!

God, my Father, my Mother, the spirit through which I live. I continue to surrender my will, my way, the fear that I won't do it right, on time, or in a way that makes people happy. Finally, I understand that God Is Enough!

The Inner Vision Spiritual Life Maintenance Team, Adara Walton, Almasi Zulu, Ebun Adelona, Erica Jackson, Gemmia Vanzant, Helen Jones, Janet Barber, Judith Hakimah, Lucille Gambrell, Mama Muhsinah Berry Dawan, and Fern Robinson, whose faith in me keeps me on target, without whose support I would miss the mark.

Joia "Louise" Jefferson, who knows everything I need to know and reminds me that I know it too! Thank you for being so willing to grow with me.

Ken and Renee Kizer, my re-birth coaches, who taught me how to breathe, who breathe with me and sometimes for me, taking me to the deepest depths of my soul, the place in me that is God. As Ken would say, "How much love can I stand?!!"

Fana Ifeula and the staff of The Other Eden, who

know how to work my kinks out and remind me to take care of the vessel.

Rev. Cochise and Vivianna Brown, who keep me cleaned out so I can go within.

Rev. Dr. Fernette Nichols, whose sermons on tape kept me grounded and in the spirit during my labor to birth this book.

Carol Ellis, an angel of God, with fingers of lightning speed, who landed in my driveway in the nick of time, to type, edit, and support the birth of this baby.

Dawn Daniels, my editor; Denise Stinson, my agent; Shaheerah Stevens, my best friend; Marge Battle, my voice of reason; you are my foundation and the fire in my spirit.

"Yu," the other half of me who keeps me praying, praising, and practicing the presence.

*Dedicated to the Memory of
the Great, Grand Diva
Miss Phyllis Hyman
and
Her Sisters
Butterfly McQueen, Rosalind Cash, Roxie Roker,
Madge Sinclair
and
My Sister-Friend
Dorothea Lois Dowell
I will always love you, my SISTAHS!*

There's a lily in the valley.

How to Use This Book

The Value in the Valley is more than just another book we can read to get hints and tips on how to improve ourselves and our lives. It is a process, with steps and principles designed to raise our consciousness and our spiritual and emotional well-being. In the book, valleys are described as, "those tight spots, dark places, uncomfortable situations we think make our lives so miserable." We all know about valleys. We have all had valley experiences: lonely, painful, confusing experiences we may believe we do not deserve, should not have, or cannot get out of. In the process of a valley experience, we often miss the lesson. A valley is a life situation designed to teach us the character traits and spiritual virtues that are undeveloped or underdeveloped during our life experiences. Valleys help us stretch, reach, and grow into our greatest potential. However, even when you know what a valley is and its potential good, you want to know what to do, how to behave in the midst of the experience. That's when you can turn to *Faith in the Valley*.

When you are trying to stay out of a valley, trying to get out of a valley, or engaging in behavior that will take you into a valley, there is probably a dominant thought raging in your mind. "Oh Lord! Why me?!!" "What the hell am I gonna do now?!!" When we are experiencing emotional stress or pressure, these thoughts become our affirmations. These are the things we say to our girlfriends when we are telling our story. They are also the things we say to ourselves when the story is too unbelievable to repeat! Unfortunately, when we are headed for or in the midst of a valley experience, we do not realize that what we think and what we say enhances the experience. The bad news is, most of the time we think and talk ourselves right into the valley. The good news is, we can use thoughts and words to get out.

Faith in the Valley is your life-support equipment. The commentaries in this book are written to support you in transforming dominant thought patterns, behaviors, attitudes, and self-defeating affirmations that can take you into the valley. Each commentary will provide you with insight about the lesson you can learn in the midst of a tragic, difficult, or frightening experience. Some commentaries will provide you with a new or different perspective on what may appear to be a problematic or confusing situation. Sometimes, a change of perspective may be all that it will take to transform a painful, frustrating, or shameful experience into an empowering growth experience. Whether you believe it or not, your thoughts and words determine your reality. When you change your mind, you can change your life.

Faith in the Valley is meant to support and enhance what you gleaned from *The Value in the Valley,* though it will work just as well if you have not read that book. The key to having faith when you are in the valley is knowing how to use the index of this book. The index in *Faith in the Valley* lists many of the things we say when we find ourselves in difficult situations. What we say is a reflection of what we think. What we think is the key to the lesson we need to learn. Because valley experiences teach us lessons, each affirmation has been ascribed to a particular valley. If you have *The Value in the Valley*, you may want to read the chapter under which the affirmation is listed in order to gain a better understanding of your particular experience. If you do not have that book, read the commentary and reflect on the message given.

At the right side of each page you will find a word or a list of words that relates to the commentary. These are lessons clues. This is what you are *growing* through. The words listed will give you a clue about the lesson you must learn or the principle you must apply to the details of your situation. In some cases it will probably be the most difficult thing you can imagine and the very thing you are resisting. DO NOT RESIST YOUR LESSONS! Resistance will push you deeper into the darkness of a valley experience. Trust Spirit! Trust yourself! Above all else, trust the process of your growth!

There will be those rare occasions when your experience is so challenging or difficult that your mind will go blank. You won't know what to think or say. You will not know what valley you are in or how you got there. In those moments you will have a particular feeling—dread, doom, hysteria, or just plain old fear. That's good enough! Turn to the index, find the word or phrase that best describes your state of mind, and read the commentary offered. This is a full service, user-friendly book. There is something here for everyone!

The commentaries offered in this book are based on spiritual laws and universal principles. If you are in a valley, these laws and principles will probably not make sense to your intellect or rational mind. In some cases, what you read in the commentary will be the last thing you want to know about. This is a signal that your resistance is rearing its ugly head, trying to keep you from getting the lesson. Life is a function of universal principles governed by spiritual laws that flow into and out of our lives. When we are unfamiliar with these laws and principles, we fight against them when they show up in our lives as experiences. We fight against them with logic, with thoughts, and with language. When we fight the universe, we end up deeper in the valley.

Because the language of the intellect and the language of spirit are not always in harmony, I offer a glossary of key terms and principles to aid in your understanding of the commentaries. When your intellect is resisting the lesson you must learn, you will believe that you do not understand the message of the commentary. I've covered that base too! Turn to the glossary, look up the lesson clue. The words listed in the glossary will provide you with a greater insight about your thinking, attitudes, and behaviors that lead to valley experiences or that will relieve a valley experience. If the lesson clue given by the commentary is not listed in the glossary, you may ascribe to it the commonly used definition. The glossary terms are provided to ensure that you have a better understanding of the universal principle or spiritual law operating in your experience. Understanding is the key to transformation. Transformation is your ticket out of the valley.

If all of the above fails to meet your needs, do not panic! Close your eyes, place the book at the center of your forehead, take a deep beath, and open to any page. Spirit always knows what you need. Rest assured that the message you open to will answer your question and point the way to a lesson. In the midst of your most difficult and challenging experience, remember—you are growing. Be gentle with yourself. Give yourself time to examine, question, and explore the principles at work and the emotions you are experiencing. Give yourself permission to fall, to get up and to do better next time. Wherever you are in your life, pray some, play some, and always have plenty of faith!

Introduction

I was ending a thirty-five-day promotional tour. Having flown all night, in a very crowded airplane, to get from Los Angeles to New Orleans, I was senseless from exhaustion and still wearing the clothes I had put on twenty-three hours earlier. I was feeling pretty ugly. After making a few telephone calls just to make sure no one wanted me to do anything for at least eight hours, I crawled into yet another hotel bed. I had only been in the bed forty-five minutes when my sister-friend staff member arrived. We decided eating made more sense than sleeping, so off we went.

Walking casually through the mall toward the food court, my companion was bringing me up to date on what was going on back at home. Then she asked me if I had heard about Phyllis. She had been found dead the day before. Beyond exhaustion there is numbness. In a state of numbness, the news that your sister-friend has left her body is called "the valley." I told my companion to shut her mouth. It was the only logical response to the feeling of pain, fear, confusion, and loss that descended over my body. I felt the pain, but I knew to go there would mean I would be subject to going crazy in a New Orleans shopping mall. I surrendered the thought. Actually, I shut down and continued the search for something I could tear apart with my teeth.

With a few morsels of food in my body, I moved out of numbness and back to exhaustion so that I could ask the question: *"Why?"* Why is not the appropriate question to ask when you are in the valley, because a mind in pain will reject everything except what it wants to, needs to hear. If the mind does not find what it needs and wants, it will ask why ad infinitum. After I asked and rejected all plausible explanations, I engaged in appropriate valley behavior: I cried.

Crying is a good thing to do in the valley because it clears the channels of communication. Crying purifies and cleanses. I once read about a scientific experiment which demonstrated that there are 38 toxic chemicals in a tear of sadness, while only one toxin exists in a tear of joy. As you cry in sadness, fear, or confusion, you cleanse the body and spirit of the toxins which cloud the mind and prevent it from accepting the truth. Once I had sufficiently purified, I asked the more appropriate question when one has fallen into a valley: "What is the lesson here?" In the quiet, undeniable way of spirit, the answer came. "She did not pass the test. The choice was hers to make." As my mind could now accept the truth, I fell into a peaceful sleep.

No matter who you are, you will have a valley experience at some time in your life. It just "be's" that way. For some, a valley will be a time of great fear, confusion, and, probably, emotional turmoil. For others, it may be a

grave inconvenience or a time of seemingly endless struggle. You may whine, complain, shut down, or beg God
for mercy. The truth is, you will only get what you need
to grow. You are not being punished, you are being forti-
fied!

In a great holy book of the Eastern tradition, the
Bhagavad Gita, there is a passage which reads, "You will
be tested! What if the Creator has a great task for you to
perform and you are unprepared? Your tests come to ensure that you will be prepared when your time comes to
serve." A valley is a testing experience which prepares you
for greater service. Serving the Creator is what life is all
about. Many of us, in the quest "to do" and "to get,"
forget service. We have not been taught that service means
to "be" the embodiment of the Creator, actualizing all
the attributes of the Creator as what we are. The Creator
is life, truth, love, harmony, balance, principle, and peace.
In living we become so busy "doing" we forget to "be."
Humans doing are not human beings.

The wise woman, mother, sister, and stage diva Beah
Richards once told me, "You are a human being, which
means you lack no thing essential to your survival. You
are whole, complete and loved just as you are. That is how
I love you." This is also how God, the Creator loves us.
Just as we are is the physical embodiment of God Itself.
What we look like, what we do, what we have, does not
alter what God made us to be. Living in a doing-made
world, confronted by rules, laws, and expectations which
force us to do, has a way of wiping the knowledge of our

divinity right out of our memory. We become indoctrinated to a process of struggle, conflict, restriction, and
denial based on what we do, what we get, and how we
look to others who try to out-do and out-get us. Then
we get mad. We get mad at the people who participate in
the struggle, conflict, restriction, and denial with us. Then
we get mad at our self for having the experience. Some of
us go so far as to get mad at God for not helping us "do"
better.

What we call living or trying to live is not life! God
is life! God is not in conflict or struggle with anyone about
anything. God is not restricted or restrictive. God cannot
deny Itself. God perfects! This perfecting presence is always with us at the core of our being, even when we are
in the valley.

With my father and mother gone from active living,
it has been easy for me to turn to God. I had nowhere
else to go! Then I realized the nowhere means, "now
here." Even after I had this revelation, there were days
when I got very busy "doing"; times when I went into
fear; moments, sometimes weeks, of total confusion. I
have even had experiences of temporary insanity. These
were my valleys. It took a while for me to realize that all
testing experiences fortify my faith, strengthen my character, and open my soul to the perfecting presence.

I have learned to breathe through those testing times.
I am no longer afraid to let go, to give up control and
allow spirit to work in my life. In those now-rare moments when I do forget to breathe or how to let go, I

grab a book. A book of spiritual truth which will jar my memory back to my divinity, the truth of who I am. This offering is something for you to grab and hold onto if you should happen to forget what else to do. Keep it near at all times. Hold it tightly in the testing times. And, when all else fails, act on faith!

I love you just as you are!

Iyanla

The Valley of Light

Teaches us the lesson of stillness, through the imposition of a state of solitude and silence which forces us to take a look at ourselves.

Let us learn to be still and let the Truth speak through us: to be still and know that the inner light shines.

—*THE SCIENCE OF MIND*

LIFE DOES WHATEVER is necessary to mold us into shape and prepare us for greatness. It does not always look or feel this way. Instead, what we experience in life seems difficult, painful, unnecessary. Just for a moment, think of the stones which were used to build the pyramids and the gems which fashion the Crown Jewels. Imagine how the stones were dug from the quarry and then hammered and chiseled into shape. Realize that each stone or gem had to be perfectly shaped before it could be set in its appropriate place. Recognize that once the pyramids were built and jewels cast into the Crown, they have never been disturbed, nor have they shifted, fallen, or crumbled.

Somehow life teaches us to understand that God has a perfect plan for us; according to that plan, we must be molded and shaped prior to being cast into our perfect place. When we truly recognize that there is a master plan, we can welcome any tool that comes to prepare us to behold our perfect place. When we are shaped and molded by life according to God's perfect plan, the world is amazed and blessed by our beauty, and longevity.

Get prepared to be prepared!

RIGHT WHERE YOU are is where you need to be. Don't fight it! Don't run away from it! Stand firm! Take a deep breath. And another. And another. Stop beating up on yourself. Don't blame anyone else. Breathe. Now, ask yourself: Why is this in my world? What do I need to see? To know about myself through this situation? Breathe again. Now, ask God:

Blessed and Divine Father/Mother, heal me of whatever thought or belief has contributed to the cause of this experience. Bring me the lesson of this experience lovingly and gently. Keep my mind and heart open that I may know the truth. Open my eyes that I may recognize your will. Thank you, God.

Now breathe. Don't you feel better already?

God is right here, right now!

BAD THINGS ARE going to happen. Painful, ugly, frustrating events are going to take place. There is no way around getting your feelings hurt, having your ego bruised, your trust weighed, your heart broken. Life has its ups and downs. If you are living, you are bound to trip or fall every now and then. There is not much you can do while you are going through your challenges and difficulties, but there is something you can remember that will make it a bit easier to bear.

The same God that was good yesterday is good today. The same God that loved you last week, loves you today. The same powerful, almighty, all-knowing God that saved you, comforted you, guided you the last time you needed it, will save, comfort, and guide you today. Right where you are, in the midst of trouble, take a moment to be loved, comforted, guided, by the good God who knows exactly what you need. God is present. God's presence is called grace.

Live in the presence of God's grace.

When my husband left, I thought I had been a bad wife. Then my son went to jail, and I knew I had been a bad mother. When my best friend and my mother died, I slipped face first into being a bad person. How was I supposed to figure it all out?

All women fall into the valley. Some fall deeper than others. The valley is a lonely place. A dark and confusing pit in the center of your brain. You can't figure it out. You can't get out. You've got a black hole in your life into which everything you've ever really wanted seems to fall, into the valley. I once thought it was cruel and inhumane punishment; now I know it is a reward. The stronger and more gifted you are, the deeper and eventually more rewarding is the valley experience.

We all have our lessons to learn in life. Most of us fail to learn unless we are in some kind of pain. The valley is your pain. The valley gets your attention. The valley lets you know what you are doing and why you just might want to try something new. The bad thing is that no one can warn you a valley is coming. You must pay attention to what is going on in your life! The good thing is that once you've been there, in enough pain, you figure it out. People begin to notice. "Hey, what's up with you?" "You look different." "Did you change your hair or something?" You haven't changed your hair, your mind has changed. You have learned a very valuable lesson. When you can't, FAITH CAN!

Faith makes the day and paves the way!

DEAR SELF,
Guilt says,
"There is something wrong with what I have done."
Shame says,
"There is something wrong with me."
You can eliminate guilt by making amends
for what you have done.
You cannot eliminate shame
until you know and believe,
"All that God is, I Am."
God is truth, mercy, wisdom, strength, forgiveness,
peace, order, justice, and love.
What have you got to be ashamed of?

God is not ashamed of me. Neither am I.

———

YOU CAN'T SHRINK into greatness. When you reflect on the things you have done and not done, there is a tendency to beat up on yourself. We criticize, judge, and condemn ourselves, much more severely than the world could or would. In response to this self-flagellation, we shrink away from doing or attempting to do. You cannot shrink into your greatness! We must use our past as a road map, a key, that unlocks our capabilities by giving us understanding of our frailties. The past simply tells us what we can do, cannot do, what we need to work on or work out.

You must know every intricate detail of yourself. Your past is like an X-ray machine. Once you see what is there, don't shrink, shine! Now you know, which means you can take appropriate steps toward healing and correction. Don't fight with yourself! Accept who you are now and all you've done. Then give yourself a big hug and kiss. You've been through a lot. A little loving tenderness could be what you need right now.

I love to love me.

REPETITION IS THE mother of skill. If you do something enough you get good at it. When what you are doing is good for you, it is pleasurable, and you want to do it often, getting better and better at it. However, when what we do is not pleasurable, we fight against it, resisting the discomfort, and avoiding the lesson we may need to learn.

When unwanted situations repeat themselves in our lives, there is something we have missed. There is a blind spot in our consciousness, something we can't see and don't know yet. Repeat performances of bad productions will continue coming up as an experience in our lives. We go through it again, again, wracking our brains, grasping at straws, trying to figure out how we got here and how we can get out.

Those repetitive issues which cause us displeasure are just like the things Mother told us over and over. We didn't want to hear them; we ignored what she said. In the end, we saw Mother's point. Finally, we realized, she only wanted us to be better; well, so does life. When you find yourself in the same situation repeatedly, do not fight against what you are going through. It is in your own best interest to look for the lesson and cultivate the skill, to do a new thing, in a new way.

I Am, I Am, I Am, I know I Am, learning something
very valuable.

———

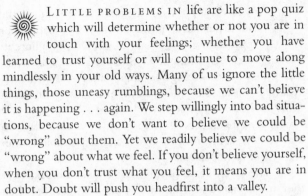 LITTLE PROBLEMS IN life are like a pop quiz which will determine whether or not you are in touch with your feelings; whether you have learned to trust yourself or will continue to move along mindlessly in your old ways. Many of us ignore the little things, those uneasy rumblings, because we can't believe it is happening . . . again. We step willingly into bad situations, because we don't want to believe we could be "wrong" about them. Yet we readily believe we could be "wrong" about what we feel. If you don't believe yourself, when you don't trust what you feel, it means you are in doubt. Doubt will push you headfirst into a valley.

Sometimes an uneasy feeling will be the normal fear or doubt associated with doing things that are different or new. At other times, it will be life warning you to get still, pay attention, remember what happened the last time you didn't pay attention to yourself, and act accordingly.

Here is a clue about life's little warnings: monsters don't have shadows! You will never see the monster coming. It will descend upon you before you recognize it. If you are feeling uneasy for no apparent reason, it means you are being quizzed about something you are adequately equipped to handle, based on past experience. Whether you pass or fail the quiz is a reflection of how much you know about and trust yourself.

Trust what you feel!

WHEN YOU GET the urge to stay home, be alone, pull back, or shut down, it is probably your spirit urging you to take a rest. Do not ignore it! Honor yourself by taking some time out. Take a day away. There may be something very important going on within you that you need to know about. You must get quiet in order to hear it. The job will be there, and people will simply have to understand; what can be done today can also be done tomorrow. All duties and responsibilities can wait. Your spirit cannot!

I have often heard people say, "I need a break!" but they never take one. I know it is no coincidence when these same people break their foot or when their car breaks down, forcing them to "be still." Often we think there is something wrong with us when we "don't want to be bothered." So we keep moving and doing. Spirit knows what we need and provides it for us. Yet when incidents force us into a needed solitude, we reach outward rather than within. Rest, Stillness, Solitude, Introspection, Reflection, are spiritual vibrations. They keep us from breaking down, falling apart, and being forced into a living deficiency.

Today is a spiritual health day!

DEAR GOD,

Today, I want to be still, to listen, to hear, and to know. Today, I want to see and know myself as a reflection of You. Today, God, I want the stillness of your love to shower me in the light of perfect peace, that I may go forth stronger, wiser, in readiness to do your perfect will. Today, God, I want to be still with you.

Lord, keep me still today! Take away all that makes me race and worry and fear and doubt and rush away from myself. Take away the need to do, be, have, know, want anything other than the grace of Your love. Show me myself today, Lord. Show me your perfect child, on a divine mission, fulfilling your perfect purpose, in a divine way. And, Lord, help me understand You and me, how we can work together in stillness to create new life.

Today, Lord, I am willing to be still in your arms, still in your light, still in your love. I am willing to see you in me and release all that is not. I am willing to know you in my life, to preserve you in my heart, to open myself to more of you as what I am. In stillness I see you. In stillness I accept you. In stillness I feel you. Lord, let me be still, just for today. Thank You, God.

Today, move in stillness.

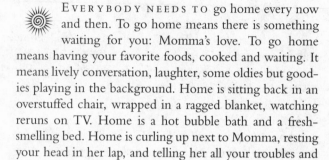 EVERYBODY NEEDS TO go home every now and then. To go home means there is something waiting for you: Momma's love. To go home means having your favorite foods, cooked and waiting. It means lively conversation, laughter, some oldies but goodies playing in the background. Home is sitting back in an overstuffed chair, wrapped in a ragged blanket, watching reruns on TV. Home is a hot bubble bath and a fresh-smelling bed. Home is curling up next to Momma, resting your head in her lap, and telling her all your troubles and fears while she gently strokes your brow. Why not go home to Momma today? You can cook. You have a radio or an old tape to play. Get that old blanket out of the box. Take a nice warm bath and curl up in the bed. God the Mother is waiting to hear from you.

Mother, I'm coming home.

IN ANCIENT TIMES, it was believed that little boys needed special protection in life. Boys were covered in blue. Blue represents the heavens. When you covered a baby boy in blue, you were providing him the energy and protection of God. It was also thought that girls did not require, or even "deserve," the same protection. Girls were fragile. Girls were meant to serve and be protected by boys. Girls were covered in pink to represent their sweet, fragile nature.

As silly as this may sound, it represents the dominant thought pattern of our culture. Boys are entitled to the world of God. Girls get ignored, pushed aside, abused, or abandoned by the boys. Don't they deserve special recognition themselves? You can begin today.

Remind your little girl, it is not what she wears, it is not the ribbons in her hair. It is not the color of her skin, the ruffles on her panties, or the neighborhood she lives in. Little girls are also expressions of God; this makes them worthy to the world. Little girls are valuable because they are; not because of what they do, what they have, or what they want to be. Little girls bring forth the grace of life in their smiles, laughter, questions, and expressions. There is a little girl in you. Have you loved her today? Have you hugged or kissed her today? Have you told her how special she is, how valuable she is, and how much you appreciate and honor her? Have you told the little girl in you how beautiful she is just because she is!

It is safe for you to be a little girl.

I'm all alone. I don't have nobody.

Fear,
Faith

NO ONE WANTS to be alone when things are not going well. Whether we fall or are pushed into one of life's difficulties, we don't want to be there on our own. In the darkness of trouble, we reach out for someone to help us. If we are lucky, they can't! They may want to, but there is simply no way anyone else can learn our lessons with us or for us.

If you are a slow learner, you might get mad at friends you think should help but don't. You may become disillusioned or resentful of the family members who always call on you but never answer when you call. If you are a spiritual special-education candidate, you may complain or whine and stamp your feet, declaring, "Why me?" "This is not fair!" "I can't take this anymore!" Oh, you can take it! We can always take the dark, lonely, frightening valley experience, because we have no other choice!

Your blessings have your name on them; so do your lessons! Your greatest blessing appears before you, cleverly disguised as your most difficult challenge, as your greatest obstacle, or as an extremely negative experience you are forced to handle all by yourself. What a blessing! What a blessed opportunity to face the truth, forgive yourself and others, practice faith, develop trust, be still, and know, "Right where I am, God is!"

I Am not alone! I Am learning!

WHERE DID WE get the idea that we must do it "all" alone? There is a guardian angel called the "Grace of God" waiting to serve us whenever we have need. So many of us struggle through life completely ignorant of the fact that the "Love of God" is sufficient protection, support, and supply under all circumstances. Far too many of us take on more than we need or want to, and by doing so, we get in God's way.

At all times, no matter what situation may confront us, "grace" is our escape route. With a long, deep breath, relaxation of the stomach muscles, and the silent affirmation "By the grace of God," we are given a clear mind and divine guidance. Often this brief exercise provides us with a new insight or renewed strength. Sometimes it lets us know that there is absolutely nothing we can do, and even this is okay. In a state of not being able to help ourselves, God's love surrounds us. This love brings us peace, contentment, and a silent strength. It brings us the ability to say no without guilt; the presence of mind to "let go" without fear; more importantly, it reminds us that with faith we can do all things.

The next time pressure, responsibilities, demands, or expectations push you to the point of overwhelm, invoke the grace; surrender to love. And let the blessings fall as they may.

By the grace, with the love of God, I Am.

———

IN THE MIDST of a valley experience, the temptation is to look at all the things you can't do and the list of reasons why. The human ego always encourages us to hold on to our limitations. It always seems easier to look at what is wrong rather than stretch to what could possibly be just fine. If we would see things as perfectly fine, just the way they are, no matter what they are, we might realize we are fine too. For some of us, this is a far stretch. But that's fine, and so are you.

If you are alive, that's fine. If you have a vision for tomorrow, that's fine. People may be pressuring you or upset with you. That's fine. You may be upset, afraid, angry, and anxious; that's just fine. You will get over it. If you can remember a time, any time when you were in a fix, a jam, a place in your life you did not want to be, that is fine. Now, can you remember that you are not where you were anymore? Or realize you made it through . . . somehow? Haven't you always gotten what you needed? And when you didn't, you made it through anyway. Perhaps things did not work out the way you wanted, but they are turning out. Most important of all, they are turning out to be just fine.

No matter what, it's fine.

———

WHEN THINGS DO not turn out the way we think they should or the way we want them to, anger, disappointment, fear, and sometimes shame or guilt are normal human responses. We want what we want, when we want it. If we do not get it, we are hurt. We try to figure out what did and did not happen; who is right or wrong; and why things never go the way we want them to go. Often, we do not realize that the moment we try to make something happen, the pain begins.

Reflect on the number of times you have asked for something and gotten it, only to realize it did not make you feel the way you thought it would. Now, reflect on those situations when things did not go your way and still turned out to be just fine. In the moment of disappointment, it may be hard to remember the good things gone bad and the bad things gone good. It is much easier to feel bad or get mad, which is exactly why we must be on guard and not do it.

There is a divine order in the universe of life which operates to protect our best interests, even when we cannot see it. Divine order will save us from ourselves. Order will bring peace. If we would "order" the brain to stop chattering, clamoring, and creating drama, the pain we think we are in would be transformed to an orderly flow of events. In the flow of life, divine order often brings our good at the perfect time in the perfect way.

Faith transforms confusion into order.

———

41

YOU HAVE A right to grieve, to be angry, to cry. You deserve a new dress, a new pair of shoes, or a new haircut. You do not have to answer the telephone or the door. You are under no obligation to show up unless you want to. If you want to stay under the covers, or sit naked in the middle of the floor and eat grapes, go right ahead and do it. Never be so responsible for the world that you forget to be responsible to yourself.

Confusing, tragic, painful events will come and go. These events cause shifts in our minds and upheavals in our hearts for which we need time to grieve, heal, understand, and accept. It is a process of taking care of one's self. While the brain is clearing, the heart mending, the body healing, it may mean taking a break from the regular routine, and moving away from the routine people. Give yourself permission to do whatever is necessary to take care of you. Take a walk. Have a cry. Break a glass. Write a letter. Pull your dress up over your head! Go ahead, do whatever it takes to help you feel better.

Today, just take care of yourself!

Some people are important because they make themselves so.
Some people are important because other people make them so.
Other people are important because God makes them so.
They are the people who never brag or boast or know so.
— REV. DR. FERNETTE NICHOLS

God makes an important difference!

SOME PEOPLE ARE compelled by the theoretical desire to live a spiritual life. These people are curiosity-seekers who will try a little of this and a little of that, never sticking to anything long enough to see if it actually works. Those who are theoretically spiritual read the books and know the language; they attend the workshops so they know what to do. However, in crisis they will panic. In disappointment they will criticize and condemn. In fear they will lie. In anger they become unforgiving and judgmental. You see, theory alone does no good. You must practice the principles in order to realize the truth. The more consistent and devoted the practice, the greater the realization and demonstration of truth.

The other telltale sign of a theoretical spiritualist is that they get full fairly quick. They have forgiven enough. They are grateful enough. They have given enough praise. The Christ said we should forgive seventy times seven. We must praise unceasingly; we must be grateful beyond measure. Isn't it interesting that those of us who have difficulty giving ourselves to one thing can measure when we have done enough of something else?

Today, I will give more, do more,
have more of one thing.

THERE DOESN'T HAVE to be anything *wrong* with you to want to do better. You don't have to be broke or brokenhearted, hated or hateful to be in search of a better way. For some reason, we seem to feel where we are is as far as we can go. We have convinced ourselves not to look for a better way; a new path is an admission that something is not good about where we are. This is simply not true.

"I can do better" does not translate to "I am doing bad." It is actually a recognition of the unlimited potential of the human spirit. The spirit within us has the ability to grow beyond all time, space, and physical matter in response to our receptivity. Our job is to remain open, to never be so comfortable where we are as to believe we cannot continue to grow. Most important of all, even when we believe we are the best we can be, we can do more, learn more, be more, by teaching what we know to somebody else.

There's more to me than this.

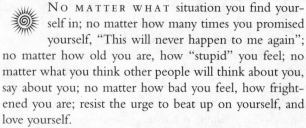 NO MATTER WHAT situation you find your-
self in; no matter how many times you promised
yourself, "This will never happen to me again";
no matter how old you are, how "stupid" you feel; no
matter what you think other people will think about you,
say about you; no matter how bad you feel, how frightened you are; resist the urge to beat up on yourself, and
love yourself.

Go ahead, love yourself right now. Touch yourself.
Give YOU a big hug. Gather yourself up in your arms
and rock yourself for a little while. Now say something
encouraging to you. Try, "I will always love you, no matter what." Tell yourself, "You're okay with me, no matter
what!" If you are really sincere, you will probably hit a
raw nerve. When you do, you will cry. Good! Love has a
way of touching the core of the being, and breaking it
down to the basic element: love. You can love yourself
into and out of anything. Perhaps you are where you are
because you need a little love. So before you try to figure
out what to do, love yourself. Nobody can do it better
than you!

Love appears as new experiences.

──────

A SPIRITUAL BROTHER and friend, Rocco Errico, explained embarrassment to me this way: It's like spilling milk. When you spill the milk, God throws you a rag and says, "Here! Clean up your mess!" The rag is truth, faith, discipline, obedience to do what you know you must, what is in your best interest. Sometimes we are courageous enough to face the messes we create in our lives and clean them up. At times we leave one mess and go create another one. When we do, God doesn't get angry. S/He says, "Here's the rag; tell the truth, admit your faults, make amends; clean it up." If we spill the milk again and again and again, God will continue to throw us the rag and wait for us to clean it up. Often, we expect God to clean up the mess for us. We beg and plead and cry. God simply waits, because God knows, when we get tired of cleaning up the mess, we will stop spilling the milk!

I will clean up after myself.

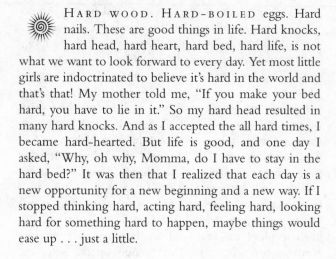 HARD WOOD. HARD-BOILED eggs. Hard nails. These are good things in life. Hard knocks, hard head, hard heart, hard bed, hard life, is not what we want to look forward to every day. Yet most little girls are indoctrinated to believe it's hard in the world and that's that! My mother told me, "If you make your bed hard, you have to lie in it." So my hard head resulted in many hard knocks. And as I accepted the all hard times, I became hard-hearted. But life is good, and one day I asked, "Why, oh why, Momma, do I have to stay in the hard bed?" It was then that I realized that each day is a new opportunity for a new beginning and a new way. If I stopped thinking hard, acting hard, feeling hard, looking hard for something hard to happen, maybe things would ease up . . . just a little.

I can hardly wait to see the good coming my way.

48

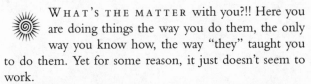 WHAT'S THE MATTER with you?!! Here you are doing things the way you do them, the only way you know how, the way "they" taught you to do them. Yet for some reason, it just doesn't seem to work.

Look at you! There you go again! Doing that, the way you think you should, the way "they" told you you should, and look at what is happening!

I can't believe you did that! Not again! Not now! But you did, didn't you? Now what are you going to do?

If I were you, I would simply "be."

Face it, no matter what you do, someone is not going to be happy. In addition to that, there is no right or wrong in doing. There simply is what "is." Whatever you do, you will continue to do it, the way you do it, until you "grow" into doing something else. You cannot be wrong. You can only be who you are, doing what you do, in order to become better.

Whatever you do is exactly what you need to do in order to learn what you need to know. As you learn, you become better at what you do. When you get better, you will do a new thing, and someone else will still not be happy. The good news is, no matter what you do, you will learn how to do it better; or you will learn what not to do in order to be better. Now there is absolutely nothing wrong with that, is there?

I am doing, learning, and growing.

———

The Valley of Understanding

Teaches us to accept ourselves, other people, and situations as they are, not as we want them to be. Understanding is the ability to get underneath the thing and stand in the truth of what it is.

Betrayal teaches that you can survive anything. All the things you thought you couldn't handle, you can.

—OPRAH WINFREY

THE QUICKEST WAY to turn a bad situation into a blessing is to get excited! Things may not look so good right now. You may even doubt your ability to hold up under the pressure or the scrutiny. It's all okay! You can still choose to be excited! Excitement is the opposite of anxiety. It brings a new energy into any situation. Excitement gives you power and puts you in charge of what you do.

Just imagine how you will feel when the situation is over. Think about what you will do with the knowledge and experience you are gaining. Think about the stories you can tell, the people you can assist, the fact that you will know what to do if you are ever in this situation again. Is that exciting?

In any situation, you have the right, power, and ability to choose your experience. Old habits and negative thought patterns will be the first to show up, but we can choose a new way in which you affect the outcome. Rather than slipping into fear, resentment, or anger, you can get excited! Be excited that this has come to an end. Be excited that you are equipped to handle it! Be excited that life is trusting you to do the right thing! Be excited that you will do your best, no matter what happens.

I'm so excited!

THE PAIN WE experience in life is not always physical. People hurt in many ways for many reasons. Unfortunately, we are programmed at a very early age to take something or to do something to make the pain go away. The taking or doing will often give us temporary relief. It usually does not root out the cause of the pain. As a result, we do what we must in the moment to find relief, and in doing so ignore the growing malignancy which initially caused the pain.

The physical, mental, or emotional shift we call pain is actually a marvelous teaching tool. When you hurt, you become acutely aware that something you are doing, or have done, is not good for you. When you are in pain, a weakened state, you want to reach out; however, life is telling you to reach within. A habitual behavior pattern, a persistent thought pattern, a response to an event or series of events is usually at the root of the pain. If you hurt long enough and hard enough, you just might be prompted to stop participating in those activities which create the pain.

No matter what kind of pain we experience in life, see it as a shift toward something better. Remember, you are equipped to handle it. Resist the urge to get temporary relief. As you learn and grow, you will realize the greater the pain, the greater the growth. The greater the growth, the less is the likelihood that you will do anything to knowingly hurt yourself ever again.

OUCH! I Am growing through this!

MOST OF US probably couldn't stand having all of our problems solved at one time. There would be so much light and power, we would be blown away. Some of us would be so frightened, we would constantly peer over our shoulder, waiting for the disaster to come. In life, we see our problems as one great big mountain. In order to move the mountain, you have to chip away one grain of sand at a time.

At certain points, you will have to move the same grain of sand several times. As you repeat the same thing over and over, you will get clear about what you do. Some parts of the mountain will fall away with very little effort on your part. Maybe that part had nothing to do with you. It got mixed in with your stuff along the way. Some parts of the mountain will resist your efforts; they will not be moved. Don't get stuck. When you are standing in front of the mountain, resist the feeling of overwhelm. Move the piece of sand closest to you; that is easy to pick up. Pay attention to how you move it. Don't forget to celebrate yourself for every grain of sand that you move.

I can do this! One step at a time! One day at a time!

WHEN YOU GET through whatever it is you are going through, you are going to be much better off. You will have firsthand knowledge of what works for you and what does not. You will have a new assessment of your strengths and capabilities. You will have greater insights about the people in your life. Perhaps you will have trimmed away some fluff, released some unnecessary baggage. In the midst of a challenge, our eyes are opened, our minds blown to new levels of awareness. When you get through this, you are going to be something else . . . a better, stronger you!

Just another growth experience, blessing me today.

YOU DID EVERYTHING you were supposed to do, the way you were supposed to do it. You even did it on time. You put your best foot forward, utilized all of your resources, followed all the rules, and things still didn't turn out as you planned. Well, don't be alarmed, angry, or frustrated; it happens to the best of us. The challenge is to realize and accept that we simply cannot see everything.

All of us have a blind spot, a weak area, a point of vulnerability of which we are simply unaware. There will be those instances in which our best efforts are for naught. When our deepest desire goes up in smoke. This will not always mean we did it wrong; it simply means we did not see it right. When we are blindsided by tragedy, disaster, or disappointment, the lesson becomes knowing that our best is always good enough, no matter what the outcome appears to be.

I should have seen it coming, but I didn't.

———

WHEN THINGS HAPPEN that upset or frighten children, they run away. When they do "bad things," they hide. Children believe "bad things" will kill them, or if they do bad things they will lose love. If there is no one around to support, protect, or reassure children, they find ways, mentally and emotionally, to escape the punishment they might receive.

When children grow up, they realize the bad things did not kill them, yet adults will still find ways to escape unpleasant or frightening experiences. Mentally we make excuses, lay blame, find fault to escape the "bad thing" that has happened or that we have done. Emotionally we create defenses, crying, swearing, lying, striking out to cover our fear or shame. It is a reflection of the little child inside trying to run away and hide.

In the midst of your most troubling time, difficult challenge, frightening experience, know that you can feel bad and recover. It is not the pain, fear, shame, or guilt which will "kill" you; it is your attempt to run away that will. When we run from our challenges, we kill off our power. We strangle our strength. We suffocate our character. We assassinate our character and the ability to grow. "Be still and know . . . no matter what, you will survive." Chances are, if you reassure yourself, just a bit, you will grow faster than you imagined.

I shall not run or hide.

WE MUST AVOID the tendency to compare ourselves with anyone else. We must resist the urge to compare where we are and what we are doing against the strides or failures of another. Comparison of self to others feeds self-doubt. Self-doubt grows into self-defeat. My grandmother always said, "Mind your own business!" I now understand what she meant in a completely different light.

Your growth is your business, and it has nothing to do with how anyone else is growing. When you do the best you can, where you are, with what you have, it does not matter what anyone else is doing. The time spent watching and comparing yourself to others is time that could be spent developing your skills, perfecting your craft, creating your visions of the future. What you are doing is your own business. When you pay attention to it, it will ultimately pay off for you—not the people you are watching.

I can grow at my own divine pace.

A COURSE IN Miracles states, "You are never angry for the reason you think." This implies that there is an underlying reason for our anger. If we extend this theory to any negative emotion—fear, shame, guilt, betrayal, rejection, disappointment—the same principle applies: we are never upset for the reason we think we are; there is always something else going on.

One challenging experience in life will always trigger our old stuff. That stuff will show up as more confusion, greater difficulty, more pain. In the midst of our challenges, we must take a moment to ask, "What am I really feeling?" An honest inquiry will undoubtedly produce, "I'm not good enough, smart enough, pretty enough," which all boils down to, "I'm not enough." If this personal lie is at the core of your challenge, ask yourself, "When was the first time I heard this? Who said this to me?" When you identify the person, forgive him or her. You must forgive that person for crippling your self-concept, self-image, self-value. After you forgive that person or those people, forgive yourself for believing them.

Forgiveness heals old wounds. Forgiveness removes us from the shadows of the past. Forgiveness helps us understand where we are, how we got there, how to shut the door and not return.

There is something here I must forgive!

───────

DEAR GOD,

Have mercy on me. Your mercy, Your grace, Your love, are my strength. Your mercy clears my mind, renews my soul, reminds me I am the loved child of a loving Father who knows my needs before I ask. Your mercy kindles love in my heart, wisdom in my mind, life in my human being. Have mercy on me.

Dear God, forgive me. I know I have not always lived according to Your word. I have not always honored Your will, but You love me anyway. Today I confess to You my frailties as a human, and ask that You send Your Spirit to heal me of the thoughts, habits, and beliefs that keep me from the full realization of You in my being and life. Forgive me for anything I have done consciously or unconsciously to push You out of my life.

Dear God, restore me. Restore me to the state of peace in my mind, love in my heart, balance in my soul with which You created me. Restore my faith in myself and my life. Restore discipline in my spirit and my deeds. My desire is to know and serve You with all my heart and soul, that I may have my eyes opened to the miraculous nature of Your being.

For this, to You, I give thanks.

I Am forgiven! I Am restored through God's mercy.

FOR MANY OF us, it is hard to believe that we have been chosen. Our lives, the circumstances and conditions in which we live, make it very difficult to believe that we have a special purpose, a special place in God's heart. Even though it is hard to believe, it is true. The chosen have many tests and trials. They also have the chosen ability.

Just for today, allow yourself to believe you have been chosen. All of the experiences you have had were your training ground. If you are still here, you made it through. Every experience you thought was a bad experience was simply a test. Guess what? You passed! All the times you were down, you got up. All the things you could not do, got done. Everything you thought you messed up worked out anyway. Why? Because you have been chosen, and the chosen have a very special ability. It's called God.

Remember that you have been chosen!

SPIRIT IS SELF-CORRECTING. If you continue to do that which you know not to be good for you, eventually it will cause you so much pain, you will stop. If you continue to eat, drink, smoke, spend without a budget, stay in toxic relationships, you will become so miserable you will find the strength, courage, willpower to rehabilitate yourself.

Spirit really is self-correcting. The longer you do a thing, the better you get at it. The more you pray, the faster your answer will come. If you increase your practice of meditation, the calmer and stiller your mind will be. If you read more, reassure yourself more, support, nurture, and honor yourself more each day you will feel better. Instead of feeling anger or confusion, you will be clearer, more focused, and peaceful. The self-correcting spirit in you will make the best of what you do more of—more destruction, greater pain; more construction, greater peace, pleasure, and plenty.

You will do it until you understand what you are doing.

IN THE REALM of human experiences, death seems to be the one thing that has the power to make us feel powerless. Whether it is the end of a physical life or the end of a situation which has meant a great deal to us, death, the end, seems so final. It may seem that way, but it doesn't have to be that way. In reality, death is simply another way the nature of life calls upon us to shift, change perspective, reach, and grow to new heights of consciousness.

It may take a little time to process the body and mind through the emotion of the experience. However, once that occurs, there is a power within the spirit capable of helping us make the shift. In the face of death, an end, or a separation, we have the spiritual power to make peace, continue communication, forgive, release, share, and find closure. Writing a letter to the departed one, letting them know you miss them and think about them is an excellent process. Mailing the letter is optional. Communicating your thoughts and feelings provides the healing.

You can mentally speak to the person. In this way you can say whatever is in your heart, all the things you did not have the opportunity or courage to say in person. More important, when we turn to spirit, the consciousness shifts an unwanted ending to spiritual closure. Closure enables you to release. With closure we can find the strength to accept; and understand, and the strength to recover from the experience and move on.

You have the power to bring closure to this experience.

REMEMBER WHAT HAPPENED the last time you second-guessed yourself, or let people talk you out of what you had decided to do? Have you forgotten what happened when you changed your mind back and forth six times and settled on doing what you thought would make "them" happy? Don't you remember what happened the last time you didn't pay attention to yourself, didn't trust yourself? You ended up in trouble!

For most of us, it is extremely difficult to believe we can really believe in ourselves. It always seems easier to trust other people, to listen to someone else. Most of the time, we never realize, when we don't trust ourselves, we are prone to let little setbacks and little people take us off our mission. As soon as things get a little tough, a little tight, a little hot, we start to worry. That worry leads to negative self-talk and ultimately to self-doubt. What will it take for us to realize how powerful we are? How powerful our minds are? Sooner or later we will understand that we are our first line of defense and reference. It would be very wise to listen to yourself very carefully. You never know when you will say exactly what you need to hear.

Self-doubt damages self-worth!

EVERYBODY WANTS EVERYTHING their way, all the time. Everybody thinks everybody else is wrong most of the time. When things don't go the way we want them to go, we get mad. Then we blame somebody or anybody for not getting our way. That is what it's about: We get angry when we don't get our way. Just like children, we pout, stamp our feet, swear under our breath, and promise ourselves that one day we will have our way. Unfortunately, we didn't know how to have our way without the pain, anger, and confusion— UNTIL TODAY!

You can have your way easily and effortlessly. You can have what you want, when you want it, the way you want it, without fighting, struggling, or being pissed off. You can have as much as you want, of whatever it is, in whatever size, quantity, or style you desire. In order for this to happen, you must fulfill one tiny requirement: make the decision. Once you decide, don't waver or falter or doubt or accept anything less than what you've decided on. Don't get mad or impatient or fearful that it won't show up. Once you make the decision, trust that things will fall into place and show up at just the right time.

You can have all things the divine way.

SOME PEOPLE HAVE a way of bringing out the worst in us. Sometimes it is the way they talk to us. For some reason they think we don't know what they know. Sometimes it's just the way they do the things they do. It just makes you crazy! Some people just show up with their face and hair and attitude and that look that makes your skin crawl. You try to be nice. You really try to like them. Yet no matter how hard you try, they just bring out the ugly in you. The next time you are in the company of someone like this, ask yourself, "Why am I giving this person my power?" Better yet, you might want to remember that God works through people —all the time!

All people, no matter what you think about them, are an embodiment of the same divine energy in you. They may not know it. You may not see it. Sometimes they may not act divine, but actions do not change the truth. People are God's hands and feet, eyes and ears. People are God's students and God's teachers. God will test you, teach you, love you through the being of another person. Your job is to honor and respect people for the part of God they are.

The next time you are challenged by one of those nerve-wracking people, remember, God is in your face! How you respond to and treat other people is always a reflection of what you know and believe about God.

I See the God in You!

JUST WHEN YOU think you have it all figured out, something will show up to make you doubt yourself. At the precise moment you think that your troubles are over and that things are finally going your way, things will appear to turn around and head in the other direction. On the very day that you are feeling up, happy, ready to go, you will get some news that will knock the wind right out of your sails. Life is just like that, so don't take it personally.

When bad times show up in the middle of good times, just sit down, get quiet, remember the truth about who you are, and pray. All things really do work together for your good. Just because things take a curve does not mean they are not on track. The curve could very well be a part of the process! Life always brings us what we are divinely entitled to, and sometimes it will not look the way we want it to look. Sometimes we are being tested. At other times we are simply being called on to surrender, to be patient, and have lots and lots of faith.

Good comes in many shapes and forms!

DEAR SELF,
People talk about you. It gets back to you.
You strike out at them;
find things wrong with them;
tell bad things about them.
But do you really look at yourself?
Sometimes talk comes to you because you need to
hear it.
But you don't want to hear anything about your "self."
You indulge your "self" in
greatness, righteousness, aggrandizement, and
ego-gratification.
If you are so great, so wonderful, so marvelous,
why is this information coming to you?
DETACH and LISTEN!
There may be something in it you can use.

Maybe you are telling me something I need to hear.

No MATTER WHO you are and how much you know, you are not always right. Even when you are not right, it does not mean you are wrong. It may simply mean there is something you cannot see, do not fully understand, or have not taken into consideration.

When we hold on to the need to always be right, we close ourselves off to the energy of Divine Mind which is always at work in and through other people. When we allow our "rightness" to cut others off, we limit the new information Divine Mind offers us.

Very often we look at what people do or how they look and determine we know or are more than they. In other cases, past experiences, what we know or have heard about a person entices us to judge them or their ability and knowledge. In a universe where we are all connected to the same life force, judging is not the "right" or the "righteous" thing to do. You may be right about what you feel, and still this does not make the other person wrong. They may have done a wrong thing, but this does not contribute to making you right.

Right and wrong are judgments we make in response to our own perceptions. The need to always be right or to prove your rightness to and above others is a reflection of the self-perception that somehow, somewhere you are not so right.

Today, do not need to be right.

PEOPLE CAN CALL you names, accuse you
unjustly, slander you behind your back, but they
cannot change who you are and the truth you
know about yourself. Very often we can get so caught up
in the injustice and unfairness of the actions of others, we
have a temporary lapse of memory. We may say or do
things which, to an uninvolved observer, give credence to
the very things people are saying.

Always remember who you are. Know that you are
never required to apologize to anyone for being yourself.
People may not like it, but they, like you, are still growing.
If you have conducted yourself honorably, with good intent, giving 100 percent of yourself and your energy to
your endeavors, do not waste time defending yourself
against what others may call you. The truth needs no
defense. It will stand on its own in the face of any opposition and against the most powerful adversary. Be willing
to make amends if you have in fact acted out of principle
or spoken hastily. Be prepared to engage in self-reflection
and correction. When you can do these things and act
with a clear conscience, you will not be derailed by what
other people call you.

Respond to the truth within yourself!

BEFORE YOUR MOTHER was your mother, she was a playful little girl who hated bugs, loved candy, and never wanted to go to bed when she was sent. She was an adolescent with zits and no breasts who wanted a boyfriend. She was a teenager who had cramps and who wanted a prom date to kiss her in the places her momma said were off-limits. She was a young woman ready to leave home but afraid to go. She had problems and fears and bad days.

Before your mother was your mother, she had dreams, she had goals, and, yes, she had a life. Then she had you. Even if she didn't expect you, she welcomed you. She gave you the best of who she was and what she had, even when it didn't look like it. She was afraid for herself and even more so for you, even if she never said anything about it. She wanted you to have things that she didn't have to give you. She wanted to tell you things she couldn't bring herself to say. There were times she hurt your feelings. At other times she made you mad. In the middle of your struggles with her, you probably never considered everything your mother was before she was your mother; she still is and will be forever.

Mothers are people too.
———

WHEN YOU ARE so sure that someone is out to hurt you, it becomes very difficult to forgive their shortcomings. It is much easier to believe that people develop clever and malicious ways to inflict wounds on you than it is to accept that they are merely human, doing what humans do. For some strange reason, it is much easier to take everything very personally rather than to accept people as they are, forgive them for what they do, and release them from our lives. We know very well how to be a victim. Being a person who refuses to be victimized seems to be where we have trouble.

Perhaps it is easier to be a victim, because if we really try to understand people we will see many pieces of our self. If we see those pieces of our self, we would have to forgive other people. Forgiveness takes courage. Courage begins in character. A good solid character requires a level of self-esteem so many of us believe we do not have. One way you can enhance your self-esteem is to stop being so willing to be a victim. In order not to be a victim, we must develop the courage to speak up for ourselves. The only way we can develop this kind of courage is to be real clear about who we are. When we know who we are, we will realize that no one can do anything to harm us unless we keep them around and allow them to do so.

Be as willing to stand up as you are to bow down.

YOUR CHILDREN'S FAILURES are not your failures, and you can't kill the kids when they mess up. For some reason, mothers believe everything the children do is a reflection on their motherhood. A mother can be totally devoted, always present, giving her best, and have a child go totally astray. Children make choices. Children make decisions. Children can and do mess up. When they do, no amount of yelling, threats, and motherly guilt will change what has happened. The best you can do is support and assist them in working through whatever it is.

Our children come "through" us into life to learn their lessons and have the experiences they need in order to find their true identity. Whatever we do, and however we do it, is the best we have to offer. Our job is to guide, support, nurture, teach, and lay the foundation for them to stand on. Sometimes we miss the mark. Sometimes we get caught up in our own lessons and experiences. Sometimes we give the best of what we have and who we are, and they still fail. It's all okay. Know that the same God who watches you watches your children. Also know, no matter what, your children are equipped to fall, get up, and fall again. If or when they do, your job is to breathe! Pray! And Have Faith!

Do your best. Give your best. Expect the best from the children.

HAVE YOU EVER been in an airplane when it is changing directions? Usually there is a drop in altitude. There may even be some turbulence which will cause your stomach to flip and your heart to flutter. There is a loss of speed. Or the plane may pick up speed and then drop, suddenly and unexpectedly, which can be very frightening. Changing directions in life is like hitting turbulence in the air, and fear is the normal response to the turbulence caused by change. Things are going to be rough for a while, but you must hold on and ride it out.

When the turbulence of change hits you, make believe you are a pilot, well trained and experienced, able to ride out the turbulence until a tailwind takes you up again. If that doesn't work, make believe you are a stewardess. Keep yourself calm, give yourself encouragement, stand firmly and confidently that all is well, no matter how rough it gets. If you are afraid of flying, just lay down on the floor, cover your head, and don't worry about the turbulence. In any case, always remember that God is your landing strip, able to handle your weight, ready to receive you; even if you fall, you will still be on solid ground!

Hold on for a change!

ON YOUR JOURNEY to do better, you are going to find obstacles. The obstacles in your path are there to make you stronger. Building a new life is hard work, and you will need muscles. Obstacles build muscles—big, strong muscles which you can flex.

On the path to empowerment you are going to be challenged. Challenges make you quick on your feet. They teach you how to bob and weave. Moving into your power is going to make people nervous. They are going to challenge your new ideas, your new approach, and the new you that is emerging. Challenges make you think and rethink what you are doing. Thinking strengthens the mind. The strong mind of a powerful person has nothing to fear when challenged. A strong mind can weave together an answer for the people who challenge it—GET A LIFE! is a good place to start.

On your climb to the top, people are going to throw stones at you. Don't worry about it; you are strong, you can bob, weave, and get out of the way. The stones they throw may be very big, and they will come at you from the most unlikely places, at the most inopportune moments. Don't stop climbing! Don't look back! Stay focused! The people who are throwing stones will be so intent on hitting you they may not realize that the stones they are throwing up at you are going to come back down and hit them on the head.

I can take it! I can make it!

THINK ABOUT ALL that God is. God is peace,
joy, strength, power, abundance, truth, and love.
God is not pain, anger, fear, confusion, restriction, or destruction. So often we find ourselves in painful,
frightening, and destructive situations that limit our freedom or make us unhappy. For some reason we convince
ourselves that where we are is where God wants us to be.
If it is not peace, joy, love, and harmony, it is not God!

God does not want us to be in pain. However, God
will not interfere with the choices we make. If we choose
to stay in an abusive relationship, an unfulfilling job, a
chaotic family environment, or any other harmful situation, God will not interfere! God cannot move us until
we are ready to be moved. God cannot help us until we
are ready to be helped. God cannot save us unless we want
to be saved. When we understand who God really is and
how that relates to who we are, we are free to choose a
better way of living. When we choose better God moves
in mysterious ways!

Today, choose God!

The Valley of Courage

Teaches us to surrender our fears and secret thoughts about ourselves and the world by developing trust in the universe of life.

*S*ee the inevitable changes not as threats
but as opportunities that can deepen
our understanding and bring us wisdom
and growth.

—*Susan L. Taylor*

DEAR SELF,
In the right moment, in the perfect way;
I will be shown what to do.
I will be told what to say.
Until then, I will love myself,
I will honor myself,
and I will be still.

I will be shown the divine way.

THERE IS A little girl inside of you who never grew up. She has been there from the beginning. She has seen, heard, experienced every aspect of your life. She knows, she really knows who you are; and she never misses an opportunity to remind you. She knows your strengths, weaknesses, fears, likes, and dislikes. She knows who you are, what you can do; most of all, she knows when and how to act up.

Children will act up at the most inconvenient times. They will lose things. They will spill things on their clothes. They will make you late. They will speak out at inappropriate times. They have temper tantrums. They overeat. They fight, argue, and take things that do not belong to them. All to get your attention.

Don't ignore your little girl. Make sure you greet her, nurture her, talk to her, every day. Find ways to reassure her, make her feel safe. Let her know she is loved, welcomed, valued. Let her play, and make sure she has plenty of toys. Don't forget to discipline her. Be firm but supportive, structured but flexible. Encourage her to try new things. Listen to her opinions. Make sure she eats well and gets plenty of rest. You may be all grown up. However, there is a little girl in you still trying to figure out who she is and what life is really about.

Honor the child in you!

WHEN THE THING that we really want finally does show up in our lives, we usually have two emotions at the same time, joy and terror! We can be so excited that we are finally getting what we want that we are terrorized by what it means. It means that life really is on our side. It means that we really do deserve to have what we want. It also means that our hard work is paying off and that things are getting ready to change . . . drastically.

The conflicting emotions of joy and terror send a message of urgency through our body that sometimes kills off our joy. We can become so engrossed in the terror of losing, of moving, and of changing that we lose sight of the answered prayer. Terror makes you busy. Busyness can lead to self-sabotage! When you find yourself in a state of urgency, check in with yourself to make sure that you are not allowing terror to steal your joy.

Do not terrorize yourself!

IT IS POSSIBLE to know the truth and not tell the truth. The line between knowledge of truth and the ability to tell it is called discipline. Truth without discipline is like wearing lead-bottom shoes. You know what to do or say, yet you cannot move to do it. The weight of the knowledge holds you down. You want to move this knowledge or information off your back, but to keep a friend, keep the peace, stay within your comfort zone, you excuse yourself from responsibility. Now you are weighed down with self-doubt, self-criticism, and self-denial.

Truth supported by discipline is like a hot knife on butter. With it you can cut through fear, doubt, and the annoying habits which erode your discipline and cast shadows on the truth. If you really want to grow spiritually, you must discipline your mind to seek truth, your mouth to speak the truth, and yourself to live in truth. Only then will your heart be opened to know the truth of God.

Truth is my first line of defense.

So many of us are afraid to die, we fail to live. We will not take chances when they present any form of risk. They are too dangerous. Danger can lead to death. We may be afraid to drive, afraid to fly. Too afraid to say yes. Even more afraid to say no. We are afraid to be alone. Even more afraid to go out. When we don't live because of the fear of dying, we die without ever having lived.

What part of life are you missing when you live in fear of dying? Are you not already dead to those experiences? You may convince yourself you can live without them, but are you really living? Are you really alive when you tuck yourself away from people or experiences you believe can hurt you, harm you, or in some way take your life away? There is a way to escape the fear of death. Consider the fact that you started dying the moment you were born.

Today, I am going to live all of life.

Dreaming can be frightening.
When you dream,
all things are possible.
I like to dream.
But it can be frightening to imagine that you can have
anything, everything that you want.
It's mind-blowing to imagine that there is a place
where all your needs are met,
where all of your wishes can come true;
that you can live the type of life
you have dreamed of without struggle or effort.
Can you imagine doing all of the things you love to do;
being paid for doing those things;
feeling good about what you are doing and yourself.
Is that frightening to you?
It's frightening to me!
That is probably why it is not happening!
I am afraid to dream.

No dream is too good to come true.

> *God is there because I am here.*
> *I am here because God is there.*

There is a very subtle difference between these two statements which can make a world of difference in the way we approach life. When we understand that we are God's eyes, ears, hands, and feet we can have a little more confidence in ourselves. From on high, God is dependent on us to demonstrate His/Her work. It's on us to give love, bring peace, demonstrate power, utilize compassion, be forgiving, show mercy, and live in grace. That is what God does up there.

When we believe the only reason we are here is because God put us here, the journey becomes overwhelming. We feel unclear and unfocused. We believe we are limited and powerless. We wait around for special instructions because we believe we have to be special. No one can tell us what to do. We are the bosses. It is your job here on earth to remind people that we all have the power to create a good life, a better life. It's not God's job to make life better for us. God sent us here to make life better.

God is present and accountable for me.

___

STAND UP! YOU have the power of Queens in your blood. The sacredness of the eagles in your bones. The fierceness of warriors in your genes. The wisdom of the grandmothers is in the recesses of your mind, accessible to you through the energy of spirit.

STAND UP! Take the responsibility for defining yourself and determining your own destiny. Believe you have the power. Understand who you are. Don't be so willing to take someone else's word about what is best for you.

STAND UP! Celebrate the wisdom of life in your spirit. Dare to do, to be, to reach and stretch beyond the boundaries of humanness to the unlimited world of spirit. The universe will back you up. The Father will hold you up. The Mother will keep you up. That means you have Holy Boldness! STAND UP and show it off.

I stand in Holy Boldness!

THE NATION, THE community, the family are all one race of people—Human! Our spirit is a holistic spirit. In our hearts and minds and from our mouths, we must begin to promote the good of the whole. One man on drugs affects the whole. One homeless woman affects the whole. One hungry child affects the whole. When we ignore what affects the whole, it weakens the nation. It undermines the community. It breaks the family ties. It destroys the spirit.

I have something to offer the whole.

SOMETIMES KEEPING THINGS inside makes them seem worse than they are. There's so much going on inside: the past, the future, the present, not to mention normal bodily functions. The weight of it all is tearing you up, holding you down; it may feel like you want to burst. If you don't talk about it, you will.

The Value in the Valley states, "A wound needs air in order to heal." There comes a time when it becomes necessary to open ourselves up for review and examination by talking about our pain. It's not easy. As a matter of fact, it's frightening. We don't want to expose ourselves to public speculation or criticism. We don't want to admit our frailties or follies. Goodness knows, we don't want to face the pain, fear, anger, shame, or guilt attached to our deepest thoughts and feelings. Yet when what is going on inside hinders what we are able to do, we must talk about it.

Find somebody you can trust. Find someone you don't know and may never see again. Call a help line, hot line, or prayer line. Find someone you can talk to about what you feel. You are not looking for an answer or a resolution; you are in search of a release. If you can't find a living person, go into a quiet place and talk to God.

I've got to talk about it.

YOU MUST KNOW at all times, in all situations, under every possible circumstance, you can depend on God. God, the good, powerful essence of life is always within you, always around you, always holding and lifting you up. The very essence and energy of God is actually what you are. Yet in times of difficulty, we forget this. For some of us, we never knew it in the first place.

You may have convinced yourself that you have done too much wrong for God to still be with you. This is simply not so. Perhaps the events of your life have led you to believe that God does not have the power to help you. Nothing could be further from the truth. Very often we blame God for what has happened to us. We get angry with God because things do not go the way we want them to go. In the end, we mentally and emotionally abandon God by resigning ourselves to pain and suffering! No matter what has happened, where we have been, or what we have done, we will not, cannot move beyond pain, fear, and disappointment until we realize in the deepest part of the soul, "I can depend on God."

God is the spirit of life. Life is not merely what we live, it is what we are. Even when we believe God cannot or will not help us, there is a ray of hope: God can and will help us. God will maintain and sustain the energy of life that we are.

I can depend on the life of God in me.

YOU DO WHAT you think is right, only to find out it is the worst thing you could have done. Somebody is mad at you. You're out a lot of money. You feel real bad, and you still have a big mess to clean up. Here's something you might want to remember: even when it doesn't look good, be conscious of God in every little thing you do.

God really is everywhere, all the time. God is always healing and teaching and loving us. Things may look pretty bleak right now. You might feel bad or foolish, but you never know how the Creator is going to show up or stand up. It may not be fancy or flashy. It may look confusing or frightening. You may be stressed or angry or teetering on the edge of disaster; just remember, God is in everything, everywhere, all the time.

God is always on time and in time.

———

DEAR SELF,
If I had to do it all over again,
I wouldn't change
what I did.
I would change
the way I felt about what I did.

What I do cannot change who I am.

No storm can last forever! It will never rain 365 days consecutively. The rain may ruin your wedding or your roof! The rain can blind you and flood out the basement. But no matter how hard it rains, one day the water will dry up. Even snow cannot fall forty, fifty, sixty days in a row. It may fall very heavy today and tomorrow. It may freeze up, creating very dangerous conditions. Just keep in mind, all the snow piled up outside your door must melt one day.

Trouble comes to pass, not to stay! Just as in a storm, you may be having a miserable time in life. Perhaps you can't get around some problem. Something or someone may have caused an incredible amount of damage to your heart, your mind, your total state of being. You may be snowed in, bogged down, flooded out by fear, anger, or emotional destruction. Don't worry! No storm, not even the one in your life, can last forever.

This storm is just passing over!

DON'T BEAT UP on yourself if you did not make it through the diet. If you cannot convince yourself that you can make it without a cigarette, a candy bar, that extra piece of chicken, or just one bag of potato chips, it's okay. Even if you hate the job and know you should leave, or love the man and know it's not going to work, try not to be so hard on yourself for staying. Whatever you are doing that you know you must stop doing, you cannot stop doing it until you are ready.

Talking ready is not enough. Thinking ready will not work. You must "be" ready in mind, body, and spirit before you can make a change. All of your circuits must be positioned on "go." Until then, people cannot convince you to do it. You cannot force you to do it. No book or song or magic potion can make you move before you are ready. Everything you think, say, and do until that happens is just preparation. So love yourself right now. Honor yourself anyway. Keep talking to yourself. Keep thinking ready thoughts. In the meantime, try to remember you will not be ready until you are ready.

Ready is as ready does!

———

COURAGE NOT ONLY means being able to do something new. It also means taking steps to "be" someone new. Some of us talk a great deal because we are afraid we won't be heard. Others never say anything in fear of saying the wrong thing. Some of us are overactive and hyperactive because we fear missing out. There are those of us who are withdrawn, lethargic, inactive, in fear of messing up.

One of the first steps in developing a courageous outlook and approach to life is being able to look at ourselves, our beliefs, attitudes, and patterns. Courage enables us to examine. Examination enables us to choose. Courage is more than forceful, aggressive, bold outward action. At its most infinite level, courage is an in-depth, inward examination which leads to alteration and application of a new way to be.

Courage creates a new state of being!

So you think you are not good enough, not "God" enough. You've been doing everything you should, the way you should, and still the changes, if any, are slow in coming, almost insignificant. You keep wondering what more can you do, how much more should you know, to get yourself, your life, to the point of peace and plenty you desire. You're asking when will it get better? When will you be better? Maybe, just maybe, things are the way they need to be. That doesn't mean things will not get better. It means they take time.

Every seed planted takes time to grow. Every thought that crosses your mind is a seed. Every word you speak is a seed. Every action you take is a seed in the garden of life. You cannot see how the seed germinates. You will not see the roots sprout and take hold in the deep darkness of the earth. Unless you watch very carefully, you will not see that first little stalk poke its head up through the earth. If you move too quickly, you will trample the first leaves of the tiny plant.

Doubt, worry, anxiety will retard the growth of spiritual seeds. You are a sprout in God's garden. Your roots are growing stronger and taking hold with every ounce of faith and trust you pour forth. God is a good gardener. S/He showers love and mercy and grace on the garden of life every day. God's seeds may grow slowly, but as long as God has anything to do with it, they grow strong in divine time and order.

All seeds take time to grow.

I've got asthma! I don't have the money! I'm not smart enough! It's too hard! I'm too old! I've got kids! He won't let me! It is very easy to find reasons not to do the things we say we want to do. Once we convince ourselves that we have a good enough excuse, we have a reason to be unhappy, stuck, unproductive.

Physical, financial, and emotional challenges are real. They create boundaries in our lives, However, no one said we cannot move beyond boundaries. Your life is a reflection of what you believe. If you really believe something or someone can stop you, it can, and . . . it will! But you already know that. What you may not know is that what you tell yourself about yourself, about your life, about your limitations, you will believe. What you believe is the foundation of what you do and don't do.

There is nothing so wrong that it cannot be made right. There is nothing so heavy that it can't be lifted. There is nothing so bad, so ugly, so horrible, so heavy, so deep, that you can't work through it, move around it, step over it, but you have to believe it. If you don't believe it, you can't do it.

You can! Yes! You can!

YOU MAY NOT own your home, a car, or a fine array clothes. You may not have stocks, securities, or an impressive amount of cash. You may work for someone you have never seen, depend on people you don't know to provide food for your table, and pay taxes to an institution that has relegated you to an identifiable number. Still, you own something that is more valuable than any of these things. What you own is your mind, and your mind produces very valuable thoughts.

Every thought you have is your personal property, to do with as you choose. Like everything else you own, your thoughts are precious. When you understand just how valuable thoughts are, perhaps you will own your home. Maybe that car you want will be yours. You may continue working for someone and paying taxes to someone else, but owning your thoughts will give you a completely different perspective. When you own your thoughts and value them, it means you realize that they are powerful enough to create any experience you want.

A thought is a valuable possession.

DEAR SELF,
When you panic, you do things in fear.
The moment you think the thoughts;
speak the words;
commit the acts;
you know you are out of balance and out of control.
Yet for some reason,
you cannot stop yourself.
When it is over, you go into remorse;
beating yourself, feeling bad, being sorry.
It is important to learn to stop yourself
at the panic stage.
When you sense the fear, panic, desperation welling up
in your heart and mind,
you must get still and say,
"STOP!"
"I will not panic!"
"I will not go into fear!"
I Will Be Still!

Please! Don't panic!

———

At the sound of the tone,
leave your name and your need;
God and Goodness
will make sure you get exactly
what you ask for.

Before I ask, God knows my needs!

The Valley of Knowledge and Wisdom

*Teaches us to develop the courage, strength,
obedience, and discipline
to act on what we know to be true.*

*There's an old saying: only little children
and old folks tell the truth.
When you get real old, you just
lay it on the table.*

—BESSIE DELANY

DEAR GOD,

Please order my thoughts today. Place in my mind those things that are a priority to you. Those things that will establish divine order in this life you have given me. Take away the thoughts, habits, attitudes which create fear and keep me from being in alignment with Your will. Help me to see things through Your eyes, according to Your law. Take away every thought, want, unconscious and conscious urge that can place me on the treadmill of pain and confusion. Fill my mind with Your will, Your way, Your desire for me today. Help me to see all things from a divine perspective today, a perspective of love, peace, and joy. And then, Lord, guide me to act accordingly. Thank You, God.

Today, my thoughts are ordered.

YOU CANNOT COME to God with your hands full. You cannot expect spirit to lift you up if you come with clenched fist. Very often we seek the assistance, support, guidance of the Most High when we are filled to the brim with our own "stuff." We come with preconceived notions; fixed ideas and opinions; judgments and criticisms of others, very structured demands of what we need, how we want it, and what we are willing to do or not do to get it. The universe cannot work that way!

If everyone got what they wanted, exactly the way they wanted it, there would be no room for divine intervention or improvement. What about the demands we make when we are angry, frightened, upset, or desperate? Very often the things we cry out for in the moment are not things we really want or need. And let us not forget those occasions when we asked for help while hiding something behind our backs. Something we didn't want anyone else to know; something we were ashamed to admit; something hidden in the subconscious mind. We may not have remembered, realized, or understood what it was, but the universe did and responded accordingly.

No matter how afraid, ashamed, angry, or upset we may be, we must empty out before we face the divine. The best way to get what you need, just in the nick of time, is to come to God with nothing in hand.

I come with open hands.

EVERYTHING IN LIFE is a process. Events occur one at a time until the process is complete. When you are faced with a difficulty in life, the question you must first answer is, what is my process? What are the steps I can take to begin working through and out of this situation? If you are an average, warm-blooded human being, you probably don't have a process. Like the rest of us, the process is to panic. Until today!

No matter what is going on, you can only do one thing at a time. If you panic, you can't think. First step, think. Make every effort to have a bite-size idea of what is happening. Ten words or less should be just fine. Look at one issue or problem at a time. Next, take yourself out of the situation. Depersonalize and defuse the situation by allowing yourself to become the third party. Think in terms of, look what is happening to her/him. Third step, examine everything you know about what is going on: who is involved, what has happened, what needs to happen. Resist blaming or imagining the worst, being angry or afraid. This is not about you; you are an observer.

Final step, without looking to outside forces, honestly place responsibility where it should be, with the resources and information available right now; advise the person how to proceed. Don't worry about what might happen. Don't take the path of least resistance. Do what is honest, just, peaceful, and in the best interest of all. After you tell the other person how to proceed, do it!

Let me get out of the way of the process!

H OW ARE YOU going to handle it this time? You have probably been here before, in this or a similar situation. You undoubtedly learned something, even if you didn't fully understand or like the lesson. Well, here you are again! The issue is, how are you going to handle it this time? What are you going to do? How will you choose to respond?

As we travel through life, the scenery changes, the players come and go, but the truth remains constant. Our lessons are consistent. Our experiences are testing tools by which life examines us and gives us the opportunity to examine ourselves. As we progress, life knows what we know, even when we think we don't know. How are you going to respond? What are you going to do this time? Are you going to pout, stamp your feet, put your hands on your hips, and create drama? Or are you going to practice what you know, follow your heart, honor yourself, and grow? The choice is yours, but remember, life is watching you. Don't fail the test!

I am willing to do a new thing.

THERE ARE MANY ways to learn your lessons and receive your good in life. Only you can determine how you will do it. Some of us get it quick! We get in a little bit of trouble or experience a little bit of pain. It will cause us to drop to one knee to pray for mercy. We get the point and move on, never to repeat that lesson again. For some of us, it takes a little longer. We will persist in doing things our way until the pain, the confusion, or the stress become so intense, we must drop to two knees to beg and plead for mercy before we get the point. Then, there are those of us who do not get the point, and are not even aware that a point exists until we are flat on our face in the mud! We are what my grandmother called "hard-headed."

When you see that things are not working out, don't insist that they do! Back up! Detach! Take some time to assess the situation. Always remember, your blessings have your name on them. No one can take them away from you. There is no need to rush, push, stress yourself out to get to your good. It will come to you at the divine time in the divine way. The condition you are in when the blessing shows up is totally up to you—on one knee, on two knees, or with your face full of mud!

When you get it, you will get it!

THE TRUTH OF the matter is, you will not always know what to do. Unfortunately, you may not know that you don't know, until you know. That can be dangerous. When you don't know that you don't know, you run around trying to convince others that you know. If they don't know that you don't know they will follow you, because they think you know. But we know that won't work because you really don't know. And if they know, but think they don't know, that you don't know, nobody knows whether or not you know what they think they don't know. Do you see how confusing it can be?

You can save yourself a great deal of trouble by admitting to yourself and them, I'm not sure I know. Actually, you do know, but you must be still in order to come to that realization. In stillness, you will know that you know, and that's all you need to know in order to move forward.

I know I'm not confused!

———

IF YOU DRIVE too fast, you might miss your turn. If you walk too fast, you might pass where you are going. If you speak too quickly, you demonstrate that you have missed the point. Slow down! You cannot arrive at your destination until you get there. Along the way, take in the scenery. Stop, sit a spell, and rest yourself. There's a lot going on in life and in you. If you zip around, you are bound to miss something. If and when you do, resist the urge to blame other people. Tell the truth! You know you were moving, talking, wanting too much, too fast.

Slowly I move, step by step!

———

D O W E Y E L L at children when they fall down and bump their heads or bust their lips? No. Do we punch guests who break glasses or spill drinks? No. Do we lash out at plants that die or flowers that don't bloom? No. Somehow we find compassion in our hearts to forgive and excuse the mishaps and errors of others. Yet we have little if any compassion for ourselves. For some reason, we tend to forget we are growing and learning, and that we will fall down and sometimes make a mess.

You may not always know what to do. It's okay! You will not always be able to find the right words at the moment you need them. It's okay! You may swear you won't and then do it anyway. It really is okay! It's okay if you do, or say, or forget to do or say the "right" thing at the "right" time. The challenge is to learn not to beat yourself up about it.

It's okay because I'm okay.

———

WHEN CHAOS, CONFUSION, difficulty show up in our lives, we must go back to the beginning. Not to the beginning of the problem, but the beginning of life; before life got messed up, got to be hard, got to be more than we could handle. We must go back to the beginning, before we got in trouble, got fired, got our hearts broken. We probably don't remember that time because we were in the womb. We were innocent, defenseless, helpless children of God. And, whether we realize it or not, we haven't changed a bit.

God is like the womb around us, squeezing, pushing, prodding us through the circumstances of life. Remember, the beginning of the birth process is painful. We are in darkness; we can't see. We are frightened; we do not know what to do. We want the pressure, pain, pushing to be over . . . Now!

But life doesn't happen like that. In the beginning of a new life, the womb must contract to strengthen our muscles and push us into alignment. The safe and familiar environment in which we have existed becomes chaotic; it becomes uncomfortable. In the beginning, we called it labor. Now it feels like confusion. We must remember, there comes a time when the womb pushes us forward from the old to the new. It may not feel good, but in the beginning God was there with us, around us and in us. When we remember the beginning, we realize that in just a little while, we will have a bundle of joy in our midst.

It is not confusion, it's birth.

YOU MUST TELL the truth! The whole truth, if you want to be helped out of a bad situation. So often we run to people, asking for their help or assistance, but we don't tell them the whole story. We leave out the pieces that could make us look bad. We skip over the parts we think will make them think we are stupid. More often than not, we conveniently forget to mention what we did that got us into the situation in the first place.

People cannot help you if you do not give them all the facts, all pertinent pieces of information. The truth is complete. It is whole. It is real. The truth, no matter how bad you think it sounds! The truth, even when it makes you look bad or foolish! The truth! No matter what you think the other person needs to hear in order to get them to help you! The truth, and nothing but the truth, will get you to the support, the help, the freedom you desire. If you only give half of the truth, you can only receive half of the solution!

What I'm about to say is the absolute truth!
———

WE DON'T GET in trouble because of what we do. We get in trouble when we do it in spite of reliable warnings and cautions, against all good advice, and in defiance of good common sense. All of us have things that we are obsessive about. We insist and push, or scheme and connive to make sure this thing will happen. Sometimes we do it to prove we are right or to prove someone else is wrong. We may do it when we are angry or afraid. Or we may do it just to prove we can do it.

We may know the behavior is unproductive or inappropriate. We may know it is foolish or dangerous. Still we insist it must be done. That is how we get ourselves in trouble or hurt or embarrassed. In response to what we do, we feel bad, beat up on ourselves, or blame others for making us or letting us do it. Whatever we do, we do it because we need to do it. No matter how foolish, hazardous, or outlandish it may be, it is simply another lesson we must learn in the classroom of life.

This is something I must do to learn my lesson!

How do you know whom to trust? When you are in a bad situation, people may offer you help or advice, but you have been led astray before. You have been hurt and lied to before. How are you supposed to know who is real and who is not real? People say things that you want to believe, but something in your gut sets off bells and whistles in your head! How are you supposed to know what to do? Is it you? Is it them? Whom do you trust?

Each of us has been faced with the dilemma of not knowing what to do and whom to trust. The easiest way to solve the dilemma is to ask yourself, "Can I be trusted?" "Have I told the truth in this situation?" "Have I honored my word?" If you have, chances are those who are coming forward to help you can and will. If you have not, you are the issue, not the other person. You are harboring old memories, old guilt, old shame. The way to resolve the issue is to confess your errors to yourself, forgive yourself, and come clean with everyone else. Until your heart and mind are cleansed, you cannot make a decision to trust others because you know you cannot trust yourself.

When you live the truth, tell the truth, and release the past, you have no reason not to trust *them* or yourself.

Trust yourself to know the truth when you see it!

DEAR SELF,
Free your mind from the dead things
you wanted to do but allowed yourself to believe
you weren't good enough, smart enough, young or old
enough to do.
Free your heart from the fear that someone
can stop you or harm you.
Free your self from self-imposed limitations
of age, color, and gender.
Free your body from the harmful things you love
even when you know they are
absolutely no good for you.
Freedom is the key.
You must not let anything or anyone
confine or define you!

Freedom is a state of mind.

───────

WHEN I THOUGHT I was fat, I could not find anything nice that fit my size. When I told myself I was ugly, people treated me in ugly ways.

In the book *Practicing the Presence,* Joel Goldsmith reminds us, "Every issue we face in life grows out of and stems from the well of our consciousness." Many of us do not realize that whatever we experience in our day-to-day lives and relationships is a mirror reflection of the deepest belief we hold about our self. Whether we are fired, jilted, or defamed, insulted or blamed, there is something that goes on in our consciousness that has attracted us to every experience we have.

Take a moment right now and ask yourself, when was the last time I complimented me? Have I told myself that I love me lately? How often do I criticize myself? Beat up on myself in thought, word, and deed? *You Are Always Your Own Experience.* It is a bitter pill to swallow. A challenging concept to examine. Just for today, pay close attention to how you think about you; what you say to you; how you behave toward you. If you do not like what is going on in your life, you may want to adjust your attitude about you.

What I think about me, I Am.

IT IS DANGEROUS, spiritually dangerous, to believe that everyone is wrong and you are right.

Granted, there are times when you go into a situation with the best of intentions, when you work hard, give your all, and things do not turn out the way you expected them to turn out. It is even possible for it to appear that people are against you, out to get you, doing their best to do you in. However, it is dangerous, spiritually dangerous, for you to believe that everybody else is wrong and you are right.

Always remember, the most difficult adversary and the biggest obstacle can teach you a powerful lesson. When we take up arms in opposition to people and conditions, we run the risk of missing the lesson. If we judge people by their behavior, criticize them because of their different opinion and approach, it is easy to become self-righteous. We can easily identify what we do that is correct in the face of others we deem incorrect. What is not always so easy to see is how challenging people and situations can strengthen us. We become frustrated, often angry, when we cannot get people to see our way or to be the way we believe they should be. In the process, we miss the opportunity to be patient, tolerant, or cooperative. In the most challenging situations, we overlook a golden opportunity to see a new way, do a new thing. That can be most dangerous and damaging to the spirit.

Every point is a good point!

SOME OF US are born into dark circumstances. As children we grow up in the midst of dark experiences. In response, we may think dark thoughts and come to the conclusion that darkness is all we can expect. In the midst of darkness we are limited as to what we can see. We see and expect very little for ourselves because the world of darkness has little to offer. It has taken all the light from our dreams.

The story of Jabez in the Bible speaks to the issue of darkness. Jabez, like so many of us, had very little to look forward to in life. What Jabez held onto, which many of us lose in the darkness, is character. Jabez's character remained strong through his faith. He kept that faith active with prayer. In prayer, Jabez did not limit his expectations to what he could see; he asked for all the goodness, grace, and favor that God had to offer in order to make him strong enough to move out of his dark circumstances into the light of Spirit.

We must remember to be like Jabez, faithful, prayerful, strong in the spirit of our character. When we find ourselves in the shadows of darkness, we must not limit ourselves to only what we can see in the glow of a 40-watt bulb! We must pray for what we know is present under the glow of 100 watts.

Darkness must give way to the light!

WHEN DIFFICULTY OR trouble shows up in your life, the first instinct is to tighten up. Your body becomes tense. Your mind closes in on the situation at hand. You may shut your eyes, grit your teeth, and clench your fists. Your tightness is probably intensified when the situation has something to do with money. Money trouble causes a restriction in the brain. You want to pinch pennies, stretch dollars, and, hold on to what you have.

Tightening up or holding on in the time of trouble, particularly financial trouble, is the worst thing you can do! You are holding onto the trouble. You are demonstrating your belief in lack. When you tighten up, you restrict your thoughts, and that may keep your good from coming in. You tighten the grip of energy around the very thing you don't want—lack! The best way, actually the only way, to get out of trouble is to give your lack a way out!

Giving activates the law of correspondence; what you give must come back to you tenfold. Giving is an act of faith. It is the only way that you can demonstrate your belief in the abundance of life, the goodness of God, and the wealth that is yours by divine right. And the best time to give is when you think you don't have enough to give. Give your time, your energy, your knowledge, your resources, and your money. Giving is a blessing, and you can never out-bless God!

Give what you have. Get what you need!

PSALM 37 IS one of my favorite passages in the Bible. "Fret not thyself because of evil doers."

We must keep this passage in mind when we see people receiving good that we may believe they do not deserve. At times it may seem that while we are doing all the work and getting nowhere, others come along, do very little, and are rewarded greatly. The truth is, we really don't know what they have done or what they deserve. Most of the time, we judge based on appearances and experience, which may or may not tell the entire story.

Then there are those times when we know that people are unethical, unprincipled, or dishonest. It may appear to us that they are getting away with it. We become upset and sometimes angry with them and with ourselves. We may question our worth and our methods. We may even question the wisdom of God. The truth is, no one gets away with anything they do in life. A few ill-gotten gains will quickly fall away when the hand of universal justice passes over. You can only have what is rightfully yours. You make the choice about how you will receive it: righteously and permanently or wrongfully and temporarily!

You get what is rightfully yours righteously.

THE ENERGY AND work required for spiritual growth and transformation offer very few short-term rewards. The work is hard, and the hours are long. There will be times when it seems as if you are getting nowhere—real fast! It will appear to you that others are passing you by and still others are gaining on you. Some will even appear to step over you or on you. You will get tired. You will get discouraged. You will want to give up . . . but you won't!

Most of us are conditioned to expect short-term rewards for the things we do in life. Study hard, get an A. Work hard, get paid. Look good, get complimented. Spiritual growth does not work like that! You must work hard and exercise what you know before you reap the benefits of what you know. And the more you know, the harder you must work to exercise the principles in all situations and under all circumstances. In the process of all of this work, no one is going to be grading you. You may never get a compliment. Your bank account may not reflect how hard you have worked or how much you know. But in the end, you will have such peace of mind and inner strength, those things won't matter to you anyway.

Spiritual work brings long-term rewards.

DEAR SELF,

Let me rememer:
The Father and I are one!
God's plan for me is my salvation!
There is nothing I want that I cannot have!
I must be willing to forgive!
I make the choice about who I am and who I become!
The time is now!
What I can't do, God can do!
I am my sister!
Right where I am, the light of God, the power of God,
the peace of God,
and the love of God are too!
I must always be grateful!

Love,
God's gift to me!

God always works on your behalf!

THE MINUTE JEAN heard there was something wrong with somebody, she had to rescue
them. She was a fixer who usually felt broken.
Carol always had an excuse for doing or not doing something in a particular way. The way she did things usually
left her feeling used up, drained, and unappreciated. Mae
was a blamer. It was never her fault. Someone had done it
to her or made her do it this time and that time. Joan
didn't do anything unpleasant. She either ate, drank, or
went to sleep. These women were totally unaware of what
they were doing to contribute to their undoing. They did
it habitually, believing they couldn't help it.

There is a price we must all pay to feel good in life.
That price is attention. We must pay attention to what we
do and what we get in return. We must pay attention to
how we feel before, during, and after we do our thing.
When we find that what we are doing does not make us
feel good or empowered, we must stop doing it. We must
not let fear for others or ourselves, excuses, or mindless
meanderings repeatedly prompt us to take unproductive
actions. Pay attention. Attention must be paid. If you do
not watchfully attend to what you do, you will find yourself where you don't want to be . . . again.

I am attending to my goodness.

———

THERE ARE TIMES when you want to make a mark on the world. You may want to make a statement. You may want to make a name for yourself. You may believe that the best way to make this happen is to take a big project and refuse to let people support, assist, or help you. You want to do it all because you have something to prove. Beneath that rationale is the truth that you want to get all the credit. There is nothing wrong with having a desire to be recognized and rewarded. What you probably don't want is the confusion and stress being in charge and in control can cause you.

The mark of a good leader is the ability to delegate and share responsibility. A good leader knows how to allow other people to do the work. A true leader is surrounded by good people who share the vision and do the work because they believe in what they are doing. Your job is to find these people and hire them. A leader can step out of the way, let the workers work, and know in the end, the leader gets the credit. What a good leader does when she gets the credit is give it away. A true leader is humble and willing to serve because a leader knows the best way to make a name for yourself is to create it within yourself. The world already knows that a good leader stands behind, not on top of those who do the work.

The work is a credit to the leader.

YOUR MOUTH IS the stable of your power. Every word that comes out of your mouth is like a horse. Some horses are well trained, well groomed, and well kept. These are the race horses. They have a strong and powerful energy, supported by their ability. When a race horse leaves the stable, it is expected that the horse will bring the owner many rewards.

Other horses are wild stallions that buck and kick. Once they are out of the stable, it is hard to catch them. It is even harder to get them back into the stable. A wild stallion can be destructive. It can run down, run over, even kill something. A stallion on the loose, which cannot be caught or brought back to the stable, will usually cause harm or bring disgrace to the owner.

Nags are kept in a stable too. These slow-moving beasts are almost useless and serve no good purpose. Nags just hang around until somebody can figure out what to do with them. A nag makes really good fertilizer and even better glue!

Any time you open your mouth, be aware of what you are unleashing from the stable. Choose your words well. It is like grooming a horse. Make sure your words are useful and purposeful. They should not nag or kick wildly. Every time you open your mouth, know what you want to say and why. In other words, bridle your tongue!

My words put me in or take me out of the race!

YOU CANNOT RUN away from your problems. You can distance yourself in order to look back and assess your situation, but you can't get away from a persistent problem. A problem is like a tennis ball. It comes at you, you hit it to deflect it, but you cannot disarm a real problem with the swat of your hand. Until you are willing to sit in the middle of the problematic situation and pick it apart, piece by piece, until you get to the core, you will not be able to resolve it. It will remain a problem that grows from a little tennis ball into a giant missile. If you make one false move, it will explode!

A problem is a problem until you get to the root of the problem.

IN THE MIDDLE of panic, crisis, or confusion, it can be difficult to listen to what is said and not to what you hear. Even the slightest emotional upheaval will not only cloud your vision, it will also clog your ears. When we are upset, we hear with *fear muffs* on our ears. We hear with our broken hearts, our shattered egos, and our anger. At times like this, harmless little words take on great big meanings, and the smallest, most innocent gestures become life-threatening movements. You may feel like you are being attacked when you are actually being consoled. You may think you are being criticized when you are really being supported. If you know you are upset or feeling vulnerable, ask people what they are saying before you jump to a conclusion about what they have said.

Listen to what is said, not to what you hear.

YOU ARE BLESSED! It may not look or feel that way right now, but it's true. If you want to know how blessed you are, think back to a situation you thought was right for you and admit how wrong you were. At the time, you may not have realized you were growing. There was no way to know back then that something bigger and better was on the other side of something painful, ugly, and uncomfortable. Now look where you are and remember where you were.

Realize that where you are right now is not where you are going to be at sometime in the near future. Whether you love it or hate it, your current condition is only temporary. Do your best. Do what you can. Give what you have to give, and remember, you are still growing. You are learning. In fact, you are earning new degrees of wisdom. Sure, you have some grief. You will have some fears. You might even have bouts of pain and sadness. However, just around the corner from where you are, you will be able to look back and see how truly blessed you are.

Whatever it is, I can do it for now.

The Valley of
O.P.P.

Other people's problems, other people's priorities, other people's principles, other people's people, can get in our way, hold us back and take us off track until we develop the strength to be honest with ourselves.

Those who watch you march to your death will salute you.

—NIKKI GIOVANNI

WHAT IS THIS business of womanhood? Is it more than softness, beauty, motherhood, and girlfriends? Is it less than manhood? The same as manhood? And who said so? How do you know? What were your models of womanhood? Were they harsh? Cruel? Unheard? Tired? Abused? What images of womanhood do you hold? Aspire to?

Every morning you wake up a woman. What does it look like? How does it feel? Do you like it? Are you afraid of it? What is this business of womanhood? Is it sold? Can it be bought? Where do you find it? How do you keep it? Increase it? Was it given to you? Did you ask for it? Is it a blessing? Or a curse?

What is this business of womanhood? Do you work on it? Play with it? Does it work on you? Does it wear you out? Do you nurture it? Embrace it? How? When? Why? What is this business of womanhood? And how close does it come to being a child of God expressing the flesh from a feminine energy?

A woman's business is God's business!

THERE ARE TIMES when you innocently fall into things you cannot seem to get out of. Perhaps to keep the peace, you said you liked something or someone when you really didn't. Or maybe you said you would do something, knowing you didn't have the resources, hoping you could get them. It may have appeared that to tell the whole truth would have created a problem, so you deleted a few facts, altered a bit of the reality. You forgot to do something but you don't want anyone to know, so you try to cover your tracks. The innocence you had at the beginning will turn on you unless you tell the truth.

My daddy said, "Either you are lying or you are not lying." There is no such thing as a little lie, a good lie, or a necessary lie. You will be held accountable for everything that flows from your mouth. If you bring forth a lie, even a little lie, it will haunt you, and maybe even bite you. The process of life is truly impartial; it does not examine why we do what we do; it looks at what we did and holds us accountable for it. Rather than unleash a dishonest word and risk being bitten, don't say anything at all. Smile and nod. Say, "I can't offer an opinion or help now," or "Oops! Please forgive me, I forgot." When we develop a good habit of telling the truth to others, we avoid the damage we can ultimately cause by lying to ourselves.

When you know the truth, you must tell the truth!

DURING AN INTERVIEW, the host referred to me as "another self-help guru" after money, who had written, "another self-help book" to get rich. As it fell from her mouth and in response to her tone of voice, my claws came out. While she continued to frame her question, with the lights and cameras shining in my face, I realized I had about thirty seconds to smooth my ruffled feathers. Breathing as deeply as I could, I realized she just didn't know. She was totally unaware of the time, prayer, and energy I put into my work. She had no idea of how many nights I sat up working, how many dates I passed up in order to work, how many meals I missed, or how seriously I take my work.

There will always be people who attempt to diminish or dismiss you. Some will not know any better, others simply don't care. A few will do it innocently. Others are consciously skeptical about, afraid of, or cynical about things they don't know about or care about. Some are afraid. None of that matters. What matters is your intent. What matters is your truth. What matters is what you know and feel about yourself. When I opened my mouth to respond, I lovingly reminded the host of the old African proverb, "It's not what people call me, it's what I answer to that counts."

I know who I Am!

VERY OFTEN WE place our trust in people, only to be disappointed. We must not allow those experiences to render us untrusting or untrust-worthy. Trust is not something we give in response to what we get. Trust is not something we can acquire by anything we do. Trust is a decision we make within our-selves when we surrender control to God. If you believe you have been betrayed, used, taken for granted, or in some other way had your trust violated, decide now never to give up on people or yourself.

Everyone is held accountable for what they do. Not to you, but to life. Always remember, no matter what happens, or how bad you feel about it, or how much you don't like it, God knows exactly where you are and what you need. If you realize that your Creator is in control, there is never a reason to not trust people or yourself. ALL you have to do is trust that God will help you understand the value of your experiences . . . no matter what they look like.

Even when I'm hurt, I will trust the process!

WHEN YOU HEAR something that upsets you, ask yourself, "Where did I hear that before?" Who told me that I was no good? Unworthy? Not pretty? Find the people and the circumstances in your mind. Allow yourself to feel once again what you felt then. Trust that you can feel bad and recover. When you identify the people, forgive them, and forgive yourself for believing them.

In the midst of your forgiveness, a lot of confusion will show up. You may feel you are not smart enough, worthy enough, good enough to forgive yourself or others. It's okay, forgive anyway. You may believe that who you are or what you have done is too terrible to be forgiven. Forgive anyway. Fill your mind with forgiving thoughts. Speak forgiving words to yourself. Remember that your psyche is fragile. It is also powerful. You can heal, strengthen, empower yourself with a thought or a word, just as easily as you can be broken by the same.

I think forgiving thoughts. I speak forgiving words.

WE ARE ALL connected to the one Mind, one Life, one Power, one Spirit which is God. God created us all. God remains connected to us all. God knows everything there is to know about you and everybody else. When we really understand and embrace this concept, we will realize there is no need to run around telling people what somebody else has done. God already knows, and only S/He has the power to heal and correct.

Usually when we criticize, judge, or complain to people about other people, they are in no position to help us. In most cases, 80 percent of the people have their own people to complain about, and the other 20 percent don't care. Our problems with each other can be solved as soon as we give up the idea of how they "should" behave and what they "should" do. God is the only one who knows for sure who we are and our individual level of development. If we can remember the connection and recognize the need for healing, it becomes easy not to be angry or upset with people. They are minding their own life business. You are free to mind yours.

The one Mind, one Life, one Power, one Spirit minds us all.

———

It is a bitter pill to swallow, but betrayal in our lives is the outgrowth of fear in our minds. People do not necessarily betray us; sometimes we just set ourselves up to be a victim. We don't like to think about it. Very often we do not realize it. Yet the law works whether we recognize it or not. People often come into our lives to demonstrate that which we think and feel.

Each time we experience some form of betrayal, we are convinced about how weak, fragile, ill-equipped, or inadequate we are. We get to feel sorry for ourselves. We get to blame *others* for taking our power and we fall deeper into victimhood. We can't help ourselves when we are a victim. It's not our fault when we are a victim. We don't have to grow when we are a victim. Betrayal is just one of the tools the ego uses to make us victims and to ease God out of our lives.

You can get to the heart of betrayal by forgiving those who have hurt you before. You can ease betrayal out of your life by forgiving yourself for allowing others to make you a victim. You can turn all experiences of betrayal into steps toward empowerment by affirming over and over and over . . .

I AM not a victim!

THERE IS SOME bad news we all must accept, which is that everyone who starts out on the journey with us is not going to make it to the end. The good news is, you can be one of those who makes it. And there's more. No matter how you want to or try to help somebody else make it, you can only do what they allow you to do. But that's okay, because every good thing you do will come back to you better than you gave it. And that's not all.

On the journey, some people will fall behind you, and you will feel guilty for leaving them. Some people will fall in front of you, causing you to stumble. Still others will fall right next to you, scaring you half to death. Always keep in mind, if you stop on the journey to worry or doubt or fear, you will create a major obstacle. Others will then fall over you!

The bad news is, the journey is long and arduous. It is sometimes frightening. Sometimes lonely. All along the journey the path is littered with the bodies and skeletons of the fragile, the fallen, the forgotten. The good news is, whenever you are on the journey, you have only just begun.

I shall not fall off the path of the journey.

———

WHEN FRIENDS, FAMILY, and loved ones are in trouble, they will run to you for help. When you see them sinking into bad times, bad situations, bad habits, you feel it is your duty to help. The question we must ask ourselves is, how much help is too much help? When do our attempts to support, assist, encourage, or motivate become rescue mechanisms which keep people from learning their lessons and growing? In her book *Lessons in Truth,* Emilie Cady says, "One of the hardest things to do is stand still and watch somebody we love fall." Often we don't realize that in saving others we keep them from their lesson, and in doing so, we are actually encouraging the destructive behavior we want to save them from. There is a thin line between support and salvation, assistance and rescue. When we love someone or feel responsible to or for them, the line becomes blurred.

We all have appendages at the ends of our arms. They are called hands. Hands are not only for giving help; they are also for "self-help." Watch the patterns in which other people live. How they do what they do is clear indication of where they are with themselves. At times, it may seem to you, where a person is, is not a good place to be. However, you must also realize, they may not want to *get* out as badly as you want them to *be* out. When you rescue people, they cannot develop hard-working, capable hands of their own.

I see the good in you!

WHAT OTHER PEOPLE are doing or have done is not something you have to be concerned with or involved in. The issue you must address is, "What are you going to do?" You can feel badly, have empathy for what someone else is going through. You can feel their pain, know their concern, but the issue remains, what are you going to do?

There are times when people will tell us their problems, knowing "how we are." They haven't figured out how to come right out and ask for what they want, so they beat around the bush until we offer. In many situations, we can get pulled off track, out of line, away from our own issues in order to help, save, or rescue someone else. When people need support or assistance, we must allow them to ask for it. Once they do, we must make an honest assessment of what is or is not possible. We offer what we have rather than what we can get. We can also hear the pain, know their worry, and still choose what is best for us.

I hear your concern: "They won't ask for help!" They don't know how to ask for help!" And maybe that's the bigger issue. However, what other people can't do, what other people do not know how to do, is not something you must address to your own detriment. The issue you must address is, "What are you going to do?"

I don't know about you, but I know what I'm doing.

―――――

HAVE YOU EVER considered that you may be the only Holy Book, sacred text, Bible that somebody reads today? Has it ever dawned on you that you may be the only sermon someone hears this week. What are you showing them? What are you saying to them? If you want to keep believing that you are small or insignificant, or that what you do doesn't matter, you go right ahead! God knows better! God knows that you have learned a great deal in life and that what you know can help somebody else. God knows that it's been rough for you at times, but even when the road is bumpy, you always get where you are going. God knows that you've been hurt, but you've healed. That you've been afraid, but you moved through it. That there have even been times that you were scared out of your wits, but you are so tough, so powerful, so brilliant, you did not let that stop you. More than that, God knows people are always listening to what you say and what you do. In other words, God speaks to other people through you.

People watch me in order to hear God.

WHEREVER YOU ARE, at any time or place in your life, you will get what you need, by doing what you need to do. Others may not like or understand it, but you are on a mission. Your mission, is etched into the essence of your being. It is called DNA, *Discovering New Altitudes;* how else will you know what you can do unless you do it? People may warn you about the dangers, discourage you from taking chances. Just remember, most missions are wrought with danger. The falls and pitfalls you encounter toughen your hide, straighten your back, and coat your booty with Teflon. If you attempt to alter or change your mission simply to please other people, you will alter your DNA and retard your growth process.

By the way, your DNA is nobody's business but yours. You are not required to discuss your lessons or growth process with anyone unless you choose to. Your growth, new altitudes, and new dimensions will be fully recognizable. It is not your mission, assignment, or responsibility to live up to, down to, or according to anyone's opinion of you. When you realize this, you will also realize how far you can soar.

I'm on a mission.

———

I CAN REMEMBER being so afraid of what someone might say, I could not do what I needed to do. I thought about how upset they would be; how I would hurt their feelings; how angry they would be. I also thought I would lose their love or respect. In fear I did nothing. I don't think I am alone in this experience.

It is foolish to say we should not be concerned about the way in which our actions affect others. It is, however, equally foolish to make ourselves miserable, hold ourselves back, deny our own truth, to make someone else happy. A method I have discovered to relieve the stress of this type of experience is to forgive the person before I say or do anything. I forgive them for being angry or upset with me. I forgive them for anything they might say in anger. I forgive them for not honoring my needs and my truth. Then I say what I must say, do what I must do.

Forgiveness keeps the channels of communication open. It eliminates stress and clarifies the truth. Honest forgiveness keeps you from being upset or derailed by the words or actions of another. You have already imagined the worst and forgiven it; there is no way you can be hurt or shocked. The most important aspect of forgiving, at the start, is the realization that you cannot lose anyone's love. Either they love you and honestly want you happy or they don't! Now, forgive yourself for believing what you must do for you means you cannot be loved.

I move forward with forgiveness.

JOY IS WHAT we are, not what we must get. Joy is the realization that all we want or need in life has been etched into our souls. Periods of success followed by long periods of unhappiness and dissatisfaction are not the natural order of life. We are not put here to suffer and then die. Yet it seems that we are unable to sustain an even flow of pleasure and ease in our daily affairs and relationships. Things never seem to add up when we make the tally of pleasure and pain, ease and difficulty, good times and bad times. Perhaps this is because we are using the wrong measurements.

Joy, not pleasure; joy, not ease; joy, not happiness. Joy is an internal mechanism which keeps us on an even plane as we move through life. Joy gives us the ability to move through an unpleasant situation, knowing that once we make it through, it is over. Joy reminds us of what we need to learn in order to experience longer periods of joy.

Joy helps us to see not what we are "going through" but what we are "growing to," a greater sense of understanding, accomplishment, and enlightenment. Joy reveals to us the calm at the end of the storm, the peace that surpasses the momentary happiness of pleasure. If we keep our mind and heart centered on joy, the joy of growing, of knowing, of living, joy becomes a state of mind, not an elusive preoccupation we choose, only to have it slip through our fingers over and over.

I Am joy!

WHAT WOULD HAPPEN if you let your dream come true in front of a million people?? What would people think about you, say to you if you started to have fun in public? What do you think people would think if suddenly you became very successful, very wealthy, very powerful right before their eyes? Whatever you think people would think is probably the thing that keeps you from doing it. Most of us are not willing to risk making people mad at us.

It may be difficult to believe, but the people around us want us to succeed. They may not act that way. They may never say a word. Some of them probably don't realize it, but it is a lot harder for them to watch you suffer and struggle than it is for you to succeed. We often get in the way of our own success by worrying about what other people will think. In the worst case, some of us hold ourselves back in fear of leaving or losing those close to us. We are afraid to outshine them. We think it will make them angry or uncomfortable.

Living your life to its fullest potential is a fun thing to do. Those around you can watch and cheer you on. If they watch carefully, they can learn something. If they love you, they too will benefit from your success.

Let's have some fun.

LIFE IS DEPENDING on you to shine. Life is waiting for you to bloom. Life is waiting for you to glorify it. Please don't let life down. Be sure not to allow other people to "should" on you. Folks are always so ready to let you know what you "should be" or "should not be" doing, they get very little done in their own lives. If your mother, father, sister, brother, friend is so sure of what you should be doing, let them do it. Remember, good advice is not always free. You pay dearly for it with little pieces of your life and your self. It may be challenging to move beyond the expectations and demands others have of or for you, but remember, a good challenge strengthens your muscles.

Please! Do not should on me!

———

✦ I T   I S   S O   easy to get caught up in being who others want you to be. It is even easier to convince yourself that who you are is not enough. If we are not careful and conscious, we can spend a good part of life acting out roles and expectations rather than living who we are. "Who am I?" is the question we should start the day with. Know that you are not your name, job, or level of education. You are not who your mother, father, sister, brother, husband, children say you are. You are not your dress size, hair length, number of credit cards. Who am I? For some of us it is a frightening question. To know who we are means we must move beyond the names and labels. It means we must shake off restrictions and limitations. To know ourselves is to love and accept ourselves as divine children of God. To know "who I am" means having no more excuses to be anything else for anyone else other than the Divine Father/Mother.

I Am who I Am.

SPEAKING FOR MYSELF, I have been made to feel responsible for so much, for so long, there was a part of me that believed I had to do it all. No matter what happened or who it happened to, I had to fix it. I had to fix my mother, my children, my friends, things that happened at work, and most other things that came along. When I couldn't fix it, I felt bad. Then I realized that even when I did fix it, I felt bad. I resented being responsible for having to fix so much and so many. As the resentment and exhaustion built up, I was forced to take a new approach. That is when I realized that by fixing everything on the outside, I was avoiding looking at those things I believed were wrong with me. As long as I could fix other things, I did not feel broken. As long as I could fix other people, I felt whole.

As women, we owe it to ourselves and life to assist, support, and serve others. We must remember, however, that we cannot give what we do not have. Give to yourself first! Do what you can because you want to, because of love. Never act from a false sense of responsibility. Fixing people and things is only a temporary relief which masks what we really believe about our self. In the end, we must come back to the mirror of self. Take time to heal the internal wounds that make you believe you are not enough. Once this is done, you will know when you have done enough!

I've done enough!

✦ WE TRY TO make everything all right for other people. When they hurt, we want to stop their pain. When they need, we do everything in our power to ensure that the need is met. When they make mistakes, we fix them and, in some cases, cover them up. We set ourselves up to be leaned on, but when people lean too hard or too much, we get angry. We feel used.

Some of us have a need to be needed. We derive self-value and self-worth from the things we do for others. We feel good when we are "doing." When the doing stops, we need more than people are able or willing to give us. Unfortunately, in the doing process we often lose sight of ourselves and our needs.

Remember that you set the standards for how you will be treated. People will treat you the exact way you treat yourself. If you don't want to be a crutch, don't set yourself up. Be good to you. Take time for yourself. Rest. Play. Shower yourself with affection, support, and gifts. Don't be afraid to be unavailable. Train yourself to know when to say no.

I have something to do for myself.

WHEN YOU MAKE a decision and a commitment to do something good for yourself, it is like dropping a pebble in a pond. It has a rippling effect. Energy vibrations are sent out into the universe that touch people and places you may not see. The firmer the decision, the stronger the frequency and wider the range of things that will be reached. Those things are being prepared to receive, support, and assist you in honoring your decision. The ripples closest to you may make you uncomfortable. They may rattle you a bit. That's okay! It is bound to happen. A decision will usually have a long-term and far-reaching affect. However, if it is for your good, all you have to do is stand firm. All that you need will find its way to you, and the unnerving ripples around you will go away soon.

I Am standing firm in this decision!

ARE YOU LIVING your life or are you living your mother's life? Perhaps you are living the life that your father told you to live. Maybe your life was custom-built for you by your husband, your sister, or the "system." Does your life suit your needs? Is it too big for you? Is it too small for you? Is your life satisfactory? Do you live in your life, or around it? Do you dare do what you want to do, or are you consumed doing what you are told you *have to* do?

It is very easy to get stuck living your life for others, doing what they want you to do in order for them to get what they need. There is a very delicate balance between *my life, our lives,* and *your life.* When you are not clear about who you are, what you need, and what you want, the balance can be tipped against your favor. If you need to reclaim your life and live it, be sure to do it! You can accomplish this by taking time for yourself to take care of yourself. You must also be sure to let people know what you need, and to be willing to say no to what they need without feeling guilty about it.

I have a life that I want to live.

THERE ARE FEW things more painful or difficult than watching a loved one go through difficulty. Chances are they will give you a blow-by-blow account of their pending demise. It is even worse when they say nothing at all and you discover how bad they are really doing from outside sources. Your first instinct is to rush to help them, to give them what you think they need to put an end to their misery. You hurt because they hurt, and you want to stop hurting with them and for them. In these situations, there are a few things you want to remember—

1. It's not your issue.
2. Don't get stuck in other people's stuff.
3. When people get tired of suffering and struggling, they stop.

Does this mean you should not help out a friend or loved one in need? Of course not! Do what you can without putting yourself in jeopardy. However, you must also realize that, in some cases, people will suffer because they know someone understands. As long as they believe someone understands their misery, they will believe they have a right to be miserable! When you run into people who are perpetually miserable, your job is to pray for them, hold them in the light of your mind, send them lots of love and . . . get out of the way!

Misery does not need company!

The Valley of Comeuppance

Teaches us that we are all held accountable to the universe for everything we think, say, and do. The energy of dominant thoughts and words creates conditions in our lives.

While I know myself as a creation of God, I am also obligated to realize and remember everyone else and everything else are also God's creation.

—MAYA ANGELOU

SOMETIMES IT'S GOT to get worse before it gets better. Sometimes it is not until the muck and mire are so deep, so thick, that we realize there has got to be a change. As long as we have little problems, we are willing and able to maneuver our way around. When the challenges are small, we can find a quick fix, a means of deliverance, without realizing there is a deeper problem, a bigger issue which requires healing.

Healing is not like fixing. Fixing is doing whatever we can to cover up, disguise, or eliminate the problem . . . temporarily. Healing cuts to the core, goes to the bone, as a means of eliminating the cause of the problem . . . forever. Band-Aids fix. They cover the problem up. Keep it clean and out of sight. When something is healing, it will ooze, cause pressure, or hurt. Stitches will fix, close up the problem, make it bearable. If, however, there is an infection under the stitches, the wound must be opened; the infection must be cleaned out before there is any relief. Healing is a great deal more painful than fixing. But think of it this way; once there is a healing, the problem goes away for good.

I Am in a healing process!

I ONCE READ that struggle, suffering, and conflict are like magnets that draw us closer to God.

It is not until we feel totally helpless, confused, sometimes desperate, that we become willing or able to turn to the awesome power of life and living our Creator offers us. We may know God exists. We may understand our connection to God. Yet it seems that it is not until we are down or on the way down that we invite God's presence and power into our life. It doesn't have to be this way. God not only offers emergency care, S/He is a source of preventive care.

Your Creator always wants the best for you. Your Creator has a mission, plan, and purpose designed just for you. Sometimes when things are going our way, when they are comfortable or easy, we forget about God. We get off track, out of line, we move away from the plan, mission, and purpose. Difficulties in life are not meant to break us or break us down. Our greatest challenge may be a simple reminder, the only way we will remember that there is a Higher Authority to whom we are accountable. The real challenge we face is to keep God, God's word, and God's way in the forefront of our mind—in good times as well as bad.

I Am a magnet for God's good!

God cannot fix the mess we create.
What God can do, will do, and does all the time
is give us the courage and presence of mind
to do whatever needs to be done
to rectify our errors.
What we must do is ask for guidance, and trust
it will be okay.

God will guide me through it.

L I N K I N G   T H E   F U T U R E to the pain of the past does not allow the light to come in. Today always offers new light; however, when you hold on to what you believe about yesterday, that belief will not allow you to explore new possibilities. Beliefs demand loyalty. If you try to move away from the things you believe in, they will punish you. The belief will make you feel guilty. Guilt is your punishment for abandoning what you believe.

Spirit is the only power which can intervene between the pain of the past and the light of the future. You must rely on the spirit of truth, love, peace, joy, and freedom to change your beliefs and free you from all guilt. What happened yesterday does not have to happen today unless you believe it must. Until you have enough faith to allow the power and presence of spirit to infuse your mind and change your beliefs, you will continue on the path of yesterday's painful darkness.

Spirit brings the light of new beliefs.

———

UNFORTUNATELY, MOST OF us have no idea of what the solution looks like because we are too busy fighting the problem. For some reason, it seems that we are prone to pay more attention to what we don't want. When difficulties and challenges confront us, the mind naturally shifts to what we cannot do, do not want to do, fear doing. In response to the dynamic power of the mind, we get more of the very thing we don't want. As the anxiety, fear, and resistance grow in our mind, the situation appears to become worse.

Any spiritual teacher will tell students, "Never focus on the problem; focus on the solution." In difficult times, the mind seems to take on a will of its own, reminding us of the possible horror we face. How are we to free ourselves of the pictures in the mind long enough to see the desired outcome? The answer is simple: go through the darkness to the light. The difficulty of any situation is not the situation; it is our resistance to it. At the time of our greatest challenge, we must allow the mind to go all the way through to the end. Give yourself permission to see the horror, feel the fear, anticipate the pain. When you've done that, it's over. Chances are if you let your mind go to where you don't want to be, you will never have to take your body through it. You can go through the problem mentally; you get a better picture of what the solution looks like. From that position, you can silently affirm:

I can do this!

EVERY NEW PHASE of life is walking up to a locked door. Some doors are poorly constructed, with locks that are easy to pick. These doors are easily opened. Other doors are very big and very well constructed, with big locks that cannot be opened without a key. Even when you have the key, a big door can still be hard to open. You have to push a little harder, and once you get it open, you must be very careful that the door doesn't close on your fingers or slam shut before you can get in.

Difficulties in life represent doors you must go through. The doors are not there to keep you out. They are there to prepare you for what you will encounter on the other side. On the other side of the door are the things that you have been looking for, waiting for, and asking for. On the other side of the door are all the things that you have been prepared to have by opening all the other doors. Why do you care if you have to push, kick, or knock the door down? You've got the keys: faith, confidence, and prayer. The only thing you have to do is remember, big doors with heavy-duty locks are used to protect very valuable things!

Big doors lead to big blessings!

EVERY MUSCLE, TISSUE, and cell in your body today is different than it was seven years ago. Every strand of hair you have today is different. Every toenail and fingernail you have today are not the same ones you had just a few months ago. Today, you are totally different in every physiological sense than you were three, five, or seven short years ago. The question is, how different is your mind?

Each moment, your physical body changes without any input on your part. Your mind, however, is a completely different issue. You must work to change your mind. You must be willing to release past pains, past regrets, and ancient resentments. You must be willing to let go of hostility, anger, and judgments about experiences and people. The people in your past, like you, have also changed. They have new hair, new tissues, new cells, new toenails and fingernails! It is up to you, however, to see them in a new light . . . even when it looks like they are doing the same thing. The only thing that will keep you stuck in the past with old experiences, useless emotions, and worn-out habits is your mind. Fortunately, you have the ability to change your mind to match everything else that is new about you.

You are renewed! Now change your mind!

MAYBE WHAT YOU really need is a spiritual diet! A spiritual diet will cut down on the excess weight you carry around in your soul. The weight of people who have disappointed you or hurt you. The weight of things you should have done, could have done, or wanted to do, but couldn't bring yourself to do. As a matter of fact, that weight around your middle could be those people you've been hanging around or allowing to hang onto you. The heaviness in your legs could be all those things you convinced yourself you were not smart enough, good enough, or ready enough to do. That sluggish, heavy feeling you have in your heart might be your dreams, goals, and fantasies. You haven't put them to use, so they've turned to weight, spiritual weight which has your whole life weighed down.

Yes! I believe a spiritual diet is exactly what you need! You can start right now with a heaping portion of forgiveness smothered in surrender. You will also need a big helping of laughter three to four times a day. Next, you must begin each day with prayer, followed by a dose of gratitude. For the next six to eight weeks, sprinkle everything with faith, wash it down with courage, and let your dessert be a swig of confidence. If you follow these directions with all your heart, you will experience a miraculous weight loss.

Lose a little weight and worry with a spiritual diet.

———

WOULD YOU LIKE to know why it is that you rarely get your bills paid on time? Does it seem that, no matter how hard you try, you can never manage to save a few pennies for that rainy day? Does your financial output exceed your financial income? Is it all making you crazy? The solution is really quite simple. You must heal your lack of consciousness.

As long as you are pinching, scratching, struggling with money, it will fight you, avoid you, and operate in a diminished capacity in your life. When it looks like you don't have enough, stop looking! Start writing the check and praising the universe for divine substance. Money is not in low supply. However, if you believe there is not enough to go around, no money will come your way. Remember, God is your Source and Supply. God is never broke. God is never late. God showers abundant riches on those who open the doors of their mind with trust, faith, praise, and a solid budget which includes giving, sharing, and receiving.

I lack no good thing. I Am open to abundance.

ALL OF US have things in our lives we would rather the world not know about. Every living being knows things about who they are which they prefer not to broadcast. No person living has not done or said something which, if they had it to do again, they would do it another way. We are not alone in the darkness of our habits, personality, mistakes, or poor choices. Yet when these experiences are revealed, we often feel alone, ashamed, guilty.

Life will not allow you to be guilty forever! No one, not even you, deserves to be punished forever! When the darkness about you or your life is revealed, rejoice! Know that it is coming up in order to move out. When darkness is revealed, it means that our consciousness is moving toward the light. It is a reflection of our inner readiness to release the past and move forward with clarity. Darkness coming to the light is a good thing. It is a God thing. And God never asks us to do more than we can, before we are able. Remember, the light of God will reveal anything unlike itself. The closer you walk toward the spirit of God, the more likely it is that your darkness will come to light.

I can see the light before me!

FEAR IS LIKE a shot of white sugar directly into the brain cells. It causes the mind to race. In fear, the mind makes you believe that something is gaining on you, about to overtake you, and that the worst thing possible and imaginable is about to happen to poor little old you. Fear is an intoxicant. It makes you high. But just as with all highs, there comes the moment when you crash.

Coming down from a fear-induced high means you will confront the very thing you were trying to get away from. All the things you kept in the back of your mind, believing you could not face, you must now face. As you crash into the situation or person feared, you may feel the need to lie your way out; fight your way around it; or simply tuck your pride between your legs and beg for mercy. If you are a student of life, on the journey of evolution and empowerment, there are two things you must do when you are in fear: (1) Breathe! (2) Surrender!

When you are in fear, take several long, deep breaths. This will help you stay in your body so you can hear your divine guidance. In order to hear what you must do, you must surrender everything you think might happen. In this way, you make way in your mind for what is divinely ordained to happen. Fear is simply a signal that you are about to embark upon a mystery of some kind. But life is a series of mysteries, isn't it?

I surrender! I surrender! I surrender!

WALLY AMOS ONCE said, "If you're going through hell, don't stop to take pictures!" But that's exactly what we do, isn't it? We maintain a mental catalog of every detail of what has happened. When the situation is over, we show off our mental pictures by telling the story over and over, embellishing the worst details. It creates pain in the brain and drama in life. We hate it, but we do it, unconsciously.

When we hold on to and mentally relieve painful past experiences, we create enemies. There is always someone to be leery of; someone or something to watch out for; what we fail to realize is that the kind of mental darkness in the back of our minds creates an *"enemy* in me."

Within you there is an awesome power, a divine intelligence, that is accessible and available, wherever you are. It is a guiding light. Unfortunately, this light can't shine when we keep ourselves surrounded in dark memories. When a photographer takes film into a darkroom, the negative images are exposed to light. The light creates a new image. Only when we expose the negativeness in our brain to light, can we create a new picture in our lives.

Let there be light!

———

Would you lie on forms you were submitting to God?
Would you keep God's change if S/He miscounted?
Would you gossip about God?
Would you criticize God?
Would you invite God over when your house is a mess
or
when you have mud on your face,
curlers in your hair, and morning breath?
No!
Then why do you do it to the world and to the people
which God created?

I see God in all things and all people.

———

LET US SAY someone has hurt your feelings. What does that really mean? What do you really feel? Feelings of being attacked, betrayed, rejected, unsupported today are usually the memories of yesterday's anger, fear, and helplessness. The challenge is to figure out what we feel; how it feels; even more important, why we feel the way we do. For many of us, it began in childhood. Yesterday's pain becomes what we "feel" today.

There is no part of the physical anatomy called "feelings." The response we have to any given situation is a reflection of what we are telling our selves about what is going on. If, as children, we believed we were unloved, unworthy, unimportant, we will continue to "feel" that way in response to whatever happens in our lives. It is an old memory wearing a new dress. But big girls have the power to change their clothes whenever they choose to do so.

The next time an old memory shows up in a new experience, do not allow it to hurt you. Take a deep breath before you say or do anything. Gently ask yourself, "What is really going on here?" "What am I remembering?" Give yourself time to get clear about where you are in your thoughts. Only with clarity about what is going on inside of you will you begin to "feel" better about what you experience outside of you.

Yesterday can't hurt me today.

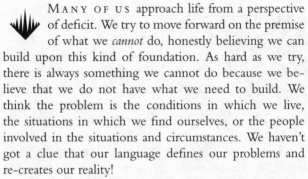 MANY OF US approach life from a perspective of deficit. We try to move forward on the premise of what we *cannot* do, honestly believing we can build upon this kind of foundation. As hard as we try, there is always something we cannot do because we believe that we do not have what we need to build. We think the problem is the conditions in which we live, the situations in which we find ourselves, or the people involved in the situations and circumstances. We haven't got a clue that our language defines our problems and re-creates our reality!

Take some time to listen to what you say over the course of the next few days. When you hear yourself say, "I'm struggling to get by!" "It's so hard out here!" "I'm just trying to make it!" remind yourself that words become conditions. Situations may be dark or dismal, but you can always speak about the good you can find in them. Conditions in your life may be challenging and difficult, but you have the ability to speak encouraging words to yourself. People may treat you unfairly, unjustly, or in the most unloving ways, but you reserve the right to counteract people with words. You're doing just fine! Hey! You keep getting better day by day! This is not as bad as it seems! You can do this! I know you can! These are just a few of the profitable things you can tell yourself to move beyond the confines of any deficit.

You can say what you want to see and be!

GOD, THE SPIRIT of life, will always meet you where you are. Never pushing, never forcing, but always reflecting back to you the level of your own understanding. If you believe in a harsh, punishing God, that is who you will meet in your time of need. If you believe in a loving, compassionate God, S/He will be your guide. If you believe in a partial, unjust God, you will experience the outgrowth of that belief if and when you turn to God for support. When you believe in a powerless or limited God, who only hears when S/He wants to hear, you will have experiences which will confirm exactly what you believe. Your beliefs and perceptions don't change the true nature of God, but they do determine the experience you will have when you seek God. One of the most important principles to remember in life is, you always get exactly what you expect!

The bigger, better, more powerful the belief, the bigger, better, more productive the experience!

DIFFICULTIES PREPARE YOU for victory. Disease prepares you for health. Confusion prepares you for clarity. Hopelessness prepares you for purpose. Failure prepares you for success. Poverty prepares you for prosperity. Criticism prepares you for acceptance. Pain prepares you for joy. Anger prepares you for forgiveness. Ignorance prepares you for truth. Loneliness prepares you for love. Love prepares you to stand face to face with God. God is the one who sends whatever it is you need to be prepared. It is called healing. Only God can heal you.

God is in the healing business.

THERE IS ALWAYS the temptation to look at
your circumstances to justify your position in life.
"I'm like this because . . ." "My parents made me
this way!" "I can't do any better because . . ." Many people fall into the trap of believing they are the way they are
because of the circumstances in their lives. What few of
us realize is that the circumstances of your life reveal who
you are, not what has happened to you!

We cannot escape the truth that every experience,
every relationship, and every aspect of our environment is
in direct correlation to how we think and what we think.
It is not the other way around. Circumstances do not
make you unless you think yourself down to them. If you
allow history, an unsupportive environment, or unsupportive people to hold you back, it is your choice! A
choice to believe you are stuck in the circumstances! A
circumstance is a creation of the mind that can always be
changed with a belief and a thought. Anytime you are
ready to get out of your present circumstances, you can
get out! The key is to fight the temptation to believe you
cannot!

A circumstance is a mental creation!

YOU DO NOT come to life totally helpless and lost. When you are born, the general direction of your journey is very clear. You have a gender. You are expressing a particular ethnic heritage. You are born in a particular location under a specific set of circumstances. These are the general parameters of your journey. It is up to you to determine the specific route you will take and what your final destination will be.

What you do with what you have been given in life is entirely up to you. You are free to move in any direction you choose, at any time you like. Keep in mind that once you start the journey you can change your mind about the direction in which you want to go. You are free to go up or down, forward or backward at any time and at your own pace. If you ever get lost or lose your footing on the journey, all you have to do is get in contact with the One who sent you here in the first place! S/He will be more than willing to help you get back onto the path of your choice.

Even if you have a map, you may need help reading it!

YOU CAN GET so caught up in being miserable that you will not see your blessing when it comes! You can become so addicted to having crisis in your life that the minute one crisis is resolved, you are on the lookout for the next one! It is very easy to miss the perfectly delightful experiences and moments of peace or joy when you are preoccupied with all of the possible tragedies that could befall you. It is quite possible that you have many of the bad situations you have in your life because you pay so much attention to them, they feel welcomed. It is also reasonable to believe that if you stopped paying so much attention to the bad things, they would feel neglected and go away! If you don't believe it, try it just to see if it works.

When a bad situation gets no attention, it becomes a better situation!

ARE YOU AFRAID of your feelings? Perhaps it is because you expect to be *caught* by surprise, or to be *thrown* into the middle. Maybe you've been *pushed* out front only to be *knocked* off your feet. How many times have you *fallen* in love only to have your heart *broken* when you were *kicked* in the face by someone you loved? When was the last time you were *stabbed* in the back by someone you trusted with your heart? If you think about it, we use such violent terms to describe our emotional experiences, it is understandable that we are afraid to open ourselves to the full range of emotions we are capable of experiencing.

Your feelings are the gauge of your life. How you express them or repress them determines the degree of your mental, emotional, and spiritual health. When we attach drama and fear to our emotional experiences, we are prone to shut down in order to protect ourselves. What you want to remember when you are on the telephone, crying your eyes out with your girlfriend, is that no matter what you feel, it is perfect! Your most heart-wrenching and painful experience is just as much part of the process of life as all the good things you have experienced. And, no matter what happens to you, it is crucial that you keep your heart open and experience your emotions. It is only when you can feel that you know you are truly and fully alive.

Be open to feel it. Use your power to heal it!

———

THE REWARD YOU receive for a job well done is getting a bigger, harder job to do. Many of us believe that once we demonstrate how strong, how good, how smart we are, life should give us a break. We believe we should be home free. Nothing could be further from the truth about the way life works. The trees with the strongest branches and deepest roots are those that have withstood the heavy winds and stormy weather, season after season.

You must never become tired of reaching, stretching, growing, and becoming better and better. The old folks called it "moving from glory to glory!" You must always keep in mind that the more you know and the more you can do, the more you will be called upon. Yes, you have a right to be tired. Yes, you are entitled to a much-deserved rest. Once you get rested, get ready! Life is going to bring you a big task to perform, a deep mystery to resolve, a harder job to work on, and a greater victory than you have ever had before.

Best to better! Biggest to bigger! Victory to victory is the journey of the great!

———

DEAR SELF,

If you have it to give, give it! If you know what to say, say it! If you know what needs to be done, do it! If there is some place you want to go, go now! If there is something you want to do, do it! What are you waiting for? Haven't you figured out yet that you are the only one who can do what you do, the way you do it? Don't you realize that the world is waiting for you?

Give it! Say it! Do it! Now!

WHAT IS IT going to take before we realize how absolutely wonderfully special and blessed we are? We are a human *being*, which means we are endowed with everything we need to master this thing called life. We are not a human *becoming* or a human *could be*. We are *being* now all that we are born capable of being. Why are we acting like there is something else we need? Isn't life enough?

Life is all that humans need to be in!

DEAR GOD,
Please remind me that my days are num-
bered. Teach me that my time here in this life is
precious so that I will not waste it. Help me to recognize
how precious every moment is so that I spend it doing
those things that will bring me closer to You. In the time
I have left, please teach me how to serve You, Dear God.
Teach me how to give joyously, share willingly, and love
totally. Remind me that I cannot serve in greed, doubt,
fear, or anger. Fill my soul with Your light, so that Your
bountiful blessings will shine through my soul into the
world. Each day that I awake, I pray that You will be
present in my thoughts, my words, and all of my deeds. I
ask that every moment that I have left in this life be a
channel through which some measure of Your love and
light may reach those with whom I come into contact.

A closer walk with God is time well spent!

The Valley of Purpose and Intent

Teaches us to be clear about our purpose and how to make a commitment to that purpose.

Don't no good come outta bad.
Can't get much bad outta real good.
Hold on to your good, your essence, until
you find the people and situations that
match it.

—*MARITA GOLDEN*, AND DO REMEMBER ME

THE QUESTION IS, what are you willing to do to get what you say you want? Are you willing to discipline your mind and your mouth? Are you willing to get up early, stay up late, and work hard all the hours between? Are you willing to work for free? Are you willing to do it with excellence? Are you willing to do it even when your best friend shakes her head, laughs at you, and tells you that you are crazy?

The question is, what are you willing to give up to get what you say that you want? Are you willing to give up bad habits, negative thinking, and negative people? Are you willing to take a risk and put your butt on the line when all the signs indicate that you are totally insane? Are you willing to stand up for yourself? To speak up for yourself? Are you willing to walk away from the people who will be very upset when you stand up and speak up? Are you willing to walk away from everything you now know to get to something and someplace you can only hope will be what you want it to be?

The question is, who are you willing to be? Are you willing to be a free and independent thinker? Are you willing to be the one who calls the shots? Are you willing to have fun? Are you willing to live in total peace and joy? Are you willing to have fun and joy in total peace all by yourself, if necessary? As long as you can find one excuse not to answer these questions affirmatively, you will never have what you say you want.

Have all that you are willing to have!

IF YOU KNOW that your life is a journey and if you want to make it to your divine destination, you must learn to travel light! Shake off all of the *nosey-know-it-alls* who try to convince you that they know what you need and how you should go about getting it! Throw away all of the *chronic-complaining-criticizers* who have never done anything except complain or criticize! Tear yourself away from the *whimpering-whiners* who have excuses for not doing all the things they have not done! Shake yourself free from the *low-life-lovers* who make many promises and keep few commitments! Unpack the abrasive attitudes, addictive appetites, belittling burdens, conflicting confusion, and frivolous fears that you have packed away in the crevices of your heart and mind. Pack a tidbit of truth, a capsule of courage, a fistful of faith, and a pocketful of prayer, and be on your way!

Pack light! Make the journey easy!

✦ THERE IS ONE sure way to know that you are doing exactly what God wants you to do: you will be at peace. Not every day, not all the time, but even in the midst of hard times and confusion you will feel good about what you are doing. Even when it seems like you are getting nowhere, you will know there is absolutely nothing else on earth you can do other than what you are doing. It's called being on purpose.

There will be times when you will want to walk away but you won't. You can't. Perhaps the money will not show up fast enough. You will figure out what you can do with the money you have. Maybe things you need will not be there when you think you need them. You will figure out how to do without them. You may even convince yourself that there is something bigger, better, more rewarding, you can be doing with your time. Just when you are about to give up, you will get a second wind, some much needed help that will keep you going just a little longer.

When you are doing what God wants you to do, the money won't matter. You will be willing to stick it out in the bad times. You will ignore the people who tell you you can't or that you are crazy. You will be so intent on finding the happiness and success you know you deserve, you will be at peace. In peace, you find God's purpose for you.

You peace is God's pleasure.

PSSSSST! I HAVE something very important to tell you. I know you are busy building a life for yourself. I realize you are working real hard to make it, to follow your dreams, and to realize some sense of personal satisfaction, but what I have to say is very important, otherwise, I wouldn't bother you. You may want to consider what I have to say before you make another move or take another step. It is something you probably know but may have forgotten to consider in all of your plans. Or maybe you have considered it but couldn't figure out how it works. What I want you to know is, unless you ask God what it is S/He wants you to do, you will never know! Once you ask, listen to your heart for the answer and watch for signs. In the meantime, if you don't get an answer, that is the answer!

God has something for you to do!

THE BEST WAY to create abundance in your life is to surround yourself with abundance. What you see, you become! If you want to be wealthy, go to the places wealthy people go. Do the things that wealthy people do. If your first thought is, "I can't afford to do that!" you will know why you do not have wealth and abundance—you don't think abundantly.

Abundant thoughts attract abundant experiences! A wealthy consciousness attracts wealth! If you don't know what wealthy people do—study! Read what the wealthy people read. Eat what wealthy people eat. Walk through wealthy environments. Save some money. Invest some money. And please, don't make the mistake of thinking that wealth has anything to do with race! Abundance is an attitude. Wealth is a consciousness. You can create an abundantly wealthy lifestyle right now, where you are, with what you have, by bringing yourself into alignment with wealth. The best part of learning to be wealthy and live abundantly when you are not is that you will know exactly what to do when the wealth shows up!

See wealth in your midst, have wealth in your life!

Money, fine clothes, fancy cars, public acknowledgment
are no substitute for purpose.
When you know your purpose,
you know you are about the business
of what you have come here to do;
you are on purpose.
With purpose,
you have vision.
With purpose,
you have clarity.
With purpose,
you have the support, power, and
blessings of the universe
at your disposal.

My purpose gave birth to me.

YOU KNOW EVERYTHING will turn out just fine. Even if it doesn't feel like it right now, you know, "This too shall pass." The question then becomes, what do you do in the meantime? How do you wait in peace and faith? Well, did you breathe? Go ahead. Take a few long, deep breaths, inhaling through the nose, exhaling through the mouth, making the sound "Ahhhh." That sound represents the name of God. That's your power. Don't forget to use it. Go ahead; breathe.

Did you pray? Did you confess from your heart to God what you are thinking, feeling, wanting right now? You know that prayer can get into places you can't; prayer changes things. Even better, prayer changes people, and people change things. So go ahead and pray.

Have you surrendered?? Have you given up your way to the will and the way of Spirit? Are you willing to give up control, realizing that whatever you want is probably far less than Spirit will do, once you get out of the way? If you are not breathing, if you haven't prayed, if you are not willing to surrender, it's no wonder you are in a panic.

I do know what to do.

196

SOME OF US want life to be like a refrigerator. We want to be preserved just as we are and to be kept crisp around the edges. We do not want to wilt or melt under the pressures of life. We want to stand in our own little space, keeping everything else in its own space so that we will not be contaminated.

I think life is like a toaster. You've got to be pushed down in order to pop up and meet the demands of life. You have to get done before you will know what to do. For most of us, unless we have a little heat under our bottoms, we will sit around and get stale. Also remember, when cold, hard things are placed on a hot piece of toast, they melt and fade away, but when you cast your bread on the waters of life, it will return to its place of origin multiplied.

The heat of light fuels the spirit to live!

———

YOU ARE A guest in this house. Life has invited you in for a while. You don't know how long you are going to be here, so while you are here you must be on your best behavior. Walk and talk softly so you don't disturb other people. Those who need to know you are here, will know. If you use something, put something back in its place. If you make a mess, clean up after yourself. Don't wait to be told what to do. If you see something that needs to be done, do it. Do it with joy and love, and please do it well. Try to leave this place in better shape than it was when you got here.

Be mindful not to whine or complain too much. Speak your mind when necessary, but do it with respect and in love. As you move through life's house, be sure to look nice. Not fancy or flashy, just neat and clean. It brings others great joy to see you look good. Above all else, always be grateful for every little thing life does for you. She could have invited anyone else, but you are someone special, so She chose you.

I Am a guest in life's house.

IN LIFE THERE are two kinds of hunters: the kind that hunts for prey and the kind that hunts for people. The difference between hunting for prey and for people is that the hunter traps the prey and kills it. The spirit captures people so that they can live. There is only one way to prevent yourself from becoming prey to the hunters; that is to allow yourself to be captured by the Spirit of life. Spirit is always on the lookout for those who really want to live. The spirit of truth! The spirit of peace! The spirit of joy and the spirit of love are searching for souls right now. Once you are caught, your life will never be the same!

Get caught up in the spirit of life!

DEAR SELF,
I will not assault my mind or spirit
with a lengthy discourse about the horror against
or the virtues of being a woman.
I will begin right now, where I am, getting to those
places
I can go if I choose to.
I will begin with the first step according to spiritual law,
doing all that is required for healing, transformation, and
evolution.
"You must bare your soul," they say.
But I know,
you cannot clean the fish and leave the water dirty.
I am the fish. I am everlasting substance.
The waters are my emotions.
They must be cleaned.
I must let the water out and fill myself
with new thoughts, new feelings, and new energy.
Then and only then will I be able to feed
the multitudes.

It is time to cleanse my mind.

There is something phenomenal going on!
I'm not quite sure what it is, and quite frankly,
I don't care!
I simply know, whatever it is,
it will be great!
It has to do with change, healing, growth, and evolution.
And
It has to do with women.
If I were pressed, I would put it in words like this:
There are changes taking place in the hearts and minds of
women
that are going to rock the world!
Women are changing their minds about who they are;
and what their role will be in the world order.
Women are learning to be responsible for the healing
of their mental, physical, emotional, and spiritual selves.
Women are learning to love themselves and each other.
Most of all, women are evolving to the point
where they are no longer willing to accept crap
from themselves or from anyone else.
I Love It!

Will the women please stand up!

✦ HOW MANY TIMES have you said, "I can't take this anymore!" but accepted it anyway? How often do you beat up on yourself, criticize yourself, belittle yourself, only to portray to the world how confident, poised, and able you are. Are you thinking no when you say yes? Do you go when you want to stay home? Have you given up when you wanted to push forward? Have you pushed forward when you felt like giving up? Do you ask for it, then doubt you will get it? Have you doubted you would get it, but asked for it anyway? If you have done any of this or any reasonable facsimile thereof, face it, you are confused.

How can we expect life to bless and support when we say one thing, think something else, and feel a completely different way. We are sending the universe mixed messages. The Bible tells us that from one's heart flow the issues of life. The mind and emotions create the "heart" of which the Bible speaks. If our thoughts are confused, our emotions full of doubt, and our action contradictory to our thoughts and emotions, just what do we really expect life to bring us?

In order to get what we want, we must say what we mean. In order to say what we mean, we must know what we want. When we know what we want, we can think and speak positively with great expectations.

Let me be clear.

———

WHATEVER YOU EXPERIENCE, whatever happens to you is merely a reflection of your need for an attitude adjustment. You can see life as a series of harsh, cruel events that push you too hard and fast; or you can see life as a process of growth and change to which you must adjust. You can see people as vicious, manipulating cutthroats; or you can see them as frightened children, searching to find their way. You can see problems as things you must fight against or struggle with; or you can see them as opportunities which pave new paths. You can see yourself as a hopeless, helpless, defenseless victim; or you can see yourself as a diamond in the rough in the process of transformation. What you see determines what you experience. What you experience is a reflection of what you need to learn. What you need to learn will show up in your life as an experience providing you with an opportunity to demonstrate a new attitude.

I Am having my attitude adjusted!

JUST DO WHAT you do and do it well. Stop worrying about what other people are doing, or what they will say about what you are doing. Just do what you do to the best of your ability. You may never get an award or public recognition or five minutes on the evening news. Just do what you do because you love to do it. Some people may not like what you do or support what you do. But some people will like it and support it, and some will pay you to do it. Whether people like or agree with what you do is not the issue. The issue has to do with what you do; just because you do it can make all the difference in the world.

I have something important to do.

WOULD YOU LIKE to know why you have not found your true purpose in life? The answer is probably in the bottom or the top of your closet. Would you like to know why you never seem to have the money to do all the things you want to do to make your life all that you want it to be? The answer is probably in your dresser drawer—you know, the one with all the junk in it. Do you really want to know why you can never seem to get anywhere on time? The answer is probably down in the basement or in the attic or in the trunk of your car. The reason you can't find the answers is because you do not have order in your life.

Order is the first law of nature. Everything in life happens in an orderly manner. Things must be in place so that when the hand of nature sweeps by it has everything it needs to leave what must be left. When your life and affairs are not in order, nature has no place to put the blessing. And even if the blessing were to be given to you, you probably wouldn't be able to find it. You must bring what you have into total and complete order before you can receive anything else. Order in the secret places! Order in the hidden places! Order in the open places! When you order your visible life, you order your mind. A well-ordered mind is fertile ground for the blessings of Spirit.

Order your life to make way for Spirit.

EVERYONE NEEDS A spiritual discipleship, just like the twelve men who followed the teachings of Christ. A discipleship brings clarity of thought. When you embrace a spiritual discipleship, you are focused and fully committed to a principle greater than yourself. As a spiritual disciple, you have something to believe in, something to work toward, something greater, more beneficial than problems to occupy your mind.

A spiritual disciple must study every aspect of principle and act upon it at all times. When people or circumstances challenge a spiritual disciple, they become the living embodiment of the principle, calling into action the energy to bring balance, harmony, and peace to the situation.

If you are ready to step over obstacles and move through challenges with grace and insight, you are ready to be a spiritual disciple. You will need a brown paper bag and twelve separate slips of paper. On each slip of paper, write one spiritual principle. You may want to choose from among love, faith, truth, acceptance, awareness, understanding, clarity, order, peace, balance, harmony, surrender, discipline, and courage. Drop the slips in the bag. Say a prayer asking for divine guidance and assurance to select the divine principle for you. Reach in and pull out a slip. For the next ninety days, study, meditate upon, and live the energy of the principle. Be that principle in action.

I Am a disciple of _____.

I WONDER WHAT would happen if you stopped worrying about your situation and prayed for somebody else. I know it seems like this is the worst time of your life; you are in pain, totally confused, and you don't know which way to turn. But perhaps if you turned away from the problem for just a minute you might have a breakthrough.

Try it. Close your eyes and pray for someone you know who is sick. Or maybe pray for someone who is homeless, jobless, helplessly locked in an addiction. Pray for someone, perhaps a mother in a war-torn country who does not know where her child, husband, or mother is. What about a mother with a sick child or one who has just buried her child? Pray for a family that is in turmoil; or a child who is lost, in trouble, or both. Pray that your mate will be strong in your times of weakness. Pray for your children, that they will be protected while you are going through this bout of temporary insanity.

I don't know what will happen to your problems while you are praying, but I do know that what you give you get . . . tenfold.

A prayer for somebody is an answered one for me!

MONEY WILL NOT ease the pain we experience in life. It may look that way; it may feel that
way; but it is simply not true. Money is *My Own
Natural Energy Yield*, a reflection of what I think, feel,
and do. It is the manifestation of our beliefs, emotions,
and dominant thought patterns. When we believe we are
in pain because of the lack of money, or if we engage in a
pattern of restrictive thinking, money will not help or
save us. It is belief in pain and lack that keeps money from
coming to us.

When our purpose in life is to be whole, peace-filled,
and loving, we generate positive energy. When we think
about how good life is, how blessed we are, how far we
have come, we realize we are not restricted. When we
seek to give rather than get; when we focus on "do"
instead of "cannot do"; when we move beyond pain, fear,
doubt, and distress, we open ourselves to a wide range of
possibilities. In most cases it is possible to get everything
we need and want, with or without money. In all cases, as
long as we remain desperate about not having money, the
money we seek cannot get to us.

I Am the soul source of my wealth!

REV. WILLIE WILSON of Union Temple Church in Washington, D.C., told his congregation to be "planted," not "potted." Potted plants can be knocked over or turned over and easily uprooted. It is very easy for a strong wind or a careless movement to demolish or destroy a potted plant. Potted plants may be beautiful to look at, but they are fragile. They require intensive care, and they die easily under adverse conditions.

Things which are planted have strong roots. They are usually outdoors and able to withstand the winds and the storms. When something is planted, it makes the best of adverse conditions, by grabbing on to whatever is available, to the ground itself, until things get better. When something is planted, it may be nibbled on by varmints; it may be stepped on by the careless; it will be pushed and prodded, but never uprooted. Planting requires reliance on God. Potting is subject to the whims of humans.

I Am planted, not potted.

•✦• THOSE THINGS THAT are going to tempt you off the path of your spiritual growth are not going to come up to your front door and ring the bell. Temptations come in through the cracks. They slide under the door! They sneak in through the windows! If you are not careful and always alert, you will be tempted to go right back to your old way of thinking, doing, and being.

Keep the cracks of your heart covered with constant prayer. Ask for divine wisdom and spiritual insight in the midst of all experiences. Seal up the windows of your mind with song. Songs of goodness, songs of praise, and songs that will keep you protected by the watchful eye and guiding ear of the Holy Spirit. Secure the door of your soul with the knowledge of who you are. You are a daughter of light, a woman of power, a child of the Omnipresence of God. Temptation may ring your door-bell, but if you are singing and praying loud enough, you won't even hear it!

Pray a prayer of wisdom! Sing a song of praise!

FINDING THE WAY to joy, peace, abundance, health, and balance requires an examination and evaluation of everything you cherish. In the midst of your evaluation, the Holy Spirit will step in and separate that which is false from that which is true; that which is necessary from that which no longer serves any purpose in your life.

Separation from that which is familiar and cherished is frightening. Yet the Holy Spirit is a spirit of light which will reveal the darkness of the things you have held on to. When the darkness is revealed, what you once cherished will look different! In some cases it will *act* different! The truth is, nothing is different. In the process of evaluation, the presence of the Holy Spirit gives you the ability to see things in a new light. Hopefully that light will set you free.

Everything looks different in the light of spirit.

The Valley of Nonresistance

Teaches us to cooperate with the flow of life and life's events by surrendering control, the demand to have things our way.

Life is not promised to you. Nor is it promised that it will go the way you want it to, when you want it to.

—ROSALIND CASH

THE OLD SPIRITUAL reminds us, "Nobody told me that the road would be easy . . ." and it's not! It is not easy to shift out of what we do and how we do it. It is not easy to shift our views in order to see new things in place of the old. It is often confusing and frightening to make a shift away from the familiar in order to embrace the unknown. Yet it is a necessary labor we must undertake in order to grow. No matter how difficult, challenging, or hard it may seem, shifts are necessary when the time comes to free ourselves from the confinement of mental, emotional, or physical boxes.

All shifts create a vibration which in turn affects everything around it. If you shift one crayon in a box, all the other crayons will move. Sometimes moving one crayon will cause a slight shift. Under other circumstances, moving one may mean the others fall, crack, and crumble. This is frightening. Sometimes, in fear of the effects our changes will create, we delay making a much-needed shift in our minds and behaviors. As a result, our lives and everything around us remain stuck. When the time comes to move, we must move. The longer we fight against it, the harder and more painful the movement becomes. There is a good thing about life and human nature that we often forget: life and the humans in it move like machinery. When you change gears, everything connected changes too! That is not necessarily a bad thing.

It's time to shift gears.

DEAR GOD,

   Into the temple of Your peace I enter to meet You; to share sacred moments in Your presence. In the sanctuary of Your presence I find the peace which heals, which strengthens; the peace which surpasses understanding. Into the womb of Your love, Dear God, I enter, so that you might nourish, protect, and embrace me, for I am Your child. In the shrine of your abundance I rest my head, wash my hands, cover myself so that You may provide for me all that I need to glorify all that You are.

   Into Your home, Dear God, I come once again, to be fed and to rest from the noise of the world. For it is in the sanctuary of Your temple, my heart, that I find You and love You, and understand how much You love me.

                                        Thank You, God
                                        Me

Come unto me all you that labor, and I will give you rest.

———

YOLANDA ADAMS SINGS a song that re-
minds us, "The battle is not yours . . . it's the
Lord's!" I love that song because it reminds us
that we are not required by life or in life to fight with
people or conditions. The only thing required of us is to
faithfully trust in the omnipresence of the all-knowing
Creator to handle every situation according to Divine
Law. Make no mistake, that in and of itself is a challenging
task. It is quite difficult to be under pressure, under attack,
by people you can see or tangible life experiences, and to
remember that God is always in charge. It takes a very
powerful person not to get sucked into the appearance of
disaster or the onslaught of trouble. It takes strength and
nerves of steel not to answer false accusations, not to
defend oneself against seeming injustices, because to the
human psyche, not to do anything is to be passive. Nothing could be further from the truth.

It's not my battle!

WHEN WE REFUSE to surrender our power when we are attacked or when we encounter trouble, we are exercising the knowledge of our authentic power. There is an old gospel song that reminds us, "No matter what you are going through, remember God is using you." God is our power, the source of our strength and our good. When we face difficulties, God will use the opportunity to demonstrate just how powerful S/He is. When we do nothing, we are doing the best thing. We are actually providing the Creator with the opportunity to do everything, according to His/Her will. It is not the Creator's will that we suffer, struggle, fight, or die in the battle to save ourselves from life. God will fight the battles on our behalf when we move out of the way. The challenge is to realize that the movement re-quired is no movement, no word, no fight. To be in trusting, faithful stillness is to be in God's powerful armor.

To do nothing is to do something with God!

ARE YOU PUSHING, struggling, trying to get something done, but getting nowhere? When it seems that nothing you are doing is making anything any better, it is time to call on Divine Mind. Divine Mind is the strength, the power, the ever-present, all-knowing energy of life within you. Divine Mind can do what you could never imagine doing. But first, you must stop doing and allow Divine Mind to work.

Divine Mind can move the mountain, part the sea, stop the turmoil. It can straighten that man right up, bring that child back into the fold, move that supervisor to another location, or find some money in the budget. Divine Mind is able to dissolve that tumor, cleanse the immune system, lower the blood pressure or the amount of sugar in the bloodstream. Only Divine Mind can destroy the dependency on drugs or food or alcohol, or eliminate any bad habit, thought, or emotion.

Now if you are truly ready to put an end to suffering, move around the obstacles, get rid of the pain, find a way out of "no way" and save yourself some grief, here's what you have to do. Give up the need to be right! Stop demanding that things go your way! Stop talking about what you don't want! Don't have! Can't do! Speak your good into existence with power, dominion, and authority! Move your limited human-self out of the way and watch Divine Mind work for you.

Divine Mind is always mine!

THE RENT IS due, and you have no cash on hand. You are hopelessly, desperately, foolishly in love, and he doesn't know your name. You have lost some important papers at work, and your supervisor is asking for them. You cleverly embellished your expenses for the year, and now the IRS is auditing you. You squeezed that new pair of shoes onto your charge account, and now the bill is due, along with the rent. What do you do? NOTHING!

No matter what is going on in your life, the planets are still moving around the sun. Seeds are turning into flowers. Embryos are turning into babies. The moon is becoming full. The sun is rising. Things are going to happen, and you have a choice: you can be a witness or a participant. A witness observes and learns. A participant creates drama and stress.

No matter what it looks like, the truth is simple: there is something you are learning or unlearning. There is some part of you that must be refined. Not fixed! Not changed! But fine-tuned in order to operate at a higher level of efficiency. You may not like what is going on, but you will live through it, if you give up the need to fix it. Surrender control with a deep breath. Forgive yourself for any poor choices. Make a commitment to work on your weak areas. Trust yourself to know that you will know exactly what to do when the time comes to do it. In the meantime, go pick a flower, hug a baby, or salute the sun.

Only good can come out of this.

MY GRANDMA ALWAYS said, "Trouble is what God uses to prepare you for better things!"

If you have trouble in your life, you are in a valley. If you are in a valley, you are being prepared for something bigger, better, greater; something you probably could not handle now.

Trouble has a way of sharpening underutilized skills such as patience, trust, and spiritual insight. Trouble disciplines the mind. When you have trouble in your life, you are forced to focus on what you must do. The best kind of trouble is the kind that strengthens the character by showing you that you really can do the very thing you convinced yourself you could not do. Most of all, trouble builds your faith. In your moment of greatest need, you have to have faith that you will be all right.

When your life is not working out the way you want it to work, faithful trust and patience lead to new insights about the power of God. If you can remember not to panic but to trust; not to get busy but to be still; not to whine or complain but to praise, you will undoubtedly remember how merciful God is. This insight will prove to be valuable, whether you are in trouble or not.

I Am being prepared for my greater good!

WHEN MY MOTHER died, I learned the value of independence. When I was raped, I learned that I was so much more than a body. When my father died, I learned about forgiveness. In an abusive marriage, I learned self-value and self-worth. Of course, I did not realize I was learning until long after the experience and the lesson were over.

Every experience, no matter how painful, traumatic, unexpected, or confusing it may seem, is an opportunity to learn. At times, we learn about our selves. In other instances, we learn about others. We learn what to do, what not to do. We learn when to wait, how long we are capable of waiting. In the midst of the most difficult lesson, we learn the tenacity of spirit and how far it will take us. At the end of it all, we have developed character.

Always remember, every experience is merely a trip through life's classroom. Some classes have big, fat, ugly, mean teachers; this does not mean they do not know what they are doing. In some classes, you will have a great deal of homework. Good! You are being forced to study, pay attention, and take copious notes. In each of life's learning experiences, our job is to get the lesson, and practice what we have learned. What will make the lessons easier is to remember, everything you learn can someday be put to good use, and you will be better because of what you have learned.

I Am a student of life!

ONE OF THE good things about valley experiences is that they remind us to take off our Superwoman capes for just a while. It doesn't mean we can't put the cape back on. It simply means we recognize the need to rest, to stop, to be still. Valleys remind us, we can't do work, the kids, his crisis, their issues, Momma, and ourselves. Since so many of us have a problem saying no, life devises clever little ways to help us say it. Perhaps that is exactly where you are now.

Think of it this way: if you had a broken leg, you would not try to run a marathon. If you had a cold, you would not walk in the rain. Yet when we are tired, confused, overwhelmed, or just plain old fed up, we often do not know how to stop. We fly around doing and giving and trying. Being in the valley is like having a big hole in your cape. You can't fly. You are grounded. You are forced to go within.

Do not resist this blessed opportunity to mend your mind, body, or spirit. Put the shades down. Close the blinds. Turn off the motor. Shake your cape out, cover your body with it, lay down, and take a nap. Everything you think you must do today will be there tomorrow. You can handle it then, when you are rested, clear, and stronger. Anything that can't wait, won't wait, and it will not be there for you to handle.

Just a minute, please!

TAKE A MOMENT to step back and watch the sun rise or set. If you can be still long enough to observe the process, you will realize it is the earth, not the sun, that is moving. What a wonderful revelation! The world is in a constant state of motion. Some things are moving, changing, turning, dying, and being born, while other things are constant. Once you realize this, you will know that (1) wherever you were yesterday you are not today and (2) whatever you are today you will not be tomorrow. Whoever you will be tomorrow you cannot be today. Whatever you know today will look different than it did yesterday. And what you don't know today, you will know tomorrow. After all, the world is in the process of being made, and so are you. Be still. Watch the process. Learn from what you see. Practice what you know. And then, watch how it all changes.

Wait a minute, let me change!

NINETY PERCENT OF what you are cannot be seen with the physical eye. You cannot see what happened to you yesterday, last week, or two years ago. You cannot see what you will be in two days, two weeks, or two months. No one can see your thoughts or your feelings. Even you can't see your own anger, fear, guilt, or shame. You cannot see most of the things you worry and fret about, and they take up so much of your time and energy that you cannot see how wonderful you are right now!

One of the things that you cannot see is the powerful energy around you. It is an awesome energy that protects and guides you. It is an energy that holds you up, lights you up, and picks you up when you fall down. It is the energy of the *Mother.* You can't see Her so you ignore her. Like the problems and the past you worry about, the *Mother* cannot be detected with the naked eye. Because She cannot be seen, you doubt that she is real. This seems to make perfectly good sense, since seeing is believing. If that is so, why do you give so much attention to other invisible things that can never do for you what the *Mother* has already done?

Don't ignore your Mother!

CAN WE JUST be blessed right now? Can we find something, some one thing to be happy about, satisfied with, excited over? It won't cost us anything to smile and pat ourselves on the back for what we have already done and overcome. If we really understood that right where we are is exactly where we need be, we would find the joy we convince ourselves we are missing.

Life is so much smarter than we are, it never moves too quickly, nor does it skip any steps. Life always shows up on time and in time to bless, teach, reward, heal, protect, or guide us. Life always knows exactly what we need, what we are ready for, and when we are prepared to receive it. We are usually so busy looking behind or ahead, we miss the flow of life passing right before our eyes. Fear, anxiety, guilt, and shame fog our vision and cause us to miss the point, the lesson, and the blessings that are present right now. Let us remember that right now is a blessing. When we understand that, we stop second-guessing life.

In the presence of now, I Am.

ARE YOU TIRED? Fed Up? Messed up in mind or body? Have you given your all, all for nothing? Do you feel abused, abandoned, generally on the downhill side of life? Well, have I got something for you! Call 1–800-SPIRIT for instant relief from the load of your life.

No other product on the market or person in the world can provide faster relief than SPIRIT.

1–800-SPIRIT is the way to permanent resolution of those pesky problems, paralyzing fears, re-occurring bouts with self-doubt and self-defeat. 1–800-SPIRIT is the key if you've tried everything else and none of it worked!

Put an end to panic!

Remove unwanted conditions and people!

Stop the merry-go-round of 2 steps up and 10 steps back!

Don't delay! Call today! 1–800-SPIRIT!

Operators are on duty 24 hours a day! 1–800-SPIRIT!

Do It NOW!

Hello, 1–800-SPIRIT—I've got a problem!

THE TRUTH OF the matter is, we cannot expect to be in control of the circumstances in our lives when we cannot control our minds for five minutes. We can spend years running around in an attempt to make certain that things happen or don't happen before we realize that nothing is getting done. While we have so much to do, we resist and in some cases refuse to spend five minutes a day trying to reach the Master Repairman, the one who is truly in control of our lives. The only one who can fix us when we are broken.

Meditation is more than doing nothing. It is the art of listening. It is a practice which enables us to tune in and fine-tune the key areas of our lives: the mind and the spirit. Meditation is the daily minimum requirement that will prevent us from breaking down and falling apart—at the most inopportune moments. Some of us are so afraid of losing control, we can convince ourselves we don't know how to meditate; we don't have time to meditate; or even if we stop to meditate, the problem will still exist when the meditation is over. These are all clever little excuses to ensure that we stay in control of things we can't control. If you are one of us who uses one of these excuses, ask yourself, what method would you suggest to give the Repairman time to work?

I believe it is time for some repair work!

THE MIND IS such a wonderful and divine instrument, it knows exactly when we need protection. In such cases, the mind will give us an excuse or rationale we can grab onto to shield us from harmful, hurtful situations. These "defense mechanisms" the mind offers us are but a temporary shelter in the midst of a raging storm. It is our duty, however, to move from beneath this shelter when it no longer serves our highest or greatest good. In other words, when it keeps us from growing.

Be sure not to tell yourself you "don't" when you do want it. Be mindful not to accept "you can't" when you know you can. Pay attention to the excuses you make not to, when you know you must. Don't settle for less when you desire more. No matter how hard you think it is, ask for what you need and what you want when you need it or want it. Pay attention to the inner chatter which will take a temporary defense mechanism and turn it into a crutch.

I will not excuse away my truth.

SPIRIT NEVER FAILS. While it may seem as if you can call out and get no answer, spirit never fails to answer a sincere call. We will call a friend ten or twenty times until we get an answer. Yet we call out to spirit once and only half expect an answer. Unfortunately, many of our calls to spirit are filled with doubt, fear, unreasonable demands, and unworthy requests. These calls will receive a busy signal. Only when we open our hearts, bring forth the pure unadulterated truth, and rely on spirit to show up, will we receive the divine response, in the divine way, in the divine time. Spirit never fails! We, however, often fail to make the proper connections.

I have a spiritual connection!

WHAT DO YOU do when you just can't shake "feel bad?" You keep telling yourself you shouldn't, because you've got so much to be grateful for. You try to smile, to laugh, to talk yourself into a better mood, but nothing works. What do you do when, for no apparent reason, you feel sad or angry or downright ugly? You find yourself snapping at people. Perhaps you feel like crying. In the back of your mind, there is a feeling of hopelessness. In the pit of your stomach, there is a feeling of helplessness. You can't talk. You don't want to be bothered. What do you do? Allow yourself to feel it!

Do not be afraid to experience your emotions; they are the path to your soul. Emotions erupt to remind us we are alive, that we are human. And to let us know we are growing. Trust yourself enough to feel what you feel. If you feel like crying—cry. If you want to scream—scream. Get right down into the pit of helplessness and hopelessness. Allow the fear to have its way with you. Stay with yourself. Be in yourself. Ride it out when you feel bad; honor it, and know, once it's over, it's over . . . until the next time.

The worse I feel, the better I get!

IT'S NOT THE problem, the people, or the situation. It is your resistance to the problem, the people, or the situation which causes pain, anger, fear, or frustration. Resistance is when an immovable force encounters an unrelenting energy. Something comes at you. You don't want to know it, see it, or hear about it. Maybe you want to be right. Could it be that you are trying to get your way, and someone or something is in the way? Perhaps you are afraid and don't want to admit it, and now something or someone is challenging you. What do you do? You could cooperate.

When resistance comes up in your body, you want to shut down or run away. It may feel like you just don't want to be bothered. Unfortunately, if you shut down, you will miss a valuable growth experience and an opportunity to get in touch with yourself. Cooperation means you do not try to block the energy, within you or in the environment. Listening to what is being said does not mean that you have to act. Allow yourself to feel it and decide what to do about it later. Make a decision. Take a risk. Whatever comes at you is coming to teach you or heal you. Whatever you do, don't push the experience away. If you do, it will show up later with more force and urgency.

I Am open to this experience.

YOU CAN'T DO anything as long as you are afraid of what might happen. Fear makes the problem seem so much bigger than it may be. Fear freezes the mind, making the challenge seem overwhelming. Fear clouds opportunities, erases possibilities, and limits the ability to move beyond the place in which the mind is stuck. Unfortunately, we don't always realize we are afraid. We may think we are protecting ourselves or taking a positive stance against a negative influence. Fear also makes us delusionary.

A friend of mine became extremely ill, but would not go to the doctor. She continued to work, having convinced herself she could beat whatever it was. She admitted she was afraid to hear what the doctor might say. She did not want to hear it. I prayed with her and convinced her she had to have a name, an idea of what the problem was. She did not have to claim it or believe it, but she had to know what she was up against. Without the name and the knowledge, fear, not the condition, was her enemy.

No matter how difficult we think the problem is, we must muster up the courage to face it. Very often we find that what we think is the matter, is not the matter at all. Fear, however, is a matter we must be willing to confront, stare down, and move around. Fear can make a small matter appear disproportionately greater than our ability. However, we have the ability to put fear in its right place, a place where we do not have to be.

I want to hear all the facts.

The Valley of Success

*Teaches us how to ask for what we want
and expect to get it, even when it makes
others unhappy.*

It's about believin' when you ain't got nothin' to believe in.

—WHITNEY HOUSTON

DEAR GOD,

There are so many good things I want, but for some reason I am afraid to ask You for them. Maybe it's because I was denied so much as a child. Or it could be that so much of the happiness I have known was closely followed by pain. I don't know why I don't ask for my good, and I don't have to know. What I do know is, God, I am ready to be healed of this affliction. I am ready to receive all the good you have in store for me because I know that what you want me to have is probably more than I would ask for anyway.

So, go ahead and bless me, God; shower your good on me so abundantly that I won't have time to protest or get in the way. Bless me right now, God, with all the good you know I can possibly manage. Shut my mouth with good. Open my heart with good. Clear my mind with good. Order my life to receive your abundant good, in the most divine ways imaginable. Go ahead God, bless me. I dare you! After all, you know what I need before I ask. Go ahead! Make my day! Bless me! Thank you, God.

I am ready to be blessed!

———

EVEN ON THE spiritual path, things are not always going to be rosy. There will be difficult situations and people, bad days and hard times all along the way. You have moments, days, sometimes weeks when you will doubt yourself, and there will be times when you doubt the power of spirit. You may get sick. You may feel inadequate. You may lose things or people you hold dear. Just know, it is all part of the process.

For some reason, we think that spirit will miraculously change everything for the better. Eventually it may; however, the search for spirit, the quest for truth, the desire for peace usually rips the foundation of our lives apart. There are thoughts, feelings, habits, and conditions we have embraced which are grounded in fear, anger, judgment, and ego. The farther we move along the path toward a more spiritual life, the more we must be willing to release. Our trying times and major challenges are a process of release.

Things must come up in order to move out.

YOUR LIFE HAS always been a process of growing and outgrowing. You quickly outgrew your clothes as an infant. You outgrew your shoes before you wore them out. You took great pride when you grew beyond that mark on the tree, the door frame, or the chart in school. You were happy when you grew through puberty into your adolescent body. However, for some reason, today it is difficult to accept you have outgrown a habit, career, relationship, or even your hometown. You hold on, afraid to let go, trying to make it work, subjecting yourself to physical, emotional, and spiritual pain. This is not a good thing!

If life is going to work in your behalf, you must give yourself permission to grow. If it no longer makes you happy; if you are searching unsuccessfully for ways to make it work; if you know in your heart of hearts that whatever it is, it's over—let go and grow. Be willing to search for new ways to grow. Be open to new environments to grow in. Always be on the lookout for people who are growing and are willing to help you grow. Never feel bad about your growth. Some people will not support you. Others will try to make you feel bad. You might be afraid. You might even experience some pain. Know that it is all a part of growing and growing up. If you need a little taste of the pain you will create when you do not allow yourself to grow, stick your feet in the shoes you wore to the high school prom.

I accept life's challenge to grow!

———

KEEPING WHAT YOU have, even when it does not make you happy, leaves no room for your good to get in. Holding on to what is old, worn-out, or unproductive, because you cannot see your good coming, delays it from breaking through to you. As hard as it may be, and as frightened as you may be, you must let go of all you don't want in order to get all that you want.

The universe does not tolerate a void where there is a need. It will fill all empty spaces with its divine substance. When you have a request and make it known, the universe gladly responds. There is more than enough of everything to go around to everyone. However, it is up to you to make space in your life and be ready to receive what you want.

You can always have what you want, exactly the way you want it. There is never a good reason to compromise or settle for less. You can have as much as you can stand, of whatever it is you want, as soon as you are ready to receive it. You can have it now, right where you are, exactly as you are. You do not have to be perfected in order to be blessed. In order for any of this to happen, remember you must fulfill one small requirement; you must say, "NO!" to what you don't want in order to make room for what you want.

I Am open, ready, and willing to receive.

———

✴ IN HER BOOK on relationships, Sonya Ray wrote, "God is the affirmative energy behind every idea and thought we have." In essence, God always says yes to our thoughts. If we think positive thoughts about our self and life, God says yes to us. If we harbor negative thoughts or damaging ideas, God does not censor us. The affirmative energy of God supports us in our self-proclaimed downfall.

Knowing that you have the power of the universe, the power of God in your corner and on your side, should make you feel better. The Bible says, "The Lord Almighty is your husband." In effect this makes each of us Mrs. Almighty! We are fully equipped, perfectly capable of facing any situation, under any circumstances, and coming out on top. The key is thinking we can, knowing we will, believing with all our hearts that all is well, no matter what it looks like. If you think it, God will always say yes to you.

When I say yes, God affirms it!

———

IF GOD WERE to tell you that all of your problems would be solved if you did one thing, would
you be willing to do it? No matter what it was?
Imagine, we are talking about God, the Creator, the
Giver, the Keeper of Life. God, who has the power to do
all things and is giving you a verbal guarantee that if you
willingly undertake one task, all the success, health,
wealth, joy, peace, and love you can stand would be yours.
What would you say? Throughout the next few pages, let
us explore some possible responses and reactions we might
have to such a challenge. We will begin with the instructions from God.

Okay, God, I'm ready!

My Dear Child,
        *I have heard your many pleas for My help. You
have asked what you should do to improve your life.
You have asked why things never go your way. I smile when you
ask these things because everything in your life is just the way
you want it. You are so powerful, you are creating every second
of every minute within the day. You have had your way, but you
are not happy with the way it looks. I am pleased that you have
finally agreed to try My way.*

*There is unlimited abundance, total well-being, and peace
beyond understanding for the rest of your life waiting for you at
the end of this task. All I ask of you is that you climb the highest
mountain, one step at a time, one day at a time. I assure you I
will be with you every step of the way. You may bring whatever
you like. It is up to you to figure out what you will need, what
you will eat, and what you will wear. You can choose to travel
alone or to bring a companion. You can begin the journey whenever you like. The only requirement I give you is, take one step
every day, until you reach the top. I will be awaiting your arrival.*

Be Blessed, My Beloved,
I Am

Come unto me all who labor. I will give you rest.

———

DEAR GOD,

I really want to take the journey up the mountain, but I don't think it's fair that I can only take one step a day. That would take forever! Why can't I walk until I am tired? Why can't I take a helicopter part of the way and walk the rest? And You know what else, God? I've never been up a mountain in all my life! I have no idea what to bring! Is it cold up there? Do I need boots or sneakers? I've heard that the air is very thin in the mountains. Does that mean I should bring oxygen? How much should I bring? Besides that, how am I supposed to carry oxygen tanks with all the other gear I'll need? I need pots, pans, clothes, books, water, my radio, and a tent. I really think You are asking too much!

Now, I know You are God and everything, but there could be wild animals along the way. Don't You think I'll need a gun or a knife or something? But then You say, "Thou shall not kill." So I was wondering, how do You expect me to protect myself? Sure, You'll be with me, but the bears aren't going to eat You, are they? Don't get me wrong, I really would like to come up the mountain. I have been waiting to have all the things You promised. But I just don't think I can do it. Besides that, how would I get down?

Love,
Me

The will makes the way!

DEAR GOD,

I was all ready to start my trip up the mountain, but my sister messed me up. She wanted to come with me, but she has two kids. I told her we would find someone to keep them, and we did. But she didn't have the money to pay them, so I did. But then her boyfriend came home. She didn't want him to know anything about what we were doing (You know how he is), so she said we had to wait until he went back down South. That guy stayed here for two weeks! He's not working or anything. I lent her some money for food. I kept the kids three days so they could, well, you know. Then they had this big fight over at my mother's house, and I told her she was a fool, so she stopped speaking to me. She always does that.

After he left, she didn't speak to me for two more weeks. Yesterday she called and said she's ready to go. Now I don't have any money to buy the things I need. So I guess I'll have to wait until next year when I get my next bonus check.

I Am,
Helpful!

Help yourself first!

DEAR GOD,

I was on my way to the mountaintop, taking one step a day, just like You said. One day, after I had stopped, I met this really nice guy. I have no idea what he was doing way up there, but he said he needed a place to stay. It was freezing that day, so I couldn't leave him outside. I invited him in. Well, we got to talking, and he really was very nice. The next morning, I got up, fixed his breakfast, and packed up so that we could move forward. He slept until 4 o'clock! By the time he got up, washed up, shaved, and ate, it was 6:30 and very dark. He promised to get up early the next day so we could take the next step together.

I can't lie to You, God, he wore me out that night! So the next day, I overslept. To make a long story short, this went on for three weeks. We stayed in the same place without moving forward. It was fun, but I finally had to put my foot down. The next morning, he told me that he couldn't go with me because he didn't have any gear. He said he would go down and get some and meet me in a week. That was a month ago. Now I have no food, and he took my hiking boots. Before I can continue, I have to go all the way down to the bottom, restock my supplies, and start all over again. Hopefully I'll see You soon.

Just a step away,
I Am

Ain't gonna let nobody turn me around!

DEAR GOD,

You will never believe what happened to me about the mountaintop thing. When I heard what You said, I called my best friend right away. We always share good news. At first, she didn't believe me. I kept trying to convince her, but she said I was crazy. Then one day her other girlfriend from down the street told her the same thing; then she believed it, so we all decided we would go together. We had a planning meeting to decide who would bring what. Sixteen people showed up for the meeting. Some of them didn't even know why they had come. By the time we explained everything, elected officers, established committees, and collected dues, it was too late to discuss travel plans. We set the next meeting for a week later.

Only eight people showed up for the next meeting, and the treasurer didn't come. Twelve people showed up for the next meeting, but the new treasurer didn't come. This week only ten people showed up, but the head of the food committee, the safety committee, and the gear committee said they couldn't go. I told them I was leaving in two weeks, with or without them. This morning I got two postcards. The first treasurer is at the top of the mountain! The second treasurer is about half way up! I'm not coming! I refuse to spend time on the same mountain with those people!

Unbelievably yours,

I Am

Fewness of words make greatness of deeds.

DEAR GOD,

How do You expect me to climb a mountain to find my good? You know I broke my leg back in '56, and my knee has been messed up since then. Sure I play tennis, but that's therapy. I do it because I have to. And what about my blood pressure? You know I'm on a special diet. I can't eat out of cans, and I can't eat charbroiled food. They give me gas. Besides that, how can I soak my feet on a mountain plateau? You know I have arthritis, and the cold just makes it worse.

I've worked hard all my life. I've raised my kids, and I help them out with my grandkids. How do You expect me to leave them? Suppose they need me? And who is going to get my retirement check if I'm not here? What will I do for money up there? And you know I have to watch the soaps! I'm too old and tired to do this, and I don't think it's fair that You are making it so hard on people like me. I sincerely hope You will reconsider Your requirements and make special accommodations for the folks like me who have special needs.

> Sincerely,
> Worn out,
> I Am

Age ain't nothin' but a number.

My Dearest Father,

I would like to thank You for this opportunity. This is an answer to my prayers. As You know, I have been homeless for a year now. This is a chance for me to do something useful with my time. Whether I make it or not doesn't matter. I am grateful for the opportunity to try. So many days I have waited for meals and leads, so I have learned patience. One step a day is just fine with me. But I do need Your help with a few things.

I own only the clothes on my back and a blanket. God, please let it be warm during my journey. I have no gear and no food. I am trusting You to provide a little something for me to eat along the way. I don't own a map or a flashlight. Please make the path to the top very clear. And if for some reason You cannot do these things I ask You to keep my body strong. I can sleep in the cold and the dark. I can eat leaves or raw meat or go hungry. What I cannot do is live one day without Your strength, Your love, Your breath in my body. I know I will see You soon. I shall not fail, and I will not falter with Your help. Please keep an eye on me, God, and know whatever good I find at the top of the mountain, I will use to help others.

Truly blessed,
I Am

All that the Father has is mine.

My Dear Child,

    Always remember I love you. I created you out of Myself; how can I abandon you? When I love you, I am loving Myself. I Am the Spirit of life within you. I can never take Myself away from you.

    You look everywhere to everyone before you come to Me. You grab hold of things and push Me away for them. I Am your good, your source, and your supply. Whatever you choose for yourself, I will always say yes. Whatever you do with your life, I will always be there. Whatever you want for yourself, I have more than enough to give you and keep you forever.

    In the midst of fear, seek My strength. In the midst of confusion, choose My peace. When your trials and burdens overwhelm you, give them to Me. I always know what to do to restore order and balance to Myself.

                    The Joy of the World,
                    I Am

God is the good in me.

PERHAPS YOU WENT to bed last night thinking about the overdue bills, the lack of finances,
the problematic people and situations you have to
face. This morning you woke up. Did you give thanks?
Maybe your back is out; your leg may be broken; your
head is stopped up, or your eye is swollen. So you are in
pain, in fear, in an uncomfortable state, but did you give
thanks? You may be alone, heartbroken, confused, or disappointed, but the issue still remains, did you give thanks?

Let's put it this way: you can think, you can feel, you
are alive. You've got a brain, a life, an idea. All of this
means that someway, someday, you can do better. So . . .
did you give thanks? If you didn't, it is probably because
you forgot that when the praise goes up, the blessings
come down. That should be enough to inspire you to be
thankful.

What a blessing! I am so thankful!

THERE IS A song sung by Darryl Coley in which he states, "He is preparing me for things I cannot handle now." That's exactly what life's tests and lessons are about: preparation. Once we understand this, we can dispense with the notion that something is wrong with us or that we have done something wrong. Life is not out to prove you wrong. Life made you—right? Just as we are divinely made, we must be divinely prepared.

Think back to the time when you were sixteen, nineteen, or twenty years old. Remember how you were convinced that you knew everything you needed to know. And weren't you always right? Now remember how your mind was changed, your attitude adjusted through various experiences, some good, some not so good. The people you "knew" and thought were so wonderful turned out to be just the opposite. The things you thought you couldn't live without are now scattered memories. Your opinions changed. Your loyalties shifted. Those experiences were preparation and training for who you are and what you do now.

No matter what is going on in your life today, remember, it is only preparation. People roam and go; situations rise and fall; it's all preparation for better things. We must stretch, reach, grow into your goodness. Without the preparation we receive through adversity, disappointment, confusion, or pain, we could not appreciate the goodness when it arrives.

On the other side of this, there is goodness.

D E A R   S E L F ,
DO IT!
Pray!
Meditate!
Exercise!
Stretch!
Take a Risk!
Then,
Pray!
Meditate!
Give Thanks!
Do it! Do it! Do it! Every day.
You'll be a lot better for it.

I Am doing it! I Am doing it! I Am doing it!

ARE YOU A Zebedee? Zebedee was a fisherman who was busy mending his nets when Christ came by. Christ invited Zebedee and his sons James and John to join him in his travels and work. James and John went with Christ and ultimately became disciples. Zebedee stayed behind. He was too busy mending his nets.

How often have you had a good idea pop into your mind, but were too busy to follow it up? How many invitations and opportunities have you passed up because you had too much to do? How many times has your soul cried out to be something, to do something, to have something, but you had too many other things going on? Sounds to me like you could be a Zebedee!

The spirit of life speaks directly into our hearts and mind. When we are disobedient it will speak to us through other people. Questions and suggestions which seem to have little significance, could be the key to your goodness. If you are too busy to listen, you just might miss your place in glory. Take time to listen to yourself. Make time to talk and listen to others. Don't be a Zebedee! Spirit may have some very important work for you to do.

I'm never too busy for Spirit.

HOW BUSY ARE you? Are you so very busy that the quality of your friendships and loveships are beginning to suffer? Are you so busy you don't have time to clean or cook or watch cartoons with the children on Saturday morning? Is your life so filled with action and activity that little details like your sister's anniversary, your daughter's tea party, a leisurely chat with your mother, just slip your mind? Well, if you are that busy, something is definitely out of balance.

The busiest people I know are the most frightened people I know. They are afraid they won't be seen. Afraid they won't be heard. Afraid they won't do enough to be seen and heard. Being busy is like flying—the harder you flap your wings, the farther you go, the more you leave behind. Unfortunately, there are times when what we are flying to is not as loving, supportive, or necessary as what we fly away from. The key is to remember balance.

It is possible to do all the things you want to do while sprinkling it with a few things you need to do. Make a list of every important person and activity in your life. Make a schedule allowing quality time for everything and everyone on your list. Give yourself time or a day you will spend on each project and with each person. People you cannot see, you can call. Things you cannot do, ask others to do them for you. Quality, not quantity, is important in our lives. A little bit of everything will still mean we are busy, but at least we will be doing all that matters.

I Am never too busy to do what counts.

DEAR GOD:

Please shut my mouth! I always seem to say things I don't want to say, in places I don't want to say them, to people I don't need to say them to. I have a habit of speaking my dreams aloud before they are ready to be born; my criticisms before I have complete information; my fears, which have no power until I utter them.

Lord, please lock my lips! I no longer want to yell when I'm angry, beat up on myself when I think I am wrong, swear when I'm afraid or talk just because everybody else is talking. This morning I asked myself, "How stupid could you be?" Yesterday I told myself I couldn't do any better. Just last week, I remember having an in-depth conversation with me about all that was wrong with me. My tongue seems to have a mind of its own, and it uses my mouth to create things I have to live down. I know words have power, but my tongue sometimes forgets.

Dear Lord, I give You permission to shut my mouth for at least twenty minutes every day. When I open it again, let it be under Your divine supervision. Let me speak words of forgiveness to myself and others. Let my mouth become a vessel of Your grace and Your love. May the words that I speak bring to life the essence that is You. From this day forward, let the words of my mouth be acceptable to You.

Thank You, God. And so it is!

What would God say in this situation?

HOW CAN YOU tell when you are being called upon to be patient and when you are being called upon to take action? There will be those situations when you will be absolutely torn and very confused about what to do. Should you be patient, seemingly passive, or should you defend your rights, your space, or your "Self"? Your heart may say that you are being tested while your ego is screaming, "You can't do that to me!" How can you determine what is the right thing to do? I have discovered that you won't know until you get still.

In all situations you must stop before you move. Not until you stop, look, and listen will you receive divine guidance. Stop worrying. Stop blaming. Stop being angry and outraged. Look at the situation from all angles and sides. Look for your lesson and your share of responsibility. Then, you must turn within and listen for the guidance of Spirit.

If your lesson is to be still or patient, miraculously you will find the strength to let go and know that God's way is always the perfect way. If it is God's will that you should act or speak, something inside your being will stand up, move your feet, and point you in the right direction. When you are patient enough to stop, look, and listen, asking what to do, you will always be shown how to do it.

Stop! Look! Listen before you act!

THE HUMAN PSYCHE is the most fragile possession we have. It doesn't take much to damage, in some cases shatter, our sense of self and security within our being. Most of the damage occurs between our birth and the age of five. The things we see, hear, and experience in our childhood create or destroy the foundation of self which we carry throughout our lives.

Because we have little conscious memory of what happened in our earliest days, many of us walk through life with a nagging, dull ache in our minds; a sense of worthlessness, valuelessness, hopelessness we just cannot seem to shake. It may show up as unfulfilling work, broken relationships, obesity, unexplained fears and apprehensions. We find ourselves on a treadmill of despair, and cannot seem to get off.

When you find yourself in a never-ending cycle of despair, do not be afraid or ashamed to seek help: get a therapist, join a support group, go for counseling. Many of us believe it to be a negative commentary about who we are if we admit we need help. Perhaps as children, our voice, our needs, or our cries for help were ignored. As adults, we repeat the pattern of neglect, unknowingly. Therapists, psychologists, psychiatrists are trained to heal the human psyche. That is their job. Your job is to bring them to the part of you they have been trained to heal.

It is okay to ask for help.

―――――

YOU BEHAVE DIFFERENTLY when you know someone is watching you. Just as children sit up straight when the teacher is in the classroom or workers exert a little extra effort when the supervisor passes by, it is human nature to do a little more and a little better when you know someone is watching you. Has it occurred to you that someone is always watching you? Have you ever considered that the someone is God?

God is always watching what you do and how you do it. S/He wants to see how you handle your tests and challenges and whether or not you are grateful for your blessings. God is listening to every word you say. How you talk to other people and what you say about other people is very important to God. Your words reveal your knowledge and understanding of the power that you have been given, the power to create and destroy with the words you speak. Most important, God is paying very close attention to how you treat *you* and what you say to *you*. God wants to know if you *act* like you know that *you* are a unique manifestation of God.

Someone is always watching you.

WHO DO YOU think you are?

> *Don't you know you are a child of God?*

What do you want to be?

> *Isn't what you are enough for you? For the world?*

Why do you think you are inadequate? Imperfect?

> *Don't you know you are too powerful to be measured or contained?*

Why are you stumbling around in darkness?

> *Could it be you are afraid of your light?*

Why do you accept mediocrity in your life?

> *Is it just to make others feel good about you?*

What could be better for you than the love of God?

> *Could it be you can't stand to be loved?*

Just who do you really think you are?

> *Why isn't being a powerful light of God's love enough to get you through?*

I Am that I Am.

IF YOU CONTINUE to think of the situation as a problem, it will continue to be a problem. If you continue to think of "that person" or "these people" as your enemy or adversary, they will continue to hound and haunt you. If you continue to say, "I can't," "I don't know how," "They won't let me," you won't, they won't, and it will never get done. If you continue to feel bad, it will only get worse. The truth is, it's your problem and your choice.

Take a moment or a day to feel what you feel, but then regroup. Realize that you are powerful! You have something to say about what happens to you! Then realize that the way a situation affects you, hurts you, frightens you, angers you, disarms you, inspires you, motivates you, transforms you, or empowers you is entirely up to you. Maybe you didn't make it happen to you, but you can certainly decide how to make it happen for you. The issue is, how are you going to deal with it?

I can turn this around for my own good.

YOUR LIFE IS your train. You are the conductor and a passenger. How your train moves and where it ends up is totally up to you. Your talents and abilities, dreams and goals are your tickets. Now don't get excited just because you have a ticket. If you do not use it, you won't go anywhere.

Opportunities are stations along the way. If you are not at the station on time, you will be left standing at the station with all the other people who merely have tickets. The train will not wait for you. You cannot hold the train for people who are late. You cannot stop the train at every station to make sure everybody who wants to ride is on the train. Keep your train well fueled, keep it clean, be on the lookout for nicks and cracks in the tracks. Above all else, be sure you don't run over people. Move out at a steady pace, slow but sure. If you are a conscientious and alert conductor, your train will never take a wrong turn.

My train is taking off.

✺ VERY OFTEN, WHEN people upset us or hurt us, it is because there was no agreement. Agreements give clarity. They bring about order and understanding. Agreements are an important element of success. Without an agreement, you can be thinking one thing while the other person has a completely different idea. In the end, you may have both lived up to your agreement; however, there was no clarity on what you were in agreement about.

Agreements are important when we are living together, working together, or trying to get to some place together. Agreements must be clear, and spoken rather than implied. Agreements must be respected. There must be a meeting of the minds which everyone can live with. Agreements must be honored. All who agree must keep their word to do what they say they will do. When there is no agreement, those who are coming together can expect to accomplish only a few things: a lot of confusion or a few hard feelings.

Agreements are the key to success.

MANY OF US have been programmed to believe that we do not have the power to choose what we want in our lives. We do. Some of us think we cannot move beyond prescribed limits, constraints, and restrictions placed upon us by others. We can. It is often difficult to see the bright side of a difficult situation. It is difficult, not impossible. We are powerful enough to move beyond limits in order to do the impossible, when we choose to. But we have to make the choice.

The law of cause and effect is a fact of life which turns our choices into a reality. Every thought we have leads to a choice. Every word we speak supports choices we make. Every action we take is a choice today which has implications on our tomorrow, next week, and next year. Nothing is impossible tomorrow when we take the time to choose, today. Today, choose to be courageous, rather than fearful. No matter what you face, choose clarity over confusion. Remember to choose discipline over habit; when things are at their worst and when you are at your lowest, choose love over hate or anger. Choices cause a mighty vibration which in effect brings back to us more of what we give out. When we fill our thoughts, words, and deeds with spiritual choices, our days are filled with spiritual light.

Today, I make the choice.

The Valley
of Love

Reminds us that the only relationship we can have
is the relationship we have with the "self."
Everyone else shows us a mirror reflection
of that relationship.

*There are some things wrong with me
that lovin' somebody else won't fix.
When I fix them, I know love
will find me.*

—PHYLLIS HYMAN

YOU DON'T HAVE to meet certain qualifications to be loved. You do not have to do anything special, in a certain way, to get love. The only thing that is ever required of you is to be who you are and feel good about it. Love is not a reward or a prize. Love is not something you can use to trap or be trapped. Love is not even yours to give, nor can it be withheld from you.

Love is the omnipresent flow of life. It is every breath you take. It is the involuntary function of the organs, systems, and parts of your body. Love is your skin, your hair, the way you hold your head, the unique way you laugh or cry and move through the world. Your Creator has never asked you for credentials you don't possess. Anyone who expects more from you than God has a great deal to learn about love.

The love I Am is the love I receive.

WHEN IS IT enough? When is there enough love, enough communication, enough growth, enough satisfaction? In most relationships, there never seems to be enough. Something is missing most of the time, and when it shows up, we want something else.

When the sex is good, the finances are bad. When the finances are in place, the communication is out of whack. Once you start talking to each other, you discover what you don't do, haven't done, and don't have. It will take a great deal of commitment and energy to work together in order to get it together, but you don't have the time. You both have to work to make the money to get more things that will make you feel satisfied.

When is it enough? When are we going to be satisfied with ourselves as whole beings and our mates as unique beings? When will love be enough to inspire us to spend more time just loving and being? When is life and the joy that being alive can bring going to be enough to keep us loving life and living in joy? When is it enough? And, when it's not enough, what do you do about it?

Life is enough! Love is enough! Living life in love
is enough!

271

THE SONG OF Solomon, Chapter 8, Verse 7, reminds us, "Many waters cannot quench love; rivers cannot wash it away." In other words, no matter what happens, love will stand. We often forget this when we are hurt or disappointed by someone we love. We may strike out or say things which we later regret, because under our hurt and anger, there is love. Even when the time comes to end a relationship, under the pain, fear, confusion, there is love.

If you love someone, do not deny it. You can be angry or hurt or even ready to move on, but let the love come through your words and actions. If you are leaving someone, do it with love. Be mindful not to allow shame, guilt, or anger to drown out the love you have shared. If you are being left by someone, stay in love. A departure of the person does not mean the end of love. Like water, love must flow. It changes forms. The tides of love must change. Always remember the way love brought you into a situation, because that same love will get you out of a situation.

The healing flow of love moves through me at all times.

WHAT DOES "MEET me halfway" really mean? When we get halfway, what are we going to do? What lies ahead of us? Who is going to take the first step beyond the halfway point? When someone tells you, "I'm here for you" or "I'll be there for you," what are they talking about? What are you doing there when I'm over here?

One of the biggest problems we face in our relationships is the failure to communicate effectively. We often say things knowing what we mean but without a clear understanding of what the other person has in mind. One of the hindrances to effective communication in a relationship of any kind is the fear that we will ask for too much. We may also be afraid that the other person is unable or unwilling to deliver what we want and need. In the end, you are over here when they are over there, or their half adds up to only one third of your half.

The only way to build strong, stable, mutually satisfying relationships is to be clear. Never be afraid to ask, "What do you mean?" Always be willing to admit, "This is not what I had in mind." Until we make a commitment to communicate clearly and effectively in our relationships, we will be halfway there with nothing happening here.

Clarity in speech brings clear direction.

IT IS ABSOLUTELY amazing that we will talk to strangers in the most polite and patient tones, while we say anything, in any way, to the people we love and care about. We would never speak to the supervisor at work the way we talk to our mates. We rarely say things to unfamiliar children that we frequently say to our own. If company is coming over, we clean up and cook. Yet we have few reservations about stepping over or around the accumulation of clutter that results from daily living.

We must learn to talk to people we love and care about the same way we talk to and treat strangers. We must learn to treat ourselves and loved ones as if we were company. The issue of life is not to impress other people and make them feel good about us. The issue is to develop the kind of character and compassion which allow us to treat ourselves and loved ones in a consistently positive way, based upon the company we are in. When we can do this, we won't spend so much energy switching on and off.

I treat everyone like company.

WHEN YOU ARE feeling down, celebrate your spirit. The essence of life in your body, celebrating your spirit, is celebrating life. The ability to have, to be, and to do is imbedded in your spirit. In this life, we are bound to earth by the physical body. In Spirit, we are bound to the sky, the moon, the stars, the universe, and the Creator. Spirit is the life force of the Creator as it uniquely expresses itself through you! Now, that is something to celebrate!

Celebration of Spirit requires reflection and anticipation. Reflection reminds you of where you've been. Anticipation allows you to keep moving forward. Spirit inspires you to do better, ask for more, expect the best for yourself. Never allow the temporary setback or minor disappointment to dampen the celebration of life. Through Spirit you are divine. In this life, you are Spirit. CELEBRATE WHAT YOU ARE!

Today, I have a reason to celebrate.

DOES IT SEEM that no matter how hard you try, you continue to attract the wrong people as your mate? Perhaps this is because you have forgotten about the Law of Attraction, which states, "What you draw to you is what you are!" We continue to ask life to send us the right person, the person who will make us happy or whole. Under this request is the belief that we are unhappy or not whole. In response, the universe brings us the person and situations to increase what we believe we are. See how it works?

When you focus on what you lack, you receive more of it. When you speak about what you don't want, you create it. The only way to attract and maintain a divine relationship is to be a divine mate. You must be all the things you seek in another person. You must nurture, support, embrace yourself, and you must enjoy your own company. You must be kind to yourself. Generous with yourself. And, most of all, you must love yourself unconditionally. Before you can attract that perfect somebody, you must believe you are the perfect you.

I am the one I am looking for.

STAYING IN A relationship for economic reasons is not a healthy thing to do. You may be able to convince yourself it's worth it for the money. However, in doing so you put your mental and emotional well-being on the sale rack. When you hang out in an emotionally bankrupt situation, your heart is being condemned in the bargain basement of someone's pocket or bank account.

Sure your checkbook may reflect wealth, but what about your self-worth and self-value? You have placed them on the reject table. Relationships are not like fire sales, where you grab whatever you can for as little as you can. A relationship must be about mutual giving and receiving, where everyone involved is increased in spiritual, emotional, and mental measure.

My heart is not for sale.

IF YOU ARE ending a relationship, be careful not to make food your substitute lover. Eating is an unconscious response that fills the emptiness we feel. We look for something to fill the void and ease the pain. Food always seems to fit the bill. It is painless. It is available. It usually looks, smells, and feels good. Food won't argue with you. It won't take anything from you. It is something you can snuggle up with and settle down with. Food always seems to be there when you need it, but don't let food fool you. It will leave you in much worse shape than your exiting lover.

Instead of a sandwich, ice cream, or pie, try running, dancing, or screaming. If none of that works, find a nice quiet place and cry. You may not feel good when you are doing it, but you will get more out of it than calories, inches, and a body to feel bad about.

Food will not fill the void.

I HAVE NEVER been in a relationship that ended when I did not know it was going to end. There were times when I knew long before it ended, and I held on waiting for the axe to fall on my heart. There were other times when I thought it would end, but I stayed and prayed that it wouldn't. I usually forbade myself to think about it. In either case, when the end finally came, I couldn't figure out if I was angry, hurt, or relieved.

By the time we see the trouble in a relationship, it is no longer trouble; it is a disease that has eaten away the core of what the relationship is about. The signs and symptoms have been present for quite a while, but the moment we see them, we fall face-first into denial. We don't want to see or know or hear anything that might confirm what we already know. Women are blessed with a wonderful gift called intuition. It is our safety net. It is like a guardian angel. It is there to protect us and guide us. Unfortunately, it won't work for us unless we pay attention to it!

Know that you know what you know and that it is okay to know! Anything you know is for your own good. Your knowledge will strengthen you. Your knowledge will protect you. Not only will intuitive knowledge open your eyes to see what you need to see; it will also let you know what to do about what you see!

Don't be afraid to see what you know!

———

IF YOU ARE so willing to be with the wrong person, imagine how wonderful it will be when the right person comes along! In order for that to happen, you must be willing to stop feeling sad, stop being in fear, and stop being in denial. It's not working! That may not be a bad thing.

When a relationship stops working, it usually means that someone has grown. Someone is now ready to receive more and have more than the relationship offers. Someone is ready to be loved, honored, and treated the way they really want to be treated. Could that someone be you? If it is you, that must mean you are ready to say good-bye, ready to dry your eyes, and ready to let go!

Please go, if you must!

A person can love you and still have
developmental problems.
A person can love you while they are plagued by
behavioral deficiencies.
A person can love you and still be
off balance, in denial, or a really bad person.
DON'T TAKE IT PERSONALLY!
Either you love them or you don't!
Either you will stay or you won't!
Make a decision and stick by it!

People do what they do because they do.

ENDING A RELATIONSHIP is never easy, and telling your partner is going to be a challenge. It always seems that one person is never ready to let go when the other one is more than ready. Taking the unready person's feelings into consideration, the words never seem to fit. No time seems to be the right time, and no matter how we do it or when we do it, it is not easy.

When the time comes to end a relationship, here are a few things you may want to consider: fairness, integrity, and honesty. It is not fair to yourself or the other person to stay in a place you do not want to be. You cannot be your best. You cannot give your best. Forestalling the good you desire and prolonging the inevitable end also erodes personal integrity. If you do not feel good about where you are, you cannot feel good about who you are there with. You begin to find fault. You lose your sensitivity. And because of this conflict of emotions, you avoid speaking the truth about what you feel. Honesty then becomes the only way out.

Honestly expressing how you feel, as soon as you feel it, eliminates the tension, anger, and fear that accompanies ending a relationship. Honesty allows you to open your heart to compassion for the other person without compromising yourself. In the end, you can make choices that are fair, from a place in your being that feels good, while doing what you honestly believe is best for you.

In all fairness to you and me, I honestly cannot be here any longer.

LOVING A CHILD and raising a child are two completely different things. Loving a child means learning how to nurture, teach, and guide. It means being free to let your child know who you are, how you feel, and what you need. Love requires truth, not just sheltering, protecting, or providing. Love means some fun, some pain, some joy, some tears, and absolutely no guarantees.

Raising a child means learning tolerance, patience, acceptance, and forgiveness. It means learning how to teach responsibility, accountability, and dependability. Raising a child requires discipline and obedience, practicing it and teaching it. It means keeping your eyes and your mind open to all things, under all circumstances. Raising a child requires trust, of yourself to do the right thing and of your child to get it . . . eventually.

Many of us love our children so much we forget to raise them. We forget they can see and think and feel. We forget they can fall and get up, with or without our help. We love them because we are afraid to lose them. Yet we lose them because we forget to raise them.

I must love my child enough to raise an adult.

THERE ARE SOME people who come into your life with "WARNING" stamped right in the middle of their forehead. Their story sounds a little strange. Their actions totally contradict their story. You may not know what it is, but you know something is not quite right. What do you do? TRUST YOURSELF!

It is not necessary to have every tidbit of information or to know every gory detail about a person, because your instincts are usually correct. People show you who they are by what they do. If it doesn't feel right, they are probably not! We want to help everybody. Those we can't help, we want to save from themselves. To accomplish this, we will often ignore our natural, self-protective instincts and buy into a sad story. Yes, we want to give everyone the benefit of the doubt, but we also want to learn to trust ourselves.

Learn to trust what your inner voice is telling you. If the person is real, you will find out. Until then, we must stop bandaging bleeding hearts; otherwise, we will continue nursing our grieving hearts.

Nothing ever strikes without warning!

IT MAY SEEM right now that someone has done something very bad to you. It may strike you that this is unfair; that you don't deserve it; or that it is just downright wickedness on their part. You are probably angry or hurt, or perhaps afraid. You may not understand how or why this has happened. All of this and more may be true about what you feel right now. However, no matter how bad it hurts or how bad you feel, you are not a victim!

Nothing in life happens passively. We are completely responsible for every experience we have, because we determine how we will respond. Sometimes we get stuck in the "Why me?" mode. Life has a way of asking, why not you? If you happen to be in the "I can't help myself" mode, you are available, that's why! Unfortunately, we believe we become victims as a result of what happens, when, in fact, believing we are victims enables things to happen.

Always remember, no matter what is going on in your life, it is your responsibility to choose how you respond. This does not mean you will not hurt. This does not translate to you should ignore what you feel. Not being a victim and taking responsibility means: feel the pain, honor the shock, look for the lesson, and keep on moving in a way that honors who you really are. You are Spirit in a body having a temporary human experience. Your experiences may knock you down, but it is your responsibility not to let them keep you down.

Actively participate in all of your life!

WHEN A MARRIAGE or relationship is about to end, one of the major challenges we must overcome is the belief that we were wrong in choosing the person we are now leaving or losing. No one wants to be wrong, particularly about the person we love. No one wants to admit they gave so much time, energy, or attention to the wrong person or that they did it for the wrong reasons. Often the fear of being wrong will render us dumb or blind to the very thing we must see—the person is no longer right in our lives.

Wrong today does not grow from being wrong yesterday. The person who was absolutely right yesterday may be totally wrong for you today. You have grown, your needs have changed, and there is nothing wrong with that. You are not who you were last year, last month, or last week. You can see with more clarity, feel with greater passion. That does not make you wrong. Nor does it mean you were ever wrong. You were younger, not as smart, a little less prepared, perhaps a bit important. There is nothing wrong with that! There is nothing wrong with you! However, the time has come for you to release what is wrong and make room for what is right.

There is nothing wrong about wanting what is right!

BEFORE YOU GET angry with someone for what they have done, not done, or done to you, honestly ask yourself, "What role did I play in this?" Before you get angry or dismiss the question, honestly ask yourself, Did I say yes when I wanted to say no? Did I say no when I really wanted to say yes? Did I really trust this person? Did I go into the situation in doubt? In fear? Before you start beating up on yourself or anyone else, honestly ask yourself, when did I see this before? When was the last time I was in this place? Feeling this way? Before you give yourself a headache, say something you will be sorry for later, or slump into the valley of depression or anger, honestly ask yourself, "What is the lesson here?"

I know I am learning something!

YOU CANNOT LOSE! It is metaphysically impossible to lose what is meant for you. One reason we stay in relationships we know are going nowhere is because we are afraid of losing something. We think we will lose the person. We feel like we have lost a lot of time. We may even believe we are losing a certain lifestyle or a part of life that has some great meaning to us. What we don't realize is . . . you can never lose!

If the universe intends that you should be with a person, you will be with that person. They may leave. You may leave. However, at the divine time, in the divine way, you will be together. You will have no other choice. If you are with someone and the universe is not in support of the union, there is nothing you can do to keep it together. You must let go! As long as you stay where you are not intended to be, your divine mate cannot get to you. When you let go of what is not working, you will make room for what is going to work. In the end, you haven't lost a thing!

Victory fills all empty places and spaces!

THE PERSON WE love is not a piece of property! They can be a friend, a lover, a husband, or a soul mate. They may be the apple of your eye, the beat of your heart, the crunch in your Cheerios, but they do not belong to you. No matter how much you love them, want them, need them, you will never get them to do what you want, when you want, the way you want. No matter what they say, or what you do, another person cannot belong to you.

A person is a child of God, free to change, able to choose. A person is a being in the process of evolution; flipping and flopping; stumbling and falling; striking out and striking back in order to determine who they are and what they want. We are all little children all grown up. We have toys we want to play with. Fears we want to hide. We may fib to get our way. You can expect a person to say they can when they know that they can't; or to say they will and then forget to do it. A person can be many things you like and even more that you don't. The truth of the matter is, the person in your life is a reflection of you. When you stop trying to own them, you can begin the process of owning up to all parts of yourself.

I will take stock of all of me.

WHEN YOU DO something for someone and their response upsets you, you probably did it for the wrong reason. So what if they didn't say thank you? Why would you expect them to call you? If you put yourself or your finances in peril by doing it, you probably did it for the wrong reason.

It is very easy to convince ourselves that we are doing something for someone when usually the truth is we do it for ourselves. We do it to feel needed and wanted. We do it to make ourselves look better in the other person's eyes. We do things to be noticed. We do other things to take attention away from something we don't want seen. There are instances when we do things because we think we "have to"; we are afraid of what will be said if we don't do it. In each of these instances, we are expecting a certain payoff or payback. If we do not receive it, we become upset with the other person. We believe we've been done, had, ignored, and abused.

We can save ourselves a great deal of grief by doing or giving purely for the joy of doing. With no expectation of reward or return, our giving and doing becomes a blessing to us. It's called service when we serve with joy; the universe, not people, pays us in kind.

I am doing this for the joy of it.

So you've just discovered that your husband, boyfriend, lover has another wife, girlfriend, lover; what do you do? Do you strike out or act out? Do you tell yourself it's not true and continue on as if it is not? The time to figure out what to do is not when it is happening. You must know what you will do before it happens. This knowing is called understanding boundaries.

How you let people into your space will determine how they behave once they get there. How you handle the little things will give you the strength to handle the big things that are bound to come up. We all need boundaries, even in our relationships. We must let people know what is acceptable and what is not, in advance of them stepping across the boundary lines. And we must know what we are willing to do once the line has been crossed.

It is crucial to your own self-worth that you have limits. Those in your life who love you, respect you, and want to be in your space will not risk losing you by crossing the boundary lines. If, for some reason, they choose not to honor your limits, you must do what you said you would do . . . draw the line and don't cross it!

Know in advance what you will and will not accept!

A SELF-RIGHTEOUS WOMAN can drive a man away by demanding perfection. A self-righteous woman actually believes that a man's sole purpose in life is to be what she wants him to be. She may forget that the man is on his own journey through life. She conveniently ignores the fact that men have the same problems, the same issues, and the same fears as most women. Some women have learned to mask their issues much better than men, but that does not give them the right to judge anyone else.

A self-righteous woman can never be satisfied. A man can never live up to her expectations. He can never give enough, do enough, or have enough. Even if he does exactly as he is asked to do, he probably did it too slow or too fast. The one thing a self-righteous woman always overlooks is her own flaws. That is probably why she has so much time to examine the man's shortcomings.

A flawed diamond is still a diamond!

WE ARE USING the wrong math in our relationships. When two people come together to share their lives, 1 + 1 does not equal 2! 1 + 1 = 1! In a relationship, two whole and complete people come together to make a whole and complete union. The parties must be loving, supportive, respectful, and generous to their individual selves before they can offer more of the same to a partner.

Wholeness in this case relates to a healthy sense of self, a wholesome sense of value and worth. Wholeness also means the parties in a relationship each have a sense of direction. Far too often, we use our relationships as a crutch. Something to hold us up. Something which makes it easier to get by. We each want the other person to make us whole. When two cripples try to stand on one crutch, there is a great likelihood that they will both fall down. It is in our own best interest to move in and out of relationships as whole people, with strengths to bring to the table. When we add who we are to who our mate is, we should come up with one wholesome unit.

Seek all that you are in the quest to make it more!

EVERYONE WANTS TO be loved. We seem to know that love heals. Love inspires. Love picks you up, puts a smile on your face, and elongates your spine! We search for love. We wait for it. Some of us are willing to do almost everything to get it. We give up on love, then we give in to love, reaching and groping for the security we believe love will provide for us.

Do you love yourself? Are you in harmony with *you?* Do you treat yourself with respect? Are you generous, kind, and supportive of you? Do you trust yourself and treat yourself as though you can be trusted? Do you accept your weaknesses and celebrate your success? Do you radiate love, or are you just looking to find love and get love? Until you love who you are—not just say it, but do it and believe it—you will never find the love you are or the love you believe someone else has to give you.

The love you are is the love you receive.

———

ALL RELATIONSHIPS TAKE work. Sometimes that work looks like a disagreement or an argument. It may also look like stress that creates tension. The work may look like a separation. Don't worry! It is all a part of the work. The key to a successful relationship is to allow the work to take place, to allow the communication to continue, and to keep your heart open to love and be loved.

A relationship is not just the place we go to find love, companionship, and intimacy. It is the place we go to heal, to grow, and to work on ourselves. A relationship is an environment which gives us an opportunity to see how much we are capable of giving, how strong we are, and how flexible we can be. The key to successfully working through the issues of a relationship are: to be willing to grow, to be ready to heal, and to keep your heart open to do the work that will be required for your growth and healing.

Love is worth the work.

Glossary of Emotions, Terms, and Spiritual Principles

The terms and principles offered here are from a spiritual or metaphysical (beyond the physical) frame of reference as explanations rather than definitions. In some cases, what is offered may seem to be in conflict/opposition to the intellect, the rational mind, and Webster. For additional research and inquiry, please refer to the following texts:

The Metaphysical Bible Dictionary.
Unity, Unity Village, Unity, MO, 1931.

Charles Filmore: *The Revealing Word.*
Unity, Unity Village, Unity, MO, 1959.

Ernest Holmes: *The Dictionary of New Thought Terms.*
DeVross & Co., Marina Del Rey, CA, 1942.

Acceptance To know that all is well, even when you do not see or understand how it will turn out.

Accountability Considering all actions as creative energy for which you must answer to a Higher Authority.

Affirmation A statement made and accepted as truth.

Aggression Pushing, forcing, moving against the natural, normal, or visible flow.

Alignment   Being in one accord, in harmony and balance with the flow of divine energy.

Anger   The emotional reaction to not having our way, or not having people and events meet our expectations.

Awareness   An inner knowing of divine principles and how they work or manifest in the physical world.

Balance   Having and making time, or spending time and energy attending to all areas and aspects of living/being.

Belief   A mental and emotional acceptance of an idea as being the truth.

Betrayal   When expectations of people and events violate trust given, or when one who is trusted is actively dishonest.

Blame   Giving someone else responsibility for your happiness or well-being. Looking outside of self for the answer or solution.

Blessings   Good fortune which comes your way without any conscious input on your part. The demonstration of God's grace and loving in the physical form.

Celebration   Freedom of the spirit. Giving praise and thanksgiving. Feeling good and demonstrating what you feel.

Challenge   A problematic or difficult situation or experience which arises in the course of life's events. Usually a test of character, spiritual strength, and faith.

Change   A shift or movement in the flow of life. The outgrowth of the natural flow of events.

Character   The basic essence of the person. What you psychologically and emotionally rely upon, stand upon, look to, hold on to within your self. The foundation of the ability to live.

Clarity   A sense of peace, a well-being in the midst of chaos or confusion. The ability to discern the truth within one's own being.

Closure   Mental, emotional, and spiritual release. A state of acceptance. Acknowledgment that something which has been a part of your experience no longer exists.

Commitment   Unwavering focus. Giving of all one has to offer. Dedication to and faith in a desired course of events.

Compassion   The ability to see error without the need to condemn. An open and understanding heart with the ability to offer mercy, truth, and love.

Confinement   Mental, emotional, spiritual, or physical impediments to movement, growth, or evolution. A test of spiritual constitution.

Conflict   Disharmony. Imbalance. Opposition between forces, energy, or people moving in similar or differing directions. A test of character.

Confusion   Mental, emotional, or spiritual darkness. Mental, emotional, or spiritual conflict. Overstimulation of the physical senses.

Consciousness The total of all ideas accumulated in the individual mind which affects the present state of being. The composite framework of beliefs, thoughts, emotions, sensations, and knowledge which feeds the conscious, subconscious, and superconscious aspects of the individual mind.

Control Aggression. Conscious attempts to direct the course of events. Unconscious beliefs which stagnate or stymie the course of events. The ability to adjust to the natural flow of events.

Cooperation The working of one accord, the being in togetherness of two or more forces. Balance, harmony, mutual recognition among forces.

Courage Freedom from fear. The ability to be, stand, move in the presence of anxiety, danger, opposition. Stepping beyond the mental, emotional, or physical state, the place where one is safe, comfortable, or secure. A test of character.

Death Spiritual transition from one form to another. The absence of life, whether physical, emotional, or spiritual. Physical dissolution of the body or a circumstance.

Decree To command with spiritual and emotional authority. Words charged with the power of faith and truth which produce and increase with usage and time.

Denial Conscious failure or subconscious inability to see, know, or accept truth. As related to affirmations or the spoken word, a denial is the soap and water of the mind which relinquishes a false belief or evil thought.

Depression   Unexpressed anger turned inward; feeling burdened or overwhelmed, powerless in the face of situations, unable to have our way.

Desperation   A belief in physical, emotional, or spiritual abandonment. Actions taken in denial of truth. Resistance to beliefs of helplessness. Failure to surrender. Relinquishing of faith and trust. A test of character.

Detachment   A mental, emotional, and spiritual construct which enables one to withdraw emotional investment in a course of events. The ability to become a witness rather than a participant. Having no mental or emotional attachment to outcome.

Disappointment   An emotional construct. Expectations based on false or uncommunicated desires which go unmet. Unfulfilled attachments to the outcome of events.

Discernment   "The ability to lay hold of truth." To see beyond appearances to that which is obscure and hidden, but divine.

Discipline   Focus. A test of spiritual constitution. The willingness to be taught. The ability to follow through based on faith and obedience.

Diversion   Action or activity which attracts one's focus or attention. A conscious or unconscious act taken in response to fear which impedes growth and evolution. A test of character and spiritual constitution.

Divine Mind   The absolute. The Alpha (beginning) and Omega (ending) of creation and life; the unlimited, ever-present, all-knowing, all-powerful Spirit of God.

Doubt   The result of trust and truth being brought into question. Lack of focus and commitment that results in fear. The root of mental and spiritual weakness, leading to indecisiveness. A test of character.

Drama   Active participation in conflict, confusion, and the appearance of that which is false. The attempt to get attention or secure control. Resistance to change. Denial of truth!

Ego   "Easing God out"; seeing our way as the way. Believing we are separate from God. The foundation of fear.

Emotions   Activity of the subconscious mind. Energy within your being that motivates all conscious thought and action.

Empathy   The ability to stand in the circumstances of another and know the truth without judgment. To give to another what one desires for oneself.

Endurance   Unwavering strength grounded in truth and spiritual principles. An outgrowth of courage. The reward of surrender. A test of character.

Evolution   The calling to a higher order. Development achieved by adherence to spiritual law. The unfolding of natural events according to the divinely ordained spiritual plan.

Excitement A lifting or rising up of the consciousness. An expression of good. The prelude to joy. An outgrowth of acceptance.

Faith Spiritual assurance; inner knowing which draws on the power of the heart's desire. Reliance on God's goodness to deliver you from all harm.

Fear False expectations appearing real. Dread, alarm, painful emotion enhanced by the belief in separation. The basic tool of the ego to find fault.

Forgiveness To give up the old for the new, the bad for the good. To allow change to take place. An appeal for healing of the consciousness.

Freedom A mental construct. The ability to know and live the truth. The ability to choose. A state of being without thought of confinement, restraint, limitation, or oppression; having a sense of well-being within which manifests into the outer world.

Grace The omnipresent, omnipotent, all-knowing, perfecting presence of God.

Gratitude Humility of the spirit which gives praise for all. The act of giving praise. The willingness to receive. A test of spiritual discernment.

Greed Insatiable appetite of the physical senses. The absence of gratitude. Belief in lack.

Guilt The belief that there is something profoundly wrong with an act we have committed. A toxic emotion which often leads to shame.

Healing Restoration of the mind, body, or spirit to a

state of Oneness with God. Belief in openness to, receptivity to the presence of God as Spirit.

Helplessness   A mental construct. Failure to recognize truth. Denying the Divine Presence. As it relates to surrender, helplessness is the admission and acceptance of the omnipotence of Spirit.

Honesty   Willingness to know, accept, and promote the truth. The conscious participation in the activation of truth, whether or not it is spoken.

Humility   Making room for the Holy Spirit, God's Spirit, to express through you. The ability to give and serve without expectations of physical reward. Acknowledging God as the giver and doer of all things.

Illumination   Divinely inspired understanding. The ability to see beyond all physical manifestations to the spiritual principle as an active presence.

Impatience   Fear. The absence of faith. The ego's active need to be in control of circumstances and people. A test of character.

Innocence   A childlike state of purity. Pure thought. The outgrowth of forgiveness. The eternal state of spirit.

Inspiration   Divine motivation from within.

Instinct (Sixth Sense)   The voice of Spirit within your consciousness. The presence of the Holy Spirit within the being. (See Intuition.)

Intent   The state of unstated expectation. The cause of all results. The subconscious motivation of all action.

Intuition "Teaching from within." The subconscious and superconscious aspect of the individual mind which brings forth information required for spiritual evolution.

Jealousy Fear. Belief in lack. Manifestation of the lack of self-value, self-worth, and self-love. The ego's need to believe, "I'm not good enough," or "I don't deserve."

Joy The natural expression of the Holy Spirit. A state of well-being and Oneness.

Judgment Fear. A mental construct which involves evaluation by comparison or contrast. The active manifestation of the need to be right. The inability to discern truth.

Justice The effects of spiritual cause. Thought and emotion are the cause of all physical realities. What has been sown in thought and feeling that is reaped through experiences.

Knowledge The scope of information gathered through exposure, experience, and perception. Acquaintance with fact which may or may not be fully reflective of truth. Intellectual knowledge is born of individual mind and subject to judgment. Spiritual knowledge is born of Divine Mind, founded in principle, based on eternal truth.

Lack Fear. A mental and emotional construct. Denial of Divine Presence. The absence of truth.

Limitation A mental construct which gives power to people and conditions. Ignorance of the truth. Relinquishing of free choice and free will. An outgrowth of drama.

Loneliness   A mental and emotional construct based on the ego's belief in separation and imperfection. Ignorance of stillness, silence, and/or solitude. A test of spiritual constitution.

Love   In its higher sense: this is the nature of reality. God is Love. Love is of God. Creates harmony and clarity, and brings about transformation and unity.

In its lesser sense: it is an emotional attachment one has for or shares with another. It comes and goes depending on one's mood or attitude.

Meditation   The conscious act of stilling the physical mind. Placing attention on inner communion. Listening within for the voice of Spirit. Cessation of all outward movement and activity.

Mercy   God's treatment toward those who suffer. Divine forgiveness which provides a new opportunity.

Mistakes   A natural outgrowth of spiritual evolution. Confusion between knowledge and truth. An act of fear based on false perceptions.

Nonresistance—Willingness to acknowledge and honor the natural flow of events. Relinquishing fear, resentment, and judgment. Fearlessness with a foundation in trust. The prelude to surrender. A test of character and spiritual readiness.

Obedience   Unwavering acknowledgment of spirit. Trust and honoring of self. An outgrowth of discipline. A test of character.

Obstacle   The appearance or manifestation of mental or physical blocks created by one's own thoughts, beliefs, or actions.

Order   The way of the universe. The system of truth by which all things must occur to create harmony.

Pain   Mental, emotional, or spiritual dis-ease. A state of unrest within the consciousness.

Panic   The inevitable outgrowth of disorder and impatience.

Patience   Inner calm in the midst of outer chaos. An act of total surrender to divine order.

Peace   Absolute harmony on all levels: mental, physical, emotional, and spiritual. Unconditional love for all things.

Perseverance   To strive to find truth which brings peace, harmony, and acceptance.

Persistence   Spiritual quality which pushes one on to accomplishment or achievement.

Personal Lies   That which we affirm to ourselves about ourselves and which serves to create belief in lack, restriction, and limitation. A defense mechanism against fear.

Personality   The physical and mental attributes developed in response to environment, experiences, and conditioning, and judgments about the same.

Power   The ability to do.

Praise   Thanksgiving. Conscious acknowledgment and acceptance of the Divine Presence.

Prayer   Communication with and consciousness of the

Divine Presence within the being. The act of communication with the Divine Presence.

Principle Truth in a universal sense as it pertains to God. The orderly working out of truth into expressions or manifestation. The underlying plan by which Spirit moves in expressing Itself. The "I AM" presence within everything living. The formless source which gives birth to all.

Procrastination The act of delaying what one is intuitively afraid to know or experience. A mental and physical defense mechanism against conscious and unconscious fears.

Purpose Actions that are in alignment with the will of God. The underlying cause that sustains all activity in your life. Active pursuit of divine principle as the foundation of your life.

Reality That which is unchanging and eternal. Spiritual presence is the foundation of all real existence; all that is external is an outgrowth of this presence.

Reflection The sum of our thought patterns, beliefs, and actions made manifest in our life, world, and affairs.

Resistance Mental, emotional, or spiritual reversion to the active pursuit of truth. Refusal to humble the spirit. Movement which creates conflict between opposing or complimentary forces.

Respect Conscious regard or consideration for the physical, mental, emotional, and spiritual presence in our world.

Responsibility   To be accountable for all that exists and occurs in our lives.

Self-Acceptance   Self-knowledge void of criticism and judgment.

Self-Doubt   Second-guessing intuitive knowledge. A reflection of low self-worth and self-esteem.

Self-Esteem   Healthy regard and beliefs about the self and the ability of the self. Self relating to the inner divinity.

Self-Love   Acceptance of all that we are.

Self-Value   A high level of regard for self and the desires of the heart. The ability to make the well-being of self a priority in all activities. Divine knowledge of self.

Self-Worth   The composite recognition of high self-acceptance and self-esteem. The ability to expect the highest for self and to give the highest of self in all affairs. Recognition of excellence within self.

Service   Giving of one's time and resources without expectation of payment or reward. Doing what one is capable of doing for the joy of doing and giving to others.

Shame   The belief that something is intrinsically wrong with who you are. A toxic emotion growing out of programming, conditioning, environment, and guilt.

Spirit   The substance of life. The supreme energy of Mind. Life, power, and the activity of truth. The Father/Mother principle that creates and sustains all life.

Spirituality A state of thought which directly links the mind to the one Creative Cause of life. A state of consciousness that grows and unfolds through disciplined activity that relates to Spirit. The active awareness and acknowledgment of the presence of Spirit. (Spirit when capitalized is a name for God.)

Stillness See Peace.

Surrender Psychological and emotional release. Acknowledgment of the power of spiritual activity. Obedience to spiritual principle which evolves into an experience of peace and well-being. An act of acceptance.

Temptation A proving or testing of your will, character, or faith. An adversarial force which causes one to question or hold on to spiritual beliefs and principles.

Transformation Change within the form, structure, condition, or nature of your being. A shift in consciousness resulting in the release of false ideas and beliefs.

Trust Unquestioning belief and fearless expectation in the operation of divine law and order. Mental and emotional commitment to the will of God.

Truth An aspect of God that is Absolute and encompassing. The foundation of spiritual principle. That which is in accord with the divine principle of God as the creative source and cause. The immutable, everlasting word that is now, has been, will ever be eternally consistent.

Understanding   Comprehension of truth and Spirit principle. Integration of intellectual and spiritual knowledge.

Wisdom   Intuitive knowing and spiritual intuition. The voice of God within the being as the source of understanding and action. The ability to act in accordance with knowledge and principle.

Index